North Carolina
ART POTTERY

1900 – 1960
IDENTIFICATION & VALUE GUIDE

SEAGROVE

CATAWBA VALLEY

PISGAH FOREST

and more...

A. Everette James

‣with Rodney Leftwich‣   ‣foreword by Charlotte Brown‣

COLLECTOR BOOKS
A Division of Schroeder Publishing Co., Inc.

Front cover, from left: Auman porch vase, 20½" (circa 1924). Piece was acquired unglazed and painted by local art teacher, Pinehurst area. Vase, North State, 9¾". First stamp (circa 1923), glazed and decorated with unusual buff clay slip dripping. Vase, three-handled (rudimentary hanging design), 10¼" (circa 1920s). Clear lead glaze over Mitchfield clay with cobalt decoration. Background: Large standing vases (page 42), A.R. Cole, 1940s.

Back cover, from left: Vase, Hilton Pottery, raised dogwood design, 9", circa 1930s; jar, 6⅝", painted by Maude Hilton, Catawba Valley; vase, 6¼", Oriental form by Walter Stephens. Unusual celadon glaze with decoration by copper red due to partial reduction, circa 1929, western North Carolina pottery. Background: The late Nell Cole Graves, working at the wheel.

Cover design by Beth Summers

Book design by Heather Warren

COLLECTOR BOOKS
P.O. Box 3009
Paducah, Kentucky 42002-3009

www.collectorbooks.com

Copyright © 2003 A. Everette James

The current values in this book should be used only as a guide. They are not intended to set prices, which vary from one section of the country to another. Auction prices as well as dealer prices vary greatly and are affected by condition as well as demand. Neither the author nor the publisher assumes responsibility for any losses that might be incurred as a result of consulting this guide.

Searching For A Publisher?

We are always looking for people knowledgeable within their fields. If you feel that there is a real need for a book on your collectible subject and have a large comprehensive collection, contact Collector Books.

Contents

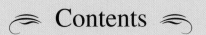

Foreword
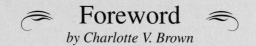
by Charlotte V. Brown

North Carolina "art pottery" is a recent concept. This familiar concept is now being used to describe and explain new information that is also the consequence of a new way of seeing things that were already there. As our knowledge of the extent and influence of the Arts and Crafts movement in the United States has increased and expanded, scholars, collectors, and museum curators have been encouraged to review attitudes that held sway for many years. In the past 10 years I have personally experienced a radical shift in the descriptions of and appreciation for North Carolina pottery made between roughly 1910 and 1950.

At the 1998 Grove Park Inn Arts and Crafts Conference, with information and images from a host of knowledgeble friends and collectors, I presented the work of the C. R. Auman Pottery in Seagrove whose glaze master, C. B. Masten, was responsible for a remarkable ware that could easily stand alongside the better known and more widely collected Jugtown ware.

O.L. Bachelder (Omar Khayyam Pottery) and Walter B. Stephen (Pisgah Forest Pottery) were also included in my talk because both makers were profoundly influenced by ideas associated with the Arts and Crafts movement, and both considered their work to be art pottery. The work of all three, seen together, was clearly derived from and was, in some modest ways, dependent on the ideals of the Arts and Crafts movement: pottery handmade and fired, simple, elegant, and decorative with functional shapes and the convincing marriage of form and color. But why had North Carolina collectors and scholars not seen art pottery before?

The axiom that a person sees what one expects to see holds true in this example. It took a new generation of collectors and scholars and a wave of new material coming from the Midwest and the Northeast to establish a different vision of pottery in North Carolina in the first half of the twentieth century. Everette James's book *North Carolina Art Pottery 1900-1960* takes advantage of this new information and incorporates the work of many stalwart and diligent scholars and collectors whose reluctance to accept established patterns of praise and evaluation have reshaped our understanding of pottery in the state. This is a good process that will force many people to ask questions about aesthetic and functional merit and will set the stage for a more forceful and forthright estimation of the quality of the work being produced today.

The sheer vitality and unending variety of pottery made in the state, whether in the west, Catawba Valley, or the sandhills, make a tangible foil for understanding and appreciating the value placed on nineteenth century production as well. Each generation learns anew. In the case of North Carolina's pottery history, this book and others will provide a viable foundation for more looking and learning.

 Biography

Charlotte V. Brown, Hon. AIA, received her B.A. in European history from the Woman's College of the University of North Carolina and her Ph.D. in the history of architecture from the University of North Carolina at Chapel Hill. After working at the North Carolina Museum of Art and teaching at Duke University, she assumed the position of Curator of Art at North Carolina State University in 1982.

In 1985 she was made Director of Visual Arts Programs which became the North Carolina State University Gallery of Art and Design. She was co-author of the award-winning *Architects and Builders in North Carolina: A History of the Practice of Building*, UNC Press, 1990, and is a contributing author to *The Humanities: Cultural Roots and Continuities*, Boston: 1979, a textbook now in its sixth edition.

The Tradition and Challenge of Collecting
North Carolina Pottery

by A. Everette James

For almost any acquisition endeavor, knowledge is power; whether one is collecting Old Masters paintings, Oriental carpets, furniture, quilts, or glass. However, if the object of one's desire is relatively fragile, condition is a judgment of great importance, and if the origin is not well known, one's personal information becomes paramount to success in the endeavor.

North Carolina art pottery has been made since the first decades of the twentieth century and was fashioned in large numbers. You would assume that finding it would not be problematic, if only you knew where to search. There is certainly an element of truth in that. The facts are that these sixth and eighth generation North Carolina potters shipped their wares all over America first by rail and later by truck. Some of the potteries shipped their "pots" in lots numbering in the thousands, so their pieces are there if you can determine where "there" is. The shapes and glazes, while not specific, were often characteristics to attribute the example in general, but the successful collector should learn to identify the individual pottery and even the potter. We have devoted chapters to this attribution process.

The art pottery movement in the Tarheel State began as an adaptation for financial survival. Progress in the form of glass and plastic containers, the availability of electricity, and even something called Prohibition led to a decline in the need and demand for utilitarian wares. The potters in North Carolina had been fashioning crocks, storage jars, churns, and jugs for over two centuries; after the turn of the century they had to make different objects if they wanted to survive for the remainder of the twentieth century. Those that were able to make the transition did, even though it was not an easy life.

The transitional forms and glazes used in the 1920s and 1930s in North Carolina provide the collector with an interesting challenge. Not a great number have survived, and the particular examples have not been systematically documented. These pieces appear crude in the reflection of the changes in turning required for decorative pieces, and the glazes were often simple and not particularly inspiring. A number of these pieces were salt glazed or used some variation of Albany slip if the potters were familiar with these glazes. Potters also tended to employ those forms that were easily translated from their former production. Many of the potters had difficulty fashioning the smaller pieces and had little, if any, experience with the decorative glazes. One can sometimes find these early examples with a crude but appealing form and wonderful patina in junk shops, in boxes at estate sales, and at flea markets.

In the 1930s the North Carolina potters became more accomplished both in the turning of these decorative wares and in choosing glazes that increased the visual appeal of their creations. Another very interesting development was the change in distribution patterns from local to national and a marked increase in the volume of wares produced so that many pieces were shipped all over the United States. This means that the aggressive collector has an opportunity to acquire examples from almost anywhere in the country, but some locations are much more likely sources than others, especially for pieces from certain potteries.

Most antique dealers that specialize in a particular form of antiquity or fine art dealers are not likely to have these hand-turned wares. The most common place to find North Carolina art pottery is in malls and in multiple dealer shops where all the dealers carry a large variety of goods to appeal to the generic desires of the public. Estate sales can also be very good sources, but one has to devote a great deal of time to this endeavor and be extremely patient. You can drive for hundreds of miles, wait for what seems to be a lifetime for the piece to come up, and then be outbid by a little old lady in tennis shoes who is reminded by the piece of her late great-Aunt Tillie — and has a $20,000,000 trust account.

Antique festivals or shows like Brimfield, Kutztown, the Charlotte Extravaganza, Greensboro Superflea, or Hillsville, Virginia, will yield good results, provided you have stamina and are willing to make your own judgment calls, and are prepared to bargain. The small shows at Liberty and Cameron, two North Carolina villages, have good examples if you are prepared to buy from dealers who are fair but well informed. More recently, special auctions and the Internet have become very popular and viable sources. Because of the escalating values of known examples, entire collections are being auctioned and extensive catalogs produced.

You will discover that there will be a substantial difference in the asking price between signed and unsigned pieces, so you should learn to identify the characteristic clay, glaze, form, and turning of the North Carolina potters. We will discuss these parameters later. For the knowledgeable, there are unparalleled opportunities in these venues for acquisition, but there are no guarantees, absolutely no warranty, and no standard return policies. While the remains of a tripod (also called a stilt) identified in the bottom glaze coupled with the uniform sanding marks of a belt sander on the undersurface suggest that the piece was made by Jacon B. Cole Pottery, such facts will be lost on 97% of antique dealers. You can thus translate this lack of information or interest on their part into your own opportunity. If you have exercised sufficient independent scholarship, the rewards may be extraordinary. The specialized pottery dealer probably knows as much or more than you will but will most often be fair because the goal of the dealer is to acquire your repeat business.

Whether a piece is signed should be neither an incentive nor a deterrent to the purchase of North Carolina pottery. If lack of signature discourages you, you have simply not been diligent in identifying the unsigned pieces, which will represent the vast majority. There are a few specialized North Carolina pottery dealers and certainly you should buy from them as well as share knowledge, but if this is your only method of acquisition, then you are going to miss a great deal of the pleasure of the hunt. Do much of your own searching, because the chase can often be as pleasurable as the catch.

Certain basics to collecting North Carolina art pottery are as fundamental as the fly rod to fishing, the wedge to the links, or the hoop to. . . hoops. You simply must be able to tell a mold-made piece from a hand-turned one. Do not believe that the turning grooves will always be prominent or the telltale joining line readily apparent. Look at the handles; could they have been shaped by the human hand and fixed to the body of the piece manually? How translucent is the glaze? Does it have the deep patina of a kiln-fired piece or a more translucent sheen of porcelain ware? Granted Pisgah Forest, a well-known line of North Carolina pottery, is fired at a higher temperature than earthenware, but the glazes are typical and almost all the Pisgah Forest pieces are marked.

North Carolina clay can usually be differentiated from other sources but not always. Mitchfield (Michfield) clay from the Auman clay pit is basically white which allows glazes to be put to their greatest decorative use. The luster from a clear glaze over the natural clay is both lovely and identifiable. Candor clay, named for a small town in south central North Carolina, is so white that it has a similar appearance to porcelain, but the effect on the glaze is different and the object does not have the very high gloss shine. The appearance of redware is red, and most of the North Carolina clay is orange. Clays from Buncombe County usually fire gray to tan while Catawba Valley clays fire darker brown with a reddish tinge.

However, it was a common practice to shellac the bottoms or to allow the glaze to run over the bottom of the piece and sand it smooth. The bottom might also become darkened by the firing process. Look at the clay and examine the undersurface of the piece, but be aware that you are not examining an object in pristine condition or understand that what you are observing might reflect some of the potting process and not just the properties of the clay. But more about the clay later.

Glazes are helpful in identification of North Carolina pottery but seldom specific. However, you certainly need to be able to identify the colors of A.R. Cole when he operated at Rainbow Pottery or the multi-glazes of C.C. Cole, Jugtown's very desirable Chinese blue, or the double dipped glaze wares of North State Pottery. If you would like to acquire some rare and very desirable North Carolina pieces, learn to identify the cream colored and cobalt decorated wares of the Aumans in the 1920s or the mottled appearance of the early Jugtown pieces.

You cannot carry in your frontal cortex all the forms and shapes of even one North Carolina pottery's ware. There are hundreds of entries in the 1932 J.B. Cole catalog alone. However, certain common forms, such as Rebecca pitchers, suggest a North Carolina origin, the specifics of form such as a "rat tail" handle, a particular potter such as Jack Kiser, or the cogglewheel decoration at the base of the handles, Joe Owen. Since this pottery was made for a national market, regional shapes were not as common as with the utilitarian goods of yesteryear. Form and shape are very important, and we will expand this discussion later.

When you begin your independent quest for North Carolina pottery, pick up every piece that might have a chance of being the object of your desire. You will get to see the bottoms of many pieces of Roseville, Frankoma, and Fulper; but gradually you will be able to eliminate them quickly. You will soon come to "feel" the presence of a mould piece, but to differentiate between Bybee wares made in Kentucky or the Gordy art pottery from Georgia and North Carolina pottery will take a more practiced eye.

The search for North Carolina art pottery can be an intellectual adventure; but you may find yourself on some remote porches, exploring a defunct florist shop, or tracing the 1930s sales of a nursery that insists that they have the records in an abandoned warehouse. The rewards are great for the informed and diligent, but the process will be pleasurable for the less successful as well.

The subsequent chapters will enlarge upon the generalizations we have presented here. The considerations are not encyclopedic, and several specialty and reference texts will be recommended for those seeking greater perspective about this process.

To the many individuals who provided information, editorial assistance, and collecting and identifying expertise as I gathered materials for this book, I am indebted, for they have helped me maintain the integrity of my information and its scholarly manner of presentation. At the ends of the chapters, I have acknowledged persons who contributed specifically to that chapter and within the text have attributed credit by listing their names in parentheses. I hope the collective wisdom here will serve to promote the historical significance and aesthetic appreciation of North Carolina art pottery.

A final word on the philosophy used in assigning values in this book. Since art pottery pieces are hand turned and individually glazed, no two pieces are exactly alike. Condition of the piece is a very important issue to consider in valuation, and there are currently no standard deductions assigned for assessing condition.

Only a limited number of the pieces shown in this text have specifically assigned values, and there are several reasons in addition to those stated above for our chosen method of presenting values. North Carolina art pottery is growing in value geometrically and for the major examples, exponentially. Price ranges assigned today will have limited value even within the next few years. In addition, the pieces photographed for this book represent both private and institutional collections from across the United States, many shown in a publication for the first time. In deference to the requests of these individuals and curators, we have chosen an alternate method of valuing the majority of pieces of this escalating collectible.

Valuation is offered in a general listing of the pieces alphabetically by shape with additional information about size, glaze, form, and pottery or potter to which or whom it is attributed, either by the presence of an artist's mark, a pottery's stamp, a style of turning, or color or type of glaze. Price ranges were assigned to this list, which was derived from the inventories of three institutional collections, by three dealers and the curator from one of the institutions. These price ranges are offered as general guidelines only.

This book is written for the initiate. Knowledge about North Carolina art pottery is an evolving process. A "truth" widely accepted today may be dismissed tomorrow in light of new data. Our attempt has been to provide valid contemporary guidance to assist in this process. Many, many contributors have assisted us in this goal, and our editors have been exceedingly helpful in presenting the material in what we trust is an enjoyable fashion.

General Concepts Regarding
North Carolina Art Pottery

The virtues of North Carolina art pottery are becoming increasingly appreciated through texts, catalogs, and exhibitions. Exhibitions and accompanying catalogs have provided the exposure for this particular genre while several reference texts have created a body of data suitable for independent scholarship by the individual collector. Dealers and auction houses such as Robert Brunk, Penland, Hollifield, Leland Little, Hussey, and the Lambert auction have also disseminated this information to the public.

North Carolina pottery as emphasized before is the symbol of a tradition that can trace its lineage seven or eight generations. These same families have been engaged in this activity beginning with the fashioning of utilitarian wares and participated in the transition to art pottery early in the twentieth century. Some of these family potteries later engaged in such volume production to make many of these wares, in general, rather commonplace. This circumstance creates a ready availability for the novice collector as well as the idea held by the general public that North Carolina art pottery is rather undistinguished. Much that was produced was made in volume to appeal to rather pedestrian tastes, but a significant number of pieces reflects the potential artistry and imagination of these extraordinary potters.

Certain examples of North Carolina art pottery were clearly made to demonstrate the facility of their maker, and commercial considerations were secondary. They reflect the independent spirit and originality that allowed the traditional potters to adapt to consumer demands in the late teens and to endure the financial hardships of the Great Depression. Unusual forms such as the "buzzard" vase and its variations demonstrate the potting abilities of families such as the Coles (both Waymon and A.R., representing two different potteries). Multi-handled vases were made in limited editions as were intricately stepped low bowls and wide mouth vases. These objects represent the very best of North Carolina art pottery and reflect the turning ability of virtuoso potters.

One of the most distinctive methods of pottery decoration in North Carolina is the cameo work of W.B. Stephen at Pisgah Forest. Brushing on multiple layers of porcelain slip, Stephen built up scenes in relief of American folklife. These freehand depictions of covered wagons, Indian buffalo hunts, square dances, and mountain cabins resembled the molded Jasperware decorations of Wedgwood potteries in England.

Another area that reflects the skill and creativity in

Vase with ring handles, 21½", Waymon Cole, rim damage and repair. Large porch vases are rare. Pristine value, $1,200.00 – 1,400.00. Damaged and repaired, $250.00 – 450.00.

Pisgah Forest Pottery cameo vase, pink interior, fine buff stoneware, 1929, h. 13".

North Carolina art pottery is the glazes. Many owners of the potteries as well as the potters made contributions themselves. The most well-known glaze was Chinese blue developed by the founder of Jugtown Pottery, Jacques Busbee. Henry Cooper of North State used "double dip" methods extensively and worked with the chemists at North Carolina State University. The Aumans invited C.B. Masten, a ceramics engineer from the University of Indiana, to come and experiment with his glazing techniques using local clay (Mitchfield from the Auman clay pit). He produced some interesting and unique wares. These are rare and highly collectible. Legend has it that Masten worked in isolation and his methods were tightly held secrets.

Despite the fact that many potteries identified their wares, several of the famous did not. Thus, stamped pieces by J.B. Cole are very rare as are those made at the C.C. Cole Pottery. A.R. Cole founded Rainbow Pottery in 1926 and used an ink stamp to identify his pottery. Many of these markings did not survive, making the identifiable stamps very desirable. The Glenn Art pottery used a paper label, making those identifiable pieces very rare. This subject will be treated in some detail later in this text.

The large planters and porch vases are elegant and impressive examples of North Carolina art pottery. Few have survived, due to breakage, and represent a highly desirable group of

wares. Some, because of their size, allowed the potter/glazer to exercise their abilities to the fullest.

Singular examples of North Carolina art pottery may be so designated by considerations of their shape and form, the glaze pattern, or uniqueness and rarity. As further scholarship is applied to this genre, rare collectible examples will be increasingly identified. Their value will increase as collectors become sufficiently informed so that they have a specific desire to acquire a rare example.

Signed C.C. Cole ware, very rare signature. Pitcher, 10". David Blackburn collection.

We are indebted to M.L. Owens, the late Howard Smith, the late Archie Teague, Charles "Terry" Zug III, Robert Lock, Joe Wilkinson, Arthur Baer, Mick Bailey, Steve Compton, the late Nell Cole Graves, Billy Ray Hussey, Sid Baynes, Bill Ivey, Tom and Cindy Edwards, Daisy Bridges, Carol Wilson, and others for the insights in this chapter and the preceding one on collecting North Carolina pottery.

An understanding of the properties of clay, the foundation element, should indeed enhance an appreciation of this art form. Historically, clays with favorable characteristics have anchored the successful production of the incredible number of potteries that have flourished in all regions of the Tarheel State. Each region, Jugtown, Seagrove, Catawba Valley, and Buncombe County, developed good deposits of workable clays in close proximity to their work.

Clay is almost infinitely variable in its natural state and responds to all manner of physical challenges, whether thrown on a treadle wheel, cast in molds, pounded, coiled, pinched, or mixed to make swirl. Left to dry and then fired or heated to maturity, the clay can become harder than some metals.

Basically, clay is created by a weathering of the earth's crust which results in two fundamental types, primary (residual) and sedimentary clay. Residual clays tend to be purer because they have been formed in place, whereas the sedimentary clays have moved from their site of origin and contain a number of impurities and debris. Folk potters in North Carolina primarily used the more plastic sedimentary clays and developed a series of procedures and devices to prepare the clay. Clay is dug, usually dried, crushed, and screened to remove pebbles, sticks, and other debris before being put into a pug mill where the clay is then mixed to an even or workable consistency.

The early North Carolina potters were primarily interested in turning properties of the clay, expressed by such terms as plasticity, fusibility, color, and strength but referred to by the potters themselves as fat and lean or conversely tough and short. Often a combination of clays was fashioned by trial and error to achieve the desired turning properties.

Certain clays from specific areas were legendary in their desirable potting qualities. Two of the best known were the Auman clay pit from the Mitchfield area (often spelled "Michfield" on nineteenth century maps) in the Seagrove region (Randolph County) and the Rhodes clay pit on the South Fork of the Catawba River. The Mitchfield clay after firing was almost white in color. While this was of little consequence in the making of utilitarian wares, it was a major advantage in the fashioning of art pottery.

These qualities were so well appreciated that the Propsts and the Reinhardts made a more than 100-mile trip from the Catawba Valley to dig in the Auman pit. Imagine the effort involved in this arduous journey in a wagon over washboard roads, digging out the clay with pick and shovel, and then retracing one's route back to the western edge of the Piedmont, to Henry, Vale, Propsts Crossroads, and the "original" Jugtown. These two families were

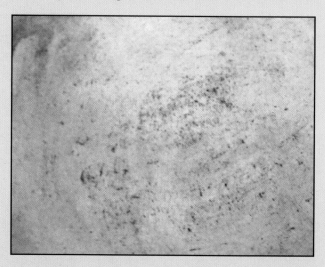

Appearance of Mitchfield or Michfield clay (also referred to as Auman clay pit). This light clay allowed the lovely transparent lead glazes to be used to create the tan or warm buff color so desired of wares made in the 1920s.

Mitchfield clay with an almost white appearance on A.R. Cole apothecary jar circa 1930s. This primary clay was the favorite during the transition period of the 1920s – 1930s in Seagrove.

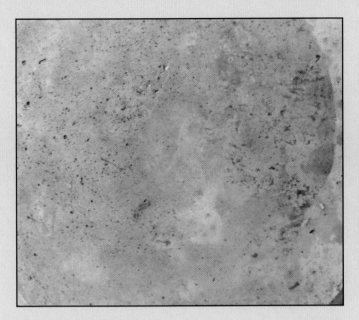

J.B. Cole, Mitchfield clay, circa 1920s. Ex-Wilkerson collection. Farmer/James collection.

Seagrove area clay. Note that it has a greater red tint than Mitchfield clay. Smithfield and Sanford area clays are often slightly darker.

Smithfield clay, inherently a light reddish color as opposed to almost white for the Mitchfield clay. With the advent of opaque glazes, this and other sedimentary clays became popular.

Low bowl with wide rim, 7½" x 9", by C.R. Auman pottery, circa 1920. This unique appearance is probably due to the Mitchfield clay and clear lead glaze with cobalt wash. $125.00 – 175.00. Ray Wilkinson collection.

Pitcher, 5½", clear lead glaze over Mitchfield clay. Numerous feldspathic flecks in well turned transitional ware (circa 1915 – 1917). Attributed to D.Z. Craven. $100.00 – 115.00. Ray Wilkinson collection.

given credit by scholar Charles Zug for developing and popularizing North Carolina swirl pottery, and their selection of clay for this process may have been the inspiration for such heroic efforts.

This Randolph County clay was not perfect, and its qualities of responding in the kiln were better than its performance on the treadle wheel. It was usually necessary to mix it with a more plastic clay to fashion the shapes and forms the pottery wished to achieve. The striking white color of the Mitchfield clay, however, gave the potter wide latitude in the choice of glazes. This allowed the use of clear lead glazes to produce the warm earth tones and mellow shades of yellow/orange and buff that make the Craven, Auman, J.H. Owens, and early Jugtown pieces so highly desirable today.

Conversely, the Rhodes clay pit in Lincoln County (just north of present day Lincolnton) had good turning properties for the fashioning of larger pieces such as the monumental storage jars of 8-, 10- or 12-gallon capacity. It allowed the pottery to control the clay when placed on the wheel so the sides

Early Moore/Randolph County pitcher, 10½" with spotting from the clay shining through the glaze. Clay was both primary and sedimentary in the North Carolina Piedmont. The patina of this example makes it collectible.

Storage jug, 12", with alkaline glaze, Catawba Valley. Note the rutile blue runs. This substance was contained in the clay used by the Hartsoe family from their property in Lincoln County.

The glaze failed to bond with the clay and with use, flaking has occurred. This early Randolph County pitcher is not collectible and should not be restored.

of the vessel would assume the vertical heights molded by the potter's hands. This quality also allowed certain potters like Daniel Seagle to fashion the bulbous shapes with very thin-walled, light storage vessels which are now so avidly collected and have become quite valuable.

Potters had to overcome problems both in the drying and firing of the clay. If clay objects are not thoroughly dry before firing, they will crack or explode in the kiln. If overfired, blisters may develop in the body or the piece may sag and collapse. A very common problem caused by most clay is the reduction in size during drying and heating in the kiln. Any debris left in the clay will dry faster than the clay itself. If water escapes the clay in an uneven fashion, this might cause cracks in the ware or inconsistency of the distribution of the glaze.

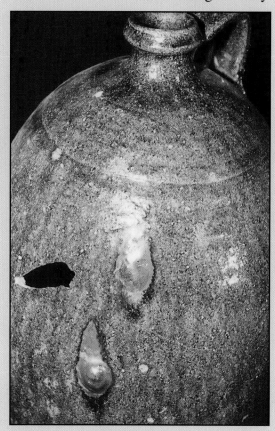

Jug, Catawba Valley. Note "blisters" and hole. The most likely cause is clay not being properly prepared, and as heat rises in the body of the ware, water becomes trapped. With kiln temperature increasing, the blisters rise to the surface and burst.

Note the raising and separating of the glaze from the clay.

Not a property of the clay itself but related to the care in preparation are large solid particles such as pebbles or wood which can separate from the body of the piece and form a crater or an actual hole. A related problem is the formation of blisters which results from clay being too "wet" (containing too much entrapped moisture) at the time of firing, the potter having made the walls of the vessel too thick, or improper and uneven firing of the kiln.

Recognizing that the very nature of the groundhog kiln meant that the heat distribution would be uneven, the potter might have a very unwelcome result after firing even if the choice of clay was generally appropriate. Certain wares because of their size and form might well be relatively unaffected by the over or underfiring which they might experience,

Storage vessel, 9¾". Early Alamance County glaze has not properly adhered to the body of the pot and blisters and separation are a result. Leland Little Auction.

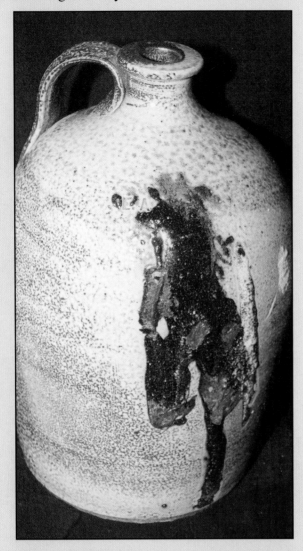

Linear grooved appearance of the "bottom cut" made when the potter passes something between the bottom of vessel and the surface of the wheel. Often a wire is used which may produce a rippled, somewhat circular appearance.

Large "kiln drip." This phenomenon was most commonly encountered when the kiln temperature reached such a high point that the bricks in the arch would have surface liquification.

Detail of Hartsoe (or Hartzog) jug with alkaline glaze on clay containing rutile which creates the blue appearance throughout the exterior surface of the vessel.

depending upon their locations in the kiln. This consideration is certainly more important in decorative ware than with the utilitarian forms where aesthetics was not the major issue.

A great deal of the mystique of hand-turned pottery of the eighteenth and nineteenth centuries as well as the first half of the twentieth involves the choice, procurement, and handling of clay. Its importance and the perception of its value cannot be overstated. Testimonials such as the 100-mile journey of the Propsts and Reinhardts are not the only examples. Aubrey Hilton felt that the determination of plasticity was so important that instead of the customary test of rolling it between his fingers, he inserted a ball in his mouth and ground it between his teeth. In Zug's text *Turners and Burners,* he relates memories by Burlon Craig of altercations

between neighbors and friends about the ownership of a new-found vein of pristine clay. The apocryphal tale of a dream leading to the discovery of the Auman clay pit is cited in the text by Robert Lock.

The mandate of the utilitarian potter was to make functional ware that came from the kiln in usable form that would withstand the rigors of its intended purpose as a churn, jug, or storage vessel. If the piece emerged from the kiln misshapen, blistered or cracked, the implication upon the potter's livelihood was immediate. However, if the flaw appeared during the use by a neighbor, it could influence business on an even longer term basis. After all, this was a cottage industry. These were the hard realities.

Decorative pottery or fancy ware was a response to an entirely different premise. These pieces were

Note small defects in glaze from clay with high feldspathic content. This appears more often in wares by Daniel Z. Craven than others such as C.R. Auman. Wilkinson collection.

Swirlware, North State. Swirl could be made from clay or from varying the glazes. Some painted wares also have the appearance of swirl.

Small shouldered vase, 8½" with excellent separation of clay in the production of swirlware. Catawba Valley, attributed to Propst family. All vintage swirlware is collectible. $175.00 – 225.00.

Early swirlware, attributed to Propst family, Catawba Valley.

acquired by the public largely for their visual appeal. Even everyday items such as cups and saucers, plates, teapots, canisters and the like should have "eye appeal" which was largely an evaluation of form and color. Jardinieres, vases, center bowls, baskets, and Rebecca pitchers were acquired entirely as an aesthetic response. The potter, if successful, must answer to the desires of these new acquirers.

A great deal is known through scientific research regarding the chemical composition and structural properties of clay. The traditional potters intuitively knew some of this data at a very pragmatic level. Much had been learned from tedious and time consuming experimentation, evaluating devastating failures, and analyzing the occasional serendipitous triumph. Procuring and understanding clay was so incredibly difficult that it sometimes formed a bond among the potters. George Donkel was thought by some to have chosen his wife on the basis of her family's ownership of his favorite clay pit.

The early potters although formally unschooled were neither unscientific nor naive; their data was

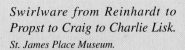

*Swirlware from Reinhardt to
Propst to Craig to Charlie Lisk.*
St. James Place Museum.

*Swirlware bottle, 6¾", by General Foister Cole (1919 – ?),
eldest son of A.R. Cole, brother
of Neolia Cole Womack and
Celia Cole Perkinson, worked
for their father from end of
WWII until 1959. In 1977
opened Cox Mill Road pottery.
Note wide separation of contrasting clays in swirl. $60.00 –
75.00.*

*Early J.B. Cole vase, circa 1920s,
11¼". Clear glaze decorated with
copper produced greens; with iron,
browns; manganese, black; and
cobalt, blue. $250.00 – 275.00.*
Farmer/James collection.

*Salt glaze, note "spots." Spots due to the
appearance of the natural clay through
the glaze are somewhat equivalent to the
"patina" of other collectibles, adding
character and interest. $200.00 – 300.00.*

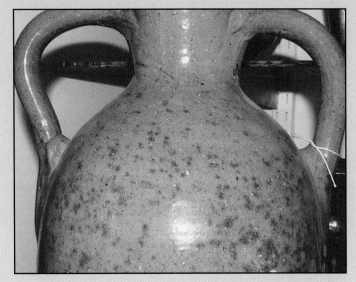

*Early transition two-handled vase, circa 1915
– 1917. Note Mitchfield clay, clear lead glaze.
"Spotting" due to clay impurities seen
through translucent glaze. Very collectible,
maker unknown. Possibly J.H. Owen or
Daniel Z. Craven.*

acquired by trial and error and the adverse consequences fundamental to their livelihood mentally recorded to alter future practices. For the folk potter, despite the backbreaking work, economic compensation was marginal, and a ruined kiln was a financial setback of major proportions. During the second decade of this century through the outbreak of the WWII, the transition from utilitarian ware to art pottery was indeed a constant struggle, and a never ending learning process about color and form, properties which were greatly influenced by the clay.

When you next have the opportunity to hold a spotted Jugtown plate or Auman candlestick in your hands, think about the clay and what it means to the process. Glaze and form, as we will subsequently consider, are very closely related to this primary ingredient, clay.

References: Rodney Leftwich, Pam and Vernon Owens

Salt glaze, Seagrove, note spotting. The grooves of the handle suggest J.D. Craven pottery, but many were influenced by his forms. $250.00 – 350.00.

Working in the Catawba valley area, Charlie Lisk has become well known for this genre. Farmer/James collection.

Swirl ware, attributed to Auman Pottery, C.B. Masten.

Swirl by C.B. Masten, Indiana chemist working at Auman Pottery. $600.00 – 800.00.

An especially attractive feature of this particular artistic form is the glazes developed by the North Carolina potteries, beginning in the early 1920s. Art pottery in North Carolina was an outgrowth of a tradition that spanned many generations and developed over almost two centuries. Many of the famous pottery families like the Owens, Browns, Coles, Donkels, Reinhardts, and Cravens could trace their potting lineage to either England or Germany, but this legacy was largely in the production of utilitarian wares. The fashioning of art pottery was quite a different process in technique, treatment of surface, and intent for the outcome.

Art pottery was truly an adaptation for financial survival for these North Carolina families and potters. While some utilitarian ware had been decorated chiefly by etching or cobalt painting, incision or scrolling, true art pottery was a different matter. In the making of art pottery, the decorative qualities became paramount. The glazing process was a very important component in this endeavor, and many transitional pieces were turned following traditional forms with decorative glazes applied as an attempt to improve the aesthetic appeal. Similarly, some art forms and shapes were glazed with traditional Albany slip or alkaline glaze.

By definition, a glaze is a liquid mixture which is applied by dipping the ware or by pouring or brushing onto the surface of a pottery object. The glaze seals the porous clay so that liquids can move neither in nor out. Seepage is a quality not desired in utilitarian ware but is an anathema to the art potter. After drying to bisque firing, the form is heated to a sufficient temperature in the kiln to bind the glaze with the surface. The melting of the glaze and its controlled movement create a glass-like coating over the object.

Another function of the glaze and probably the most important is the aesthetic quality it brings to the object, a consideration central to the making of art pottery. The variety of pigments in the glaze allows the potter great decorative latitude — for example, nickel oxide produced greens; iron oxide, browns; cobalt oxide, blues; and copper oxide, blue, green, or red, depending on the method of firing.

Certain mixtures and compounds, fluxes added to or inherent in the glaze, can lower or raise the melting point, allowing for either matte or glossy surfaces. To overcome problems with solubility, fluxes may be melted or "fritted" with the rest of the glaze ingredients to form a low temperature glass which after cooling and grinding can be applied with other materials to the surface of the vessel. These added substances create the colors and surface qualities which make North Carolina art pottery unique as well as attractive and collectible.

The common technique for glazing pottery is immersing the ware in the liquid glaze and rotating it so the surface is evenly covered. If different interior and exterior colors are desired, the inside must be glazed first. The glaze will dry rapidly, usually within minutes, binding to the body surface of the vessel.

If potters wish, they can overglaze a part of the object, or even dip the ware again after the first glaze is allowed to dry. Small areas can be glazed by digital application of a contrasting color, a technique widely employed in North Carolina art pottery, especially Seagrove. Colorful images could be achieved by brushing or dripping multicolored glazes. They are often described as variegated or as Mason (mason) stained. A.R. Cole and C.C. Cole were probably the leaders in this technique.

Lead, which allowed development of intense colors, was a common ingredient of many North Carolina glazes until the 1970s. Lead cannot be used at high temperatures as it tends to volatilize above 2100°F. Thus, wood-burning kilns were appropriate. With the realization of the minimal risk for lead poisoning from ingestion, lead was discontinued and "lead free" glazes developed. The Teagues even wrote "lead free" on the bottom of their wares.

In addition to the control of the constituents of the glaze, the potter could bias the outcome of the visual presentation by altering the firing process. The final color and even the texture of the object could be altered by the effect of the firing, especially in the reduction mode. Reduction involves a surplus of fuel or a shortage of oxygen to consume the available fuel (Ben Owen III). Reduction can be controlled to some extent by altering the openings on the vents. Again wood-burning kilns were favored for this manipulation of heat. Chrome red glazing, for example, is a heat-dependent reduction process, and overfiring of this popular glaze will lead to a dull or even blackened appearance rather than the brilliant orange/red color when it is not so reduced. However, one of the more aesthetically pleasing images is the chrome red glaze in which the top of the object is a warm brown and the lower part of the body red to orange.

Some potters may also define differences between oxidation and reduction firing, controlling the amount of oxygen in the kiln during firing. Reduction firing is believed to have been an important part of the process leading to Jugtown's, or some would say, Jacques Busbee's "Chinese blue," a glaze that has not been duplicated successfully since his death in the 1940s.

The position of the ware in the kiln during firing will also affect the appearance of the glaze as it may well determine the heat distribution across an object. This observed change in the glaze is a combination of the effect of the overall heat and the air currents inside the kiln. One side of a vase or other object may vary slightly in temperature, resulting in a variation in color. Fly ash from the firebox can also affect the color, making the pot lighter or more textured on the side facing the firebox. This is especially true of wood-fired kilns which were commonly used in North Carolina for all of the nineteenth century and through the first half of the twentieth century. Groundhog kilns are particularly susceptible to drafts which will affect glaze color and movement.

As noted previously, the color of the underlying clay can significantly affect the appearance of the glaze. Mitchfield clay from the Auman pit was almost white and imparted little color to the glaze, allowing the use of transparent or translucent glazes for a rich, natural effect. Darker clay bodies frequently produced darker or less brilliant glaze surfaces. Mitchfield clay provided a background for the compelling earth tones and striking pattern contrasts with cobalt decorations that were seen in the early North Carolina art pottery.

The production of "swirl" in the classic sense involves the use of different colors of clay, but this process can be accentuated by glazing as well as the use of contrasting clay.

Certain potteries used such unique glazes that their wares were clearly identifiable. For over a decade, A.R. Cole operated Rainbow Pottery, and his specialty during that time was the uniform, rich, lustrous colors of his glazes. These were most commonly turquoise and aqua but included yellow, mauves, and pinks as well. After he changed the name of his firm to A.R. Cole Pottery in the early 1940s, he continued

some of these glazes but added rutile and mason stains to produce wares with a less "ceramic" appearance. These colors were given such names as crystal green, mistake crystal blue, and mirror black. J.B. Cole Pottery had their signature gunmetal as well as mottled green glaze.

Multiple glazing probably reached its zenith at the C.C. Cole Pottery. This was especially true of the small Rebecca pitchers and jugs they made by the thousands and shipped to the tourist areas of western Virginia, North Carolina, and eastern Tennessee. Many were filled with honey or vinegar, corked, and sealed, providing the collector a common and relatively inexpensive example of multiple glazing as well as decorative memorabilia. Multiple glazing can especially provide a dramatic addition to one's collection if it is applied to a large format such as a vase or a tall Rebecca pitcher. Large multiglazed wares from the time period between the 1930s and the 1950s are relatively rare.

Some potteries have the equivalent of a signature glaze while others seem to be shared among families and are thus seen in several potteries. When most collectors see the orange of Jugtown, they do not need to look for the stamp, and their frog skin, "tobacco spit," and Chinese white glaze are distinctive as well. Auman pottery with the cream or tan/yellow ground and superimposed cobalt blues, nickel and copper greens, to blacks in abstract patterns is clearly identifiable which contributes greatly to their desirability. The wares of Daniel Z. Craven are similar but tend more toward an orange overall hue and are even more rare. Misfires, misadventures, and other "accidents" in the process may even produce unique collectible glazes.

The variety of glazes in North Carolina pottery is truly astounding. This can partly be explained by the large number of potteries that were and are currently existent. Another factor has been the changing desires of the public and the response of the potters to these anticipated needs. Several of the potteries either collaborated with or hired chemists to assist in the glazing experiments. The Aumans hired C.B. Masten of Indiana and Alfred University (1929 – 1936). He developed a technique of glazing stoneware with salt and colored oxides and at that time produced some of the only salt glazed decorated stoneware in America. There is the apocryphal story that his work was sequestered in a small shed and guarded under lock and key. Henry

Cooper, who owned North State Pottery, worked with the faculty at North Carolina State College to produce some extraordinary glazes and patterns. The "double dipped" wares seem to be, if not his own invention, most clever in adaptation.

In the Catawba Valley, the art pottery movement was led by E.A. Hilton (1878 – 1948) and in the west by Oscar Lewis Bachelder (1852 – 1935) and Walter B. Stephen (1875 – 1961). Bachelder, an itinerant potter for much of his career, was known for the wonderful results he achieved using variations of traditional glazes. Walter Stephen duplicated Oriental celedon and crackle glazes as well as producing the first crystalline glazes in the South.

The aesthetic qualities and appeal of pottery do not come exclusively from the glazing process or any other single characteristic for that matter. The shape, form, and balance as well add to the aesthetic and public appreciation of this art form. The combination that results in an object with a lovely and different appearance should be the aim of any collector. However, much of one's first visual impression will be because of the glaze. This response will likely remain important in the long-term enjoyment of the acquisition. Thus, one should carefully analyze the glaze and understand its character and properties.

Crackle might result in the transition pieces from the use of stoneware clays and their being fired at earthenware temperatures. The stoneware clay might not contract evenly under the earthenware glaze, causing it to form "spiders" or cracks. The glaze would come under tension as it solidified with cooling, and these shearing forces produced the crazing phenomenon. This may well have been how "antique" glaze was discovered, by pure serendipity.

The color of early wares reflects the arduous transition to fancy art pottery and the development of the new earthenware glazes. Many early North Carolina potters used a clear glaze over the light local clay which became a luminous orange when fired. You can see examples in the Craven, Jugtown, Auman, Teague, and North State pieces turned in the early to mid-1920s. When they added decoration of copper, iron or manganese, contrasting patterns of green, brown or black could be produced. If this were part of the primary glaze, it would be reflected by an overall change of coloration. The truly magnificent early greenish dark brown pieces with the translucency of a visionary painting by Albert Pinkham Ryder or Ralph A.

Blakelock are very collectible and highly valued. The covering by a clear glaze will often bring out the subtle tonalities on the surface beneath, much as varnish affects an oil painting.

Occasionally you will encounter a vessel with random small areas devoid of glaze. Some describe this as "the body doesn't fit the glaze." (Vernon and Pam Owens) If these are speckled and widely separated, the pattern produced can have visual appeal and will be collectible by even the most discriminating acquirer. Peeling usually means the glaze was too large for the clay. Pinholes are most often a result of release of water in the clay as steam or by the release of gases in the clay.

The formula for glazes and technique of application were shared by some and closely guarded by others. Henry Cooper, owner of North State, worked with ceramic engineers and shared his knowledge with Walter, Cecil, and Elvin Owens. Local lore suggests association of the C.R. Auman shop with the work and experiments of C.B. Masten, "They boarded up this little building and locked it when he left". (Womack) While the formulas of buff, orange, and the lead-glazed earthenware of Jugtown were well dispersed, Chinese blue remains somewhat of a mystery to this day.

Many potteries benefitted by the number of potters they employed who had worked at several other venues. Herman Cole at Smithfield employed such well-traveled turners as Bill Gordy, Charlie Craven, and Jack Kiser. Certain potters were journeymen because they enjoyed the turning and glazing process only. As they moved from one operation to another, they acted as bees in the pollination of information. With their employ would occur the attendant knowledge from the previous to the next employer, and a major benefit might be the potter's prior experience with glazes.

While the stories of secrecy regarding glazes abound, there was also a great spirit of cooperation among the potters, and sharing of knowledge about glazes was a common practice. This flowed from lineage, common ancestry, and traditions as well as practical needs such as the acquisition of clay, and the fashioning of kilns, and the one-day community erection of pottery sheds. Potters evidenced both sibling competitive behavior as well as family pride, and these can be seen in the development of the glazes, especially in the 1920s and up until the WWII. In fact, the war acted as a bonding experience when glazes and other materials became scarce and the young potters went off to military duty. A number of potteries went out of business, and many barely survived. The traditional family potteries seemed to rely upon their heritage to endure these challenges and as in times of mutual hardship glazes, formulas, and techniques were readily shared (M.L. Owens).

In the 1970s the "lead scare" also evoked a somewhat group response as the need to develop lead free glazes was imperative. Different glazes not including lead had to be developed but not at the sacrifice of the brilliant dynamic colors that had made the North Carolina art pottery attractive to the public. Some potters such as Archie Teague (interview) attempted to develop glazes used indigenous materials, based upon calcium borate as a substitute for lead. Others adopted these glazes and made substitutes from commercially available ones.

The artistry of glazing by North Carolina potters will be demonstrated in every chapter of this text and was used in every facet of the process to produce visually appealing pottery.

References: Ben Owen III, M.L. Owens, Pam and Vernon Owens, Archie Teague, Neolia Cole Womack

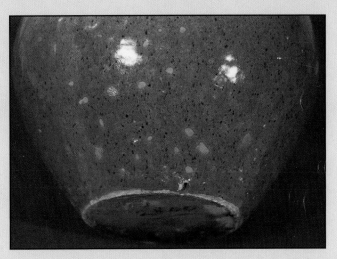

Three-handled vase, Pisgah Forest. The surface is roughened and there is some glaze loss probably caused by clay inappropriate for the glaze used and firing temperature. Walter Stephen experimented with local clays which would not fire at high temperatures.

Lower half, body of vase from Carolina Pottery turned by Lorenzo "Wren" Cole. The glaze is quite thin and the shine-through of the reddish sedimentary clay imparts a rosy hue to sky blue glaze.

Basket, J.B. Cole Pottery (1920 – 1930s). "Crackle" or antique glaze. Glaze was mixed to exhibit this appearance shortly after the piece was removed from the kiln.

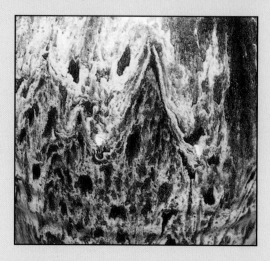

Exquisite double glaze, thick white glaze over mirror black.

Stoneware salt glaze pitcher, 12½", rim chip. The decoration was also done with salt glaze. Such Auman Pottery is attributed to C.A. Masten. The unique glazing of Masten has been recently appreciated. An exhibit at North Carolina State University Gallery of Art and Design featured this potter. Provenance: Mebane Auction, Compton collection, Wilkinson collection. $350.00 – 450.00.

Ovoid vase, 6". Modified salt glaze (blue), J.B. Cole Pottery.

Small basket, maker unknown, unusual glaze, initial glaze thinly applied with thick black overglaze or secondary glaze. Attributed to C.B. Masten (similar example in NCSU Gallery of Art and Design collection).

Brown glaze over white clay slip, 4¼". The decorated abstract design is unusual. Interior bears glaze seen in North State wares (Rinzler-Sweezy SFPCS Catalog B-1). Unknown maker, circa 1930s. Probably A.R. Cole Pottery.

Low bowl, 12", with fluted edges. Unusual and effective glaze pattern of fritted (alkaline flux melted at low temperature to facilitate mixing) green with runs over chrome red. The chrome red glaze on the undersurface is a dull brown while that in the interior is brighter and more true to color. Could this appearance be attributed to chrome red glaze alone?

Chrome red glaze on two-handled vessel. Note prominence of handles and graceful undercut of rim. Attributed to J.B. Cole Pottery, 1930s. 14". The combination of dark contrast glaze runs and orange overall color is particularly appealing. $275.00 – 350.00

On the undersurface of the low bowl above there are traces of stilt posts and peripheral smoothing from a belt sander. Attributed to J.B. Cole, circa 1940s.

Large apothecary jar, circa 1930. Double glazed with thick green glaze over chrome red or reaction of chrome red glaze. Most commonly associated with North State Pottery, double glazing was practiced by others as well. $225.00 – 350.00. Farmer/James collection.

Bottom of apothecary jar, double glazed. Note chrome red underneath. According to Vernon Owens, chrome red can exhibit such a variety of appearances alone. The firing temperature could result in the dark green.

Chrome red storage vessel, two handles. Smithfield Pottery, attributed to Herman Cole, 1930s. $325.00 – 450.00.

Vase, 16", rope handles by Waymon Cole, circa 1940, "gunmetal" glaze. $475.00 – 650.00. Farmer/James collection.

Undersurface of vase above right, showing edge removal of bottom glaze (probably with belt sander) and faint traces of ceramic stilt marks.

Example of mirror black glaze. Oriental design, earthenware. Circa 1930 – 1940. Attributed to J.B. Cole. Mirror black was used by a number of Seagrove potteries.

Large opening, fluted pot, mirror black glaze, A.R. Cole Pottery, circa 1940. $95.00 – 110.00.

24

Note smooth angles and graceful shape of handle of refrigerator jar at left.

Refrigerator jar, dark green glaze. Attributed to Smithfield Pottery. $150.00 – 225.00.

Interior grooves in basket at left, from potter's hands, note interior glazing. More rutile present than on exterior surface. See p. 35 of J.B. Cole catalog. (Copies available from Richard Gilson, Holly Hill Pottery, 625 Fork Creek Mill Road, Seagrove, NC.)

Basket, 7", yellow glaze with rutile, made by Bascomb King at J.B. Cole. The specific potter can often be determined by researching old catalogs. $145.00 – 165.00.

Detail of rutile on basket at left.

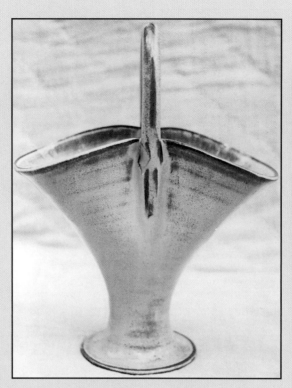

(Right) Basket, 6½", aqua glaze with rutile decoration, unsigned, attributed to J.B. Cole, circa 1940 – 1950, probably turned by Philmore Graves by virtue of the graceful pedestal. $110.00 – 145.00. St. James Place Museum.

(Far right) Two-handled vase, 13", with sophisticated form and handles and variegated blue glaze, unsigned. George Viall collection.

(Right) Vase, 13¼", double glazed with variegated glaze over mirror black by Farrell Craven. Sometimes it is difficult to determine who turned a particular ware from Smithfield Pottery. Herman Cole employed 3 to 5 potters at a time. Some would stay a month, others years. $275.00 – 350.00.

(Far right) Two-handled vase, 14½", unsigned, attributed to J.B. Cole Pottery or Smithfield. Interesting and unusual variegated glaze. North Carolina pottery glazes are sometimes aesthetically pleasing, while others are interesting and collectible. This is probably a commercial glaze.

North State three-handled vase with unusual double glaze. North State was responsible for some of the most compelling glaze combinations seen on North Carolina art pottery.

North State Pottery (1924 – 1959), second stamp. Henry Cooper glazed, W.N. Owen turned. $250.00 – 300.00. Farmer/James collection.

North State Pottery, Rebecca pitcher, 7", double dipped (glazed), second stamp, probably 1930s, rim chip. $125.00 – 150.00. Farmer/James gift to Chapel Hill Museum.

Hanging pocket vase, 4¼", double glazed by North State Pottery (third stamp).

Vase, egg bowl, and shoulder bowl with thick white glaze. Thin areas are often due to brushing on of the glaze. Jugtown Pottery.

Vase, 9½", black ankle glaze. Difficult glaze made by painting white glaze over chocolate base. May fire to many colors, including green, but this is the desired appearance. $350.00 – 400.00. Bailey collection.

Jardiniere, four handles. This represents the most desirable mixture of this glaze. The contrast between the oxblood color of the reduced glaze and the aqua is truly spectacular. North Carolina State University Gallery of Art and Design.

Ovoid vase, 6½". Jugtown first stamp. Chinese blue glaze. Note that the glaze only covers four-fifths of the body. Allegedly this was Juliana Busbee's preference because it detracted from undersurface problems and more accurately portrayed the Oriental form (Vernon Owens). $425.00 – 600.00.

Small green glazed teapot, 4¾", by J.B. Cole. Note how closely the thick color resembles frogskin glaze popularized by Jugtown Pottery. The spout and handle are J.B. Cole. Most teapots had lids which are often lost or broken.

Low bowl, Chinese blue, Jugtown, circa 1930. The appearance depends upon a reduction phenomenon to produce the marginal red decorations which are the desired combination. Since the founder of Jugtown, Jacques Busbee, died in 1948, the glaze formula has not been successfully duplicated. $800.00 – 1,100.00. Farmer/James collection.

Three-handled hanging vase, 12¾", Jugtown, with the well-known "tobacco spit" glaze. Tobacco spit is a black-speckled, medium to dark glossy glaze. It resembles "spit" from a fresh tobacco chew, the rich, dark liquid glistening in the noonday sun. $350.00 – 475.00. Farmer/James collection.

Two identifiable glazes of Jugtown pottery. Left: Chinese blue glaze, the reds are made from a process of burning to produce heavy smoking or reduction firing. Right: Frogskin glaze is produced by exposing Albany slip to salt in the kiln to bring out the green color.

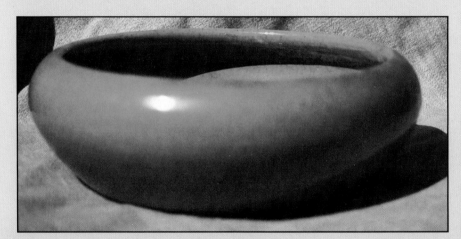

Low bowl with wide opening, 12". Note the intensity of the green glaze. Many potters believe the intense colors were facilitated by the lead in the glaze. After 1970 there was a restriction on the use of lead. $110.00 – 135.00.

Well-controlled contrast glaze giving the stripe pattern to this wide, low bowl from J.B. Cole Pottery, circa 1950 – 1960. $75.00 – 90.00.

Clearly identified ceramic tripod stilt marks on bottom of J.B. Cole bowl at bottom of page 30.

Two-handled vase, 13½", Mason stains applied over white base by A.R. Cole. Reverse is shown on page 152. $350.00 – 425.00.

Low, oblong bowl, 8" x 14", with Mason stain decoration of varied colors. A.R. Cole, circa 1940s. The inward curvature of the walls of the bowl and rudimentary handles combined with the white base glaze and decoration make this an outstanding and distinctive example of A.R. Cole ware. $135.00 – 165.00.

Vase, 8", C.C. Cole Pottery (1938 – 1973), Moore County. This pattern of glaze distribution is most often attributed to C.C. Cole Pottery. $60.00 – 75.00 (rim chip). St. James Place collection.

Vase with double loop handles, 9", J.B. Cole, made by Philmore Graves. Note thick glaze and slight separation. $150.00 – 175.00.

Rebecca pitcher, multiglaze, 14", probably made at Glenn Art Pottery (1946 – 1958) by Joe Owens. The cogglewheel decoration along with "stout" shape allows positive attribution. $225.00 – 350.00. Farmer/James collection.

Undersurface of J.B. Cole vase, above right. Note the glaze on the bottom which suggests the thick, white glaze has been applied over chrome red or the reaction of this glaze to the kiln temperatures.

Tall vase, interior glaze, exterior paint decoration of unglazed surface. 10¼". Much of this ware was made for the tourist trade, but major examples demonstrating such striking creativity are rare. $125.00 – 175.00. Farmer/James collection.

Painted vase, 8¾". C.R. Auman Pottery, unglazed exterior. Expertly painted by individual after purchase from pottery. Bailey collection.

Ovoid vase, 4¾", might this be E.A. Hilton, Hilton Pottery Company (1918 – 1934), Oyama? The foot would be unusual for Hilton, although the vase was purchased in the area and the clay appears to be Catawba Valley. St. James Place Museum.

"Dirt" dish, early nineteenth century, Randolph County, 12" across x 3" deep. $200.00 – 225.00.

Two vases by O.L. Bachelder. Bachelder used simple compounds to fashion subtle and unique glazes. George Viall collection.

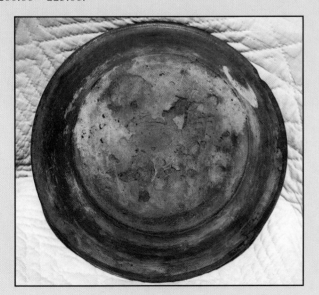

Bottom of dirt dish above, Randolph County.

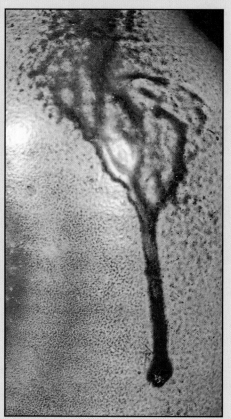

Two-handled storage jar, 12⅛", by Paschal McCoy (1816 – 1876). Signed and impressed. Two incised lines are on the shoulder of this salt glaze example of utilitarian ware. Graceful rolled rim, smeared handle ends. $900.00 – 1,200.00. Farmer/James collection.

Kiln drip during burning (firing) the salt glaze due to heat of the bricks in the arch of the kiln.

Molasses jug, at left, detail of the excellent turning done on handles and rim.

Molasses jug, 19", stoneware with alkaline flux. Buncombe County, 1890 – 1910. The small amount of crushed iron rock or ore colors the body of the vessel with a very attractive contrasting pattern. $325.00 – 475.00. Farmer/James collection.

Contrasting streaks of chrome red glaze. Chrome red is a very popular glaze. It is difficult to identify the pottery on this parameter alone. The brilliant orange/red color with striations is most characteristic of J.B. Cole pottery. This is a very desirable pattern, according to the tastes of most collectors.

Detail of unsigned small vase at right, probably by J.B. Cole. Note small rim chips which represent minimal defects and would slightly devalue the object.

Small 5" reverse ovoid vase with excellent contrast in chrome red glaze. Just as with Chinese blue (the variation between aqua and the red color from reduction), the mixture of brown and orange is important when establishing value.

Jug, 12", Albany slip, Trull family, circa 1900, Candler, Buncombe County. St. James Place Museum.

Jug, alkaline glaze. Note the very dense runs. This finish is much more common in wares made in South Carolina and Georgia than North Carolina.

Standard form with two handles, Bristol glaze. Is this an early attempt at art pottery and an effort to produce Oriental white or buff? North Carolina provenance, but probably not North Carolina pottery.

Identifiable mark of George Donkel. Note gallonage is also indicated. Characteristic dark glaze favored by their pottery. Crushed iron rock or ore was added to glaze to produce this dark color.

Bottom of variegated glaze vase. The glaze by accident has not been properly removed from the bottom of the ware. When the vase was placed in the kiln, the surface on the floor was incorporated into the glaze. At this point, the kiln material probably cannot be removed.

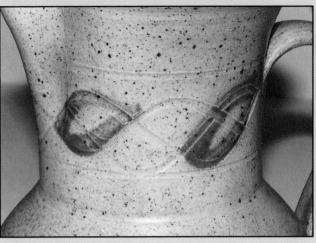

Pitcher with salt glaze sine wave and cobalt decoration. Early examples during the transition from utilitarian to art pottery are quite valuable.

Auman pottery. This particular two-handled vase was listed in Auman's "The Clay Crafters" catalog of the late 1920s. Sizes ranged from 4½" x 6" to 5½" x 7½". All are very collectible. $350.00 – 475.00.

Large 8¾" ovoid vase, 7" h. Attributed to J.B. Cole Pottery, circa 1930. Glaze is irregular, exhibiting some glaze loss. Vase is shown upside down to demonstrate blistering on the lower surface.

Double glazed, two-handled vase, 11".
Possible glaze separation of second glaze.
Seagrove area.

"Blisters" on vase at left (also called "craters")
which occur when the glaze is fired beyond its
maturing point to a very high temperature. (Teague)

Two-handled vase showing glaze openings or "skip" areas. If areas are small and fairly cir-
cular, they are due to excess water in the bisque ware or rarely, to clay impurities. This is
more likely a problem with glaze and clay not binding well, and glaze passing over small
areas of clay without adhering properly. (V. Owens)

The Forms of North Carolina Art Pottery

The aesthetics of North Carolina art pottery can be appreciated from several perspectives, including its rather unique shapes and forms. While it is well established that certain of these are derivative, especially the distinctly Oriental designs and specific European shapes and designs, nonetheless they represent original adaptations. Additionally, the images created by the North Carolina potters are often identifiable as distinct interpretations of other art forms.

An interesting and important evolutionary process occurred internally among the established potteries and the accomplished potters in North Carolina, especially in the Seagrove region. The transition from traditional utilitarian ware to fancy wares was not an easy one nor did it occur quickly.

This metamorphosis was a progression from simply glazing the older, traditional forms with new and colorful patterns to the turning of decorative fancy wares. The first attempts were simply decorating churns, crocks, and storage jars with sine wave patterns and splashes of cobalt gradually to the use of a colorful overall glaze.

However, it soon became apparent that these more decorative household wares were not going to satisfy the wishes of the new art audience although the items had some visual appeal. The forms needed to be changed as well.

Jacques Busbee, founder of Jugtown, and an artist trained in New York who became an expert in glazes, was so committed to the importance of form that he took his young potter Ben Owen to museums throughout the Northeast to observe the traditional forms that had been successful in Europe and Asia. He and his wife Juliana Royster also studied museum catalogs and ceramic texts to determine which images they wanted to emulate.

Juliana Busbee used her Greenwich Village tearoom as a showcase to evaluate which wares the public would be attracted to buy. One might well imagine that the Coopers at North State Pottery were engaging in the same type of activity in their Washington area showroom.

The J.B. Cole Pottery published a detailed catalog (circa 1932) in which the various forms they produced were illustrated. The pieces of Waymon Cole, Philmore Graves, Bascomb King, and Nell Cole Graves were identified. In fact, these catalogs have been reprinted several times because they are so useful in identification of wares and the documentation of shapes.

C.C. Cole made thousands of small, rather stereotyped forms for the tourist trade. However, the larger pieces were made for a more specific market by potters employed by Cole such as Truman Cole. Royal Crown Pottery had a catalog. Jack Kiser was a potter there and made vases with unusual handles. Since Kiser was a journeyman potter, he may have made his so-called "rat tail" handles at other potteries as well. Certain of these forms were so successful that potters might take them with them as they changed venue.

Victor Obler was a silver merchant from New York and the owner of Royal Crown Pottery (1939 – 1942). He was certainly attuned to public desires in shape and form. Potters would teach each other and would discuss among themselves the complexity of turning certain forms. The Aladdin lamps of Waymon Cole are an example of a form not often accomplished by other potters. The complicated convex strap handles of A.R. Cole are another tour d'force not often matched by his contemporaries. The progression of form in the transitional pieces (1915 – 1930) mirrors the struggle of these potters in their artistic development and adaptation for survival. Turning became a more artistic endeavor after the transition to art pottery production. The clay in most instances proved of assistance but sometimes had its limitations, and innovation and creativity might assume a very practical consideration.

It is interesting that the catalogs of these potteries illustrated the forms and not the glazes since these were not published in color. Thus, the decision to purchase wares from the catalog was primarily based upon considerations of shape and form. Since the wholesale business was mainly national, this commerce based on form was essential to the livelihood of the pottery. For this most fundamental reason, form was important to both producers and customers of the wares. The variety of forms offered in these catalogs was truly extraordinary.

Importantly for the collector, these references provide the basis for a method to characterize the wares from specific potteries and potters. One can also analyze the forms in their historic and cultural context. A Han Dynasty vase turned by Ben Owen at Jugtown and a swirl teapot by Enoch Reinhardt or Auby Hilton in the Catawba Valley or a cameo vase by Walter Stephen at Pisgah Forest will reflect not only a different visual image but a different cultural inspiration as well.

Certain forms generically sold well and were collected by the public from their inception or first public introduction. Examples of this phenomenon were baskets and Rebecca pitchers. For this reason they were made by nearly every North Carolina pottery. Other forms became signature pieces for potteries and even individual potters. For example, Jugtown was the most successful with a variety of Oriental forms, and many of the monumental vases from Seagrove were made at J.B. Cole Pottery by Waymon.

A.R. Cole was one of the most innovative potters and fashioned very distinctive pieces as both Rainbow Pottery (1926 – 1941) and as A.R. Cole Pottery until his death in 1971. The handles of his bowls, vases, apothecary jars, and larger pieces were ingenuous combinations of clay and manual dexterity. The marriage of Cole's glazes and forms provides the collector with pieces that have wide appeal and are readily identifiable. His son, General Foister Cole, was known for his Roman pitchers. Joe Owen decorated many of his wares with cogglewheel designs.

Form was not exclusively the interest of the acquiring public but was also an expression of the abilities and desires of the potter. For example, Nell Cole Graves had the ability to turn wares that had thin edges and smooth, delicately curved surfaces, a property considered very desirable in smaller pieces of fancy ware. To fashion large pieces of pottery, such as a porch vase, requires the potter to lift many pounds of wet clay off the wheel and control it or to make the ware in parts by stacking. Physical strength was necessary for this.

Certain potters like J.H. Owen, Jack Kiser, A.R. Cole, Joe Owen, and Waymon Cole fashioned large wares in which the heroic appearance was the message of the piece. These will be illustrated throughout this text.

Undoubtedly there may be some objection to the analysis of art pottery, considering a single aspect as if it contributed to the aesthetic value in isolation. The artistic evaluation of this eminently collectible art form must indeed include an appreciation of color as a reflection of the glaze as well. However, emphasizing one particular aspect of any art form only enhances one's appreciation of it a whole. Form is truly the testament to the physical skills of those accomplished North Carolina potters of yesteryear and places the present work in a historical perspective. Form is a fundamental element in the identification and documentation process and establishes a foundation for the appreciation of the individual potteries and potters.

References: Nell Cole Graves, Pam and Vernon Owens, W.N. Owens

Multiple baskets by various potteries. These are very difficult to differentiate by pottery. St. James Place collection.

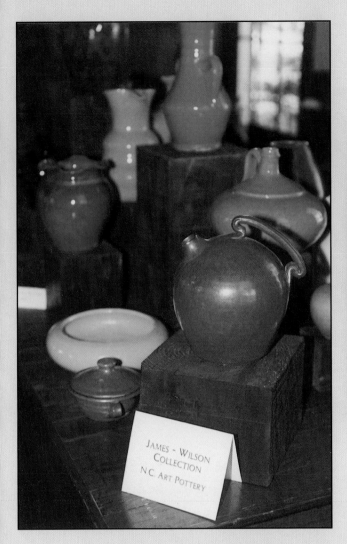

Multiple candlesticks, Seagrove area.

J.B. Cole wares. St. James Place Museum.

Multiple versions of Rebecca pitcher, Seagrove pottery area.

Detail of handle of A.R. Cole porch vase at left. Note handle's insertion at juncture of the neck and body of vessel at the precise level of incised ring.

Porch vase, 19¼" by A.R. Cole, Sanford, circa 1940s. Many of these well-turned, exquisite vases were shipped elsewhere, often to florists. The majority that have survived are in warm weather areas such as Florida. $625.00 – 750.00. Farmer/James collection.

Mouth and lip placement in relation to well-turned handle by Waymon Cole (J.B. Cole Pottery). This magnificent vase, 24" in chrome red, is rare and quite valuable. Probably valued in the thousands today if in excellent condition.

Complex and sophisticated handles, 22" vase, circa 1940. These double handles are a testament to the artistry of A.R. Cole (1892 – 1974).

Large, unglazed two-handled vase. Auman Pottery, 1924. Note the intricate handles. Shown on the cover, this vase was painted by the artist who also painted the parrot (one vase of a pair). St. James Place Museum.

Vase showing sophisticated turning and deliberate use of glaze movement. The pinched indentation at the base of split handles was often used by A.R. Cole.

Note the very sophisticated upper part of this 24" Royal Crown vase with shelved rim and rope handles. George Viall collection.

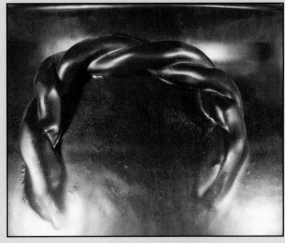

Detail of rope handle on large, bulbous porch vase made by Waymon Cole at J. B. Cole. Glaze is described as gunmetal.

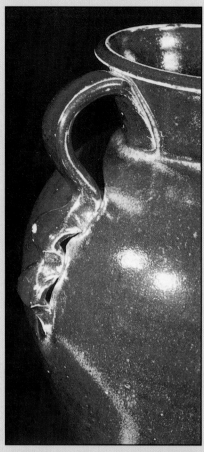

Detail handle of porch vase (Seagrove 1930s). Double grooved strap extending from rim to impressed seating along the body of the vessel. Alignment and sophistication show work of an experienced potter.

Unusual handle formation. Stamped Sunset Mountain, fashioned by J.B. Cole Pottery. George Viall collection.

Vase on pedestal with three rings, 14". J.B. Cole, made by Waymon Cole (circa 1940 – 1950s). Glaze was allegedly developed by Nell Cole Graves to be brown over white, but the white often became tan or light yellow. $350.00 – 500.00.

Two-ring handled floor vase, 22⅜". The ring handles in a loop were made by most pottery shops including J.B. Cole and C.C. Cole. This example was thought to have been made by Jack Kiser (1910 – 1985) but was in fact made by Farrell Craven at Smithfield. The contrasting cream and lime colors are particularly attractive. Provenance and sine wave decoration identify Craven as turner. $425.00 – 600.00.

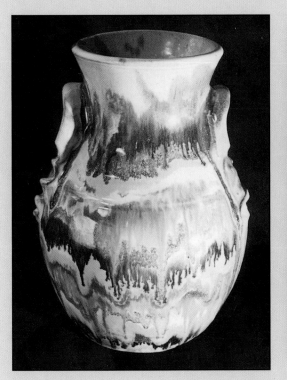

Two-handled vase, 12½" by A.R. Cole. The varie-gated glaze of brilliant colors contrasted on a white underglaze creates a dramatic visual effect. $350.00 – 450.00. Farmer/James collection.

Unusual thumb-imprinted handles. Mason stain glaze technique.

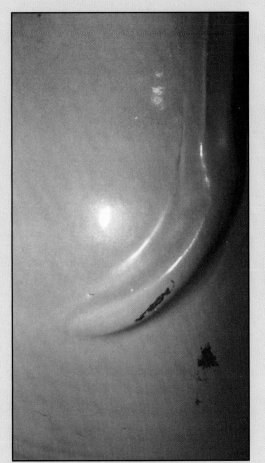

Porch vase, 27", double-handled by Waymon Cole at J.B. Cole, circa 1930s. See 1930s catalog. North Carolina Pottery Museum collection.

Curved end of handle attributed to Waymon Cole but used by a number of other potters, including Jack Kiser.

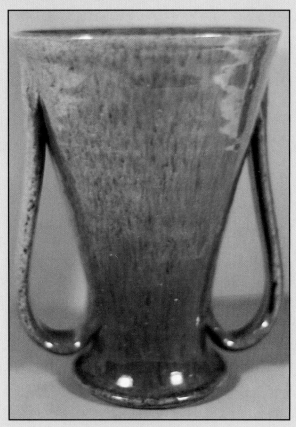

Vase, 10½", two graceful "inverted" handles. Blue glaze with rutile, attributed to J.B. Cole. $145.00 – 175.00. Farmer/James collection.

Round two-handled vase, 13", by Waymon Cole at J.B. Cole Pottery. Waymon Cole was among the most accomplished North Carolina potters. He was especially adept at turning large wares. Even though J.B. Cole was a volume operation, Waymon exercised a great deal of creativity. Note external grooves. After the death of their father, Waymon and his sister Nell took over the administration of the pottery. $195.00 – 300.00. St. James Place collection.

Two-handled vase, 12¼", by A.R. Cole, 1940s. Green glaze with rutile. $175.00 – 225.00. Farmer/James collection.

Detail of handle, note the small size with deep arch and impressed thumbprints. The utilitarian nature of these handles has been almost entirely replaced by decorative considerations.

Apothecary jars are popular and uncommon but not a rare form. This is as large as a porch vase, made by Jack Kiser at Royal Crown Pottery, probably for New York Florists Association, circa 1939. George Viall collection.

"Buzzard" vase, 16" aqua glaze by Waymon Cole at J.B. Cole, circa 1930s – 1940s. $375.00 – 500.00.

Makers of apothecary jars and Rebecca pitchers are difficult to identify as these were very popular forms and made by many potteries. This example was made in the 1930s at Rainbow Pottery by A.R. Cole. $110.00 – 175.00.

Apothecary jar made in 1930s at J.B. Cole Pottery by Waymon. This and the jar at left were unsigned but are differentiated by glaze and subtle pottery characteristics.

Two examples of handle insertion on apothecary jars. More traditional insertion on right (attributed to A.R. Cole, circa 1930s). Jar on left is by an unknown North Carolina potter but form is one used by J.B. Cole.

Water pitcher, 6¼", earthenware, double glazed, unmarked. Tan or light turquoise with deeper turquoise overglaze. Incised shoulder lines, cut-away top. Attributed to North State Pottery, early 1930s, or Auman Pottery. $125.00 – 160.00. Farmer/James collection.

Detail of refrigerator jar, below left. Slotted opening made by cutting with potter's instrument.

Two chrome red items for the icebox. Left: Refrigerator jar (sometimes referred to as medicine or elixir jar). Right: Elephant trunk (sometimes called goose neck) jar. Both forms are quite collectible.

Pitcher, 11", with glaze loss on rim. Dusty gray undersurface. Attributed to Smithfield Pottery, early example. Smithfield presents an interesting variety of patterns as many different potters worked at that site located along North/South Highway 301. $110.00 – 125.00 (spout chips).

Rebecca pitchers. Left: Joe Owen, multiglaze, coggle-wheel decoration. Right: M.L. Owens, Seagrove area.

Unglazed Rebecca pitcher by Joe Owen. Glaze would enhance the beauty of the form and dexterity of the turning. Note characteristic cogglewheel decoration.

Grecian (sometimes described as "Roman") pitcher, 13", A.R. Cole, circa 1930s, turned by eldest son General Foister Cole. $150.00 – 200.00. Farmer/James collection.

Roman (Grecian) pitcher, 16¾", A.R. Cole Pottery, turned by son Foister Cole, circa 1950s. Double groove to neck and lower belly. Thumb groove handle. $175.00 – 250.00. St. James Place Museum.

Handle insertion can be an important feature in identifying the maker.

"Drooping spout" pitcher. J.B. Cole, circa 1930s. Identified by Nell Cole Graves.

Pitcher, 10½", circa 1930s by J.B. Cole Pottery, turned by Waymon Cole (see p. 7 of J.B. Cole 1930s catalog). Note the ring indentations somewhat akin to "Futura" style. $75.00 – 115.00. St. James Place collection.

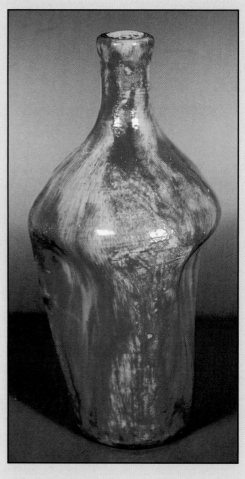

Pinch bottle with chrome red glaze, 8¾", has the appearance of J.B. Cole pottery. This shape was more a part of the art pottery phenomenon than a development of the utilitarian tradition. $115.00 – 125.00.

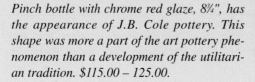

Pinch bottle, 7½", probably alkaline glaze with added crushed iron rock. Overfiring could produce this same appearance. Attributed to Brown Pottery. Wilkinson collection.

Double outlet, so-called "monkey jug" (circa 1950s, maker unknown). Due to the unique shape and use as a beverage container for several persons, this form has been repeatedly copied.

Left: Designated as Hilton pieces, dated circa 1940. Thick cobalt blue vase glazed by Auby Hilton. Almost unglazed top rim edge. Fluted opening on right pot suggests it might have been used as a vase. A "pencil holder" often has a handle.

When does a "flower vase" become a "pansy pot" or a "pencil holder?" This example of double glazed ware bears the second North State pottery stamp. Note the recessed rims of the holes. $125.00 – 175.00. St. James Place Museum.

Square 8" bowl with single handle, indistinctly stamped but appears to be characteristically the glaze and shape of North State Pottery. Attribution by W.N. Owens. $75.00 – 95.00.

Small vase with pinched center, 5¼", clear lead glaze over white or tan clay (probably Mitchfield). Early transitional piece with simple but unique lines. $110.00 – 150.00. Wilkinson collection.

Aladdin's lamp by Waymon Cole, circa 1930 – 1940. This is a difficult form to produce, and most were made by Waymon at J.B. Cole Pottery. $225.00 – 350.00. Farmer/James collection.

Tall vase, 14¾", with three pairs of incised lines. Matte light green glaze. Attributed to James Goodwin "Jim" Teague (1906 – 1988). Worked in father's shop with Rufus Owen. Turned for Fulper Pottery (New Jersey) in 1950s and 1960s, worked at Glenn Art Pottery. Also potted at home. Son Archie with wife Yvonne had a shop on Old Plank Road. Daughter Laura operates Pot Luck Pottery. $225.00 – 250.00. Bailey collection.

Accordion or multi-stepped vase, 5½". Made by Waymon Cole. Waymon, son of Jacon B. Cole, made Aladdin lamps, large porch vases, and this form as a testament to his facility as a turner. Ref. 1930s catalog J.B. Cole, p. 8 W 80. $225.00 – 275.00. Farmer/James collection.

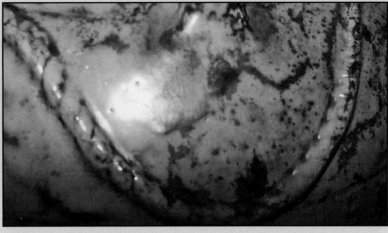

Detail: Rope decoration of a Persian jar. Jugtown, original stamp, attributed to Ben Owen, master potter. Photo of full jar is on page 219. North Carolina State University Gallery of Art and Design.

Stepped (accordion) two-handled low bowl. 12¼" w x 4" h. Flat or matte blue glaze. J.B. Cole (circa 1930s). Jacon B. Cole (1869 – 1943) had four children, Waymon (1905 – 1987), turned most of the large wares at J.B. Cole Pottery; Herman (1895 – 1982) operated Smithfield Pottery; Vellie, married Bascomb King, potter at J.B. Cole; and Nell, North Carolina's first female potter, married Philmore Graves. They both turned at J.B. Cole. $175.00 – 225.00. Farmer/James collection.

Tall bottle, A.R. Cole, 11" x 4", glazed with copper green with rutile, circa 1940s – 1950s. Fashioned into lamp. Lamp construction requiring drilling holes devalues the piece.

The struggle of the potters to adapt their efforts and change their output from utilitarian to decorative wares produced some of the most interesting, exotic, and highly collectible North Carolina art pottery that is currently both underappreciated and undervalued. The historic significance alone makes these wares valuable, but their aesthetic appeal is just as compelling. Only when these symbols of both collective and individual change are seen in their proper context can their importance be truly assessed.

As we have observed in the first two decades of the previous century, the livelihood of the traditional potter in North Carolina was severely challenged to the point that he was literally threatened with extinction. The churns, storage containers, crocks, and jugs were replaced on the one hand by paper, plastic, and glass, and on the other rendered obsolete by the mandates of Prohibition. However apparent the circumstance and the need for change might be, the response was an extremely difficult one. The potters of North Carolina were part of a tradition that spanned as many as eight or nine generations and represented a heritage lasting over two centuries. This fashioning of objects from clay did not include decorative wares. Change also was not their natural inclination, and the expression of creativity in a decorative manner was not an easy transition for them.

The potters at that time were almost exclusively males who were also farmers, practical men who through hard, physical labor provided for their families. Despite the difficulty of this backbreaking work, they managed only a marginal existence. There were few economic alternatives where they lived; one was simply to close the pottery and work in a nearby textile mill or tobacco factory or to attempt to make a living as a full-time farmer on very small acreage. Some apparently gave up and did this. Others took jobs out of the traditional pottery locations if they could find them. However, a few with the longest family tradition who were also the most enterprising, tried to determine what would be an appropriate response to the new demands of the marketplace. They sought such temporary solutions as maintaining use of the traditional forms and decorating them with incised sine waves or applied cobalt. Soon it became apparent that the product of

their labor had to be decorative and not necessarily functional if they were to have public appeal. Thus, the premise of the entire pottery endeavor changed. Certain of the accomplished utilitarian potters simply could not or would not make the changes in technique, while others modified their form only slightly and covered the piece with a nontraditional and more decorative glaze. These efforts proved insufficient, and they found a markedly reduced marketplace for their wares early in the second decade of the twentieth century (circa 1915).

Men of vision within the tradition like Jacon B. Cole and James Owen emerged as the patriarchs of the reshaped dynasties in the eastern Piedmont. The Hiltons in the 1930s and the Browns in western North Carolina achieved similar status. In the mountain region around Asheville, utilitarian potters George Donkel and Marion Penland added art wares to their repertoire, and O.L. Bachelder converted almost entirely to the production of art pottery.

However, some of the most significant innovations in product and production in the Seagrove area came from outsiders such as Jacques and Juliana (sometimes spelled Julianna) Busbee, Henry Cooper, and Victor Obler. Auman Pottery hired C.B. Masten from Indiana whose glazing techniques were very innovative. These individuals contributed significantly to the success of the Seagrove transition to decorative ware. They assisted with the application of state of the art technology in introducing the new forms and glazes and employed marketing techniques that were heretofore unprecedented in the world of the North Carolina pottery industry.

Despite the fact that some of the attempts at fancy ware were tentative, the examples produced by these exploratory endeavors are very appealing to collectors, even though they may not be elegant in comparison with other pottery traditions. Sometimes the variation of the shape of the handles on a trophy vase might provide just enough of a decorative change to impart an extra attractive feature to the piece. Some of these attempts at form and decoration were not evidently regarded as successes by the potters themselves and may represent unique examples for the collector as they were not reproduced, thus, making them quite rare. Aesthetics aside, these pieces are truly collectible as they represent documentary evidence of an extraordinary time in the history of North Carolina pottery. Holding an object from their struggle provides almost a tactile revisitation of the emotional message of this adaptation.

The traditional potters of North Carolina had previously added some decoration to even the most basic of utilitarian ware usually in the form of symbols or signs. These did not make any of these pieces or the later compromises, however, decorative wares. Some of the transitional pieces consisted of glazed interiors with unglazed exteriors, which made attractive examples especially by the Hiltons in the Catawba Valley and the Browns near Asheville. The Aumans produced wares also devoid of exterior glazing to provide the canvas for the painting of amateur artist/housewives. (Zug, Turners and Burners, UNC Press.)

As the potters became more confident with the new forms and glazes in the early to mid-1920s, double dipped (glazed) pieces and graceful shapes began to appear in the late teens and early 1920s. As time went by, the halting attempts evolved into intricate, graceful wares that retained some of the utilitarian character. The glazes that were developed responded to more flexible and sophisticated firing techniques. For example, chrome red evidenced a demonstrable color difference, depending upon the reduction firing which was somewhat under the potter's control. In the transition pieces one can see unsuccessful examples as well. Some of these unusual pieces are so unconventional they are collectible for that reason.

In the early 1920s or even a few years before, the local pottery shops in Seagrove used simply a clear lead glaze over the local clay which was naturally a light buff or slightly orange color to form the background color that might be decorated with cobalt or manganese. Early Craven, Auman, and Teague pieces demonstrate this technique.

In western North Carolina the art pottery movement was biphasic or at least had two distinct components. There was the transition engaged in by the old potting families, which was somewhat like the pattern seen in the Seagrove area. (Examples include George Donkel, Marion Penland, O.L. Bachelder, and Brown Pottery.) In the Asheville area, the work produced by Nonconnah and Pisgah Forest was decorative from their inception. This does not diminish the value of the contributions of Stephen but does emphasize that these potteries evolved in a different manner. Some believe Bachelder made the transition first; but since it was an evolutionary process, it is difficult to establish a fixed date with certainty (Leftwich).

The potters of western North Carolina and the Catawba Valley were able to sell their traditional wares at least a decade longer than their counterparts in the East. Some never made the transition. For example, the Penland family who had been very successful as traditional potters never fully changed their output to the quality production of art pottery nor did the Donkels, the Seagles, or Hartsoes. However, the few extant examples of their attempts are attractive and collectible. The Browns in the Asheville area and the Hiltons near Hickory were much more committed to the art pottery movement than their contemporaries. The Browns' primary production through the 1940s and early 1905s was jiggered dinnerware, churns, pitchers, and feeders for dogs and rabbits, but they also made art pottery.

By the end of the second decade of the twentieth century, a number of very elegant forms and glazes that were both sophisticated and beautiful were produced by a number of different potteries in North Carolina. Over the next several decades the potteries of the Tarheel State produced some of the most distinctive forms and glazes in the history of American pottery.

For a number of reasons detailed elsewhere in this text, the output of the North Carolina art potters was much more widely distributed than both the utilitarian and transitional wares. However, the earlier successes at this transition created an accepting public, already aware of the merits of North Carolina art pottery. The transitional pieces are on a relative basis: rare and somewhat underappreciated by the uninformed but pieces highly desired by astute collectors and knowledgeable dealers. They may, for this reason, be inexpensive in some circumstances, if the seller is not aware that they are historically important. They may be expensive in other circumstances; if the seller is aware that they are historically important, relatively rare, and have a unique beauty, the price will reflect that knowledge.

Collecting transitional pieces alone is probably of less merit than acquiring them as a part of a collection to place them in context. Juxtaposed or interspersed in a survey collection from traditional vintage wares to examples of the era of high style art pottery is an appropriate setting to fully appreciate the importance and aesthetic value of this desirable genre. Many of these examples will not be signed, adding to their mystique and to the challenge in acquiring them. In subsequent chapters in this text, we will comment upon and illustrate certain of these bridging manifestations of the courageous and determined North Carolina potters.

The transitional pieces are a symbol of change, which to a greater or lesser extent is a constant in all societies. At times change may be so rapid, it obscures or extinguishes the earlier cultural fabric. In this circumstance, it provided a complete new set of operating principles. These objects allow us to truly experience the transition.

Reference: Rodney Leftwich

Small Moravian jug, 6". Whether this is early Randolph County or truly "Moravian" is a difficult attribution. St. James Place Museum, gift of Clinton Lindley.

Tall vase, 19½", with extensive lug handles, unsigned transitional ware, circa 1917 – 1930. Monumental and unique example of this era. George Viall collection.

Note detail of extensive lug handles on the vase at left. Very important and unusual form. George Viall collection.

Early salt glaze vase, 20", cobalt and sine wave decoration.

Note decoration of cobalt and sine wave. J.H. Owen (1866 – 1923) opened his own shop in 1910. $475.00 – 600.00. Farmer/James collection.

Detail of rim and opening on vase above right. Note cobalt runs. J.H. Owen was an important figure during the transitional years, 1915 – 1925.

Two-handled vase, 11¾", light blue glaze. Turned by Jonah Owen at father's pottery. J.H. Owen stamped. George Viall collection.

Pitcher, 11" with clear lead glaze and decorated with applied runs of second glaze, probably manganese. Maker unknown, possibly very early Teague. George Viall collection.

Undersurface of pitcher at left, demonstrating light clay as seen with Mitchfield clay, used principally by Aumans, Cravens, and Teagues. George Viall collection.

Small jug, 5½", clear glaze, cobalt decoration, Auman Pottery, transitional example, script "August 15 1925." Courtesy Phillip Fulton.

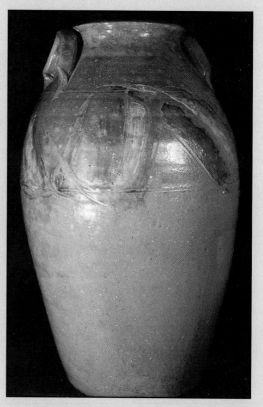

Candlesticks, 15", clear glaze, some cobalt decoration. Unusual form in excellent example of transitional pieces. Attributed to Daniel Z. Craven. Courtesy Phillip Fulton.

Two-handled urn by J.H. Owen. Owen made some of the first North Carolina art pottery. He sold wares to Jacques Busbee in the 1917 – 1923 period. Danielson collection.

Bowl, 14" with base, clear glaze over Mitchfield clay, early transition ware (1915 – early 1920s) by J.H. Owen. Danielson collection.

Early transition two-handled urn (circa 1915 – 1920s). Sine wave and glaze decoration by J.H. Owen. Owen was a pioneer in Seagrove art pottery. Danielson collection.

Two-handled vase, 6¼", with so-called "volcanic lava" glaze. Turned by Jonah Owen at J.H. Owen pottery (stamp shown at right). George Viall collection.

J.H. Owen pottery stamp.

Early cup and saucer, clear lead glaze with cobalt or manganese wash. Transitional piece, maker unknown. Probably Auman Pottery, early 1920s. $75.00 – 125.00.

Early vase, 12¾", incised rim (circa 1920 – 1925). Maker unknown, attributed to Craven Pottery. $125.00 – 150.00. St. James Place Museum.

Bottom of vase at left, Mitchfield clay with clear lead glaze.

Vase, 8", unusual form and handles. Transitional example (circa 1917 – 1925), clear lead glaze with Mitchfield clay "spots." May be early Teague, C.R. Auman or D.Z. Craven, attributed to Teague. Bailey collection.

Unusual ovoid vase, 6¾", transitional form, attributed to Auman Pottery, circa 1920. Probably cobalt wash over Mitchfield or other local clay. $325.00 – 400.00. Ex-Blount collection, Arthur Baer.

Low wide bowl, 9¾" earthenware, clear glaze over Mitch-field clay. The cobalt decoration is so extensive, it is almost a second covering glaze. True transition piece (1917 – 1925) by the C.R. Auman Pottery. Note the glazed interior of the bowl. Ray Wilkinson collection.

Cup, 6¼", clear glaze over Mitchfield clay. Transitional form (circa 1915 – 1920). Attributed to J.H. Owen. $110.00 – 125.00. St. James Place Museum collection.

Bulbous vase, 7¼" clear lead glaze over Mitchfield clay. "Speckle" from feldspathic clay. Attributed to Daniel Z. Craven. Bailey collection.

Early North Carolina art pottery pitcher, 9" (circa 1917 – 1920), double glazed with clear lead, translucent surface. Light buff body color proba-bly due to Mitchfield clay. Maker unknown. $125.00 – 175.00 (rim chips).

Same pitcher as above right, transitional piece. Note small round defects in upper glaze either due to escaping steam from clay or extension of particles in the clay. There are rim chips. Still an important example of rare early North Carolina pottery.

(Right) Early decorative wares with clear glaze over Mitchfield clay. The warm tonalities are created by the firing of the blue/gray Mitchfield clay, that turns buff or white. When covered with clear lead glaze, such an object is strongly representative of the highly collectible transitional pottery of Piedmont.

(Far right) Vase, 11¼", with fluted rim. The firing has created muted differences in glaze color from the upper body and more bulbous lower portion (late transitional piece, North State, second stamp). $275.00 – 325.00. Arthur Baer, ex-Blount collection.

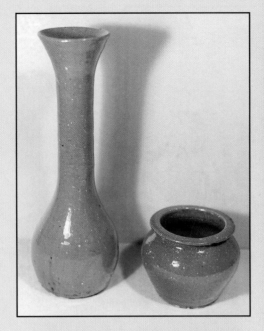

(Right) Vase, 9½", green glaze, probably cobalt wash, incised lines, unsigned, maker unknown, circa 1920s. Transition piece, probably J.H. Owen. Edwards collection.

(Far right) Vase, three-handled, double glazed, first stamp, North State Pottery, circa 1925. Courtesy Phillip Fulton.

Small cup and saucer, transitional ware, Seagrove area, circa 1915 – 1920, probably C.R. Auman pottery or J.H. Owen. $90.00 – 115.00. St. James Place Museum collection.

Identification Of North Carolina Pottery:
An Inexact Science

The potters of North Carolina from the mid-1700s to the present day have produced hundreds of thousands of wares from simple, utilitarian crocks and churns to exquisitely glazed, intricate, decorative turning patterns. Much of the production was not stamped or signed in the conventional sense. However, it may be identifiably "signed" by its composite appearance if one is aware of the components of this signature.

The form, glaze or details of the turning provide a signature analogous to the brushstroke pattern of a painter or the carving technique of a decoy carver. For example, a collector once asked Ned Burgess, the famed North Carolina waterfowl decoy carver, if he signed his decoys. Burgess simply said, "I signed every one I ever made," meaning, that he felt the Burgess style speaks for itself, and experts agree. Pottery collectors and experts can read without the letters. Style and form, however, can be simulated as we know from current revelations regarding the downgrading of paintings previously ascribed to Rembrandt. Thus, attributions are sometimes difficult, but we trust this chapter will be helpful in that regard.

As noted, with the introduction of refrigeration, glass containers, plastic cartons, improved methods of transportation, and Prohibition, the demand for utilitarian North Carolina pottery declined in the first several decades of the twentieth century. Many potters and cottage industry potteries went out of business while others began to produce fancy ware which later came to be known as art pottery. Through adoption of Oriental and European forms and decorative glazes, markets for North Carolina art pottery were created. Certain shops had a number of potters working together, and some division of labor was achieved. Artware pottery from these cottage (often family owned) shops was shipped throughout the country by truck and rail. Florists in Richmond and Miami received vases, Marshall Field and Co. in Chicago sold North Carolina pottery, North State had a salesroom in Washington, and Jugtown had an outlet in Greenwich Village. Pisgah Forest sold lamps to a New York department store and vases to Yellowstone Park. C.C. Cole supplied the tourist resorts in Virginia and A.R. Cole in the mountains of North Carolina.

J.B. Cole had the largest, most multifaceted operation with an extensive catalog (1930s), offering pieces of almost every conceivable shape, size, color, and type. Because of the volume of production, specific arrangements with purchasers or the fact that attribution simply did not matter, most pieces were not signed or stamped until recent times, but there are exceptions. Pisgah Forest Pottery signed and dated almost all wares, and most Jugtown wares are signed but until recently were not dated. Given all these circumstances, the identification of North Carolina art pottery is still an interesting and challenging endeavor.

One might logically assume that if you have a stamped piece you can date it — but this is not always the case. For example, North State had at least three stamps, and A.R. Cole changed the name of his business from Rainbow Pottery to A.R. Cole. The Rainbow rubber stamp was ink applied so it could be washed or rubbed off. The incised "A.R. Cole" had at least five versions. Glenn Art made it especially difficult for future collectors with a paper label often affixed to the pieces in such a position that prompted immediate removal.

Some potters felt their product alone was what was important, that the object spoke for itself, and identification of the maker was neither desirable nor necessary. Charlie Owen, for example, signed very few pieces in his lifetime. At Seagrove Pottery, his employer Walter Auman did it for him. Conversely, the Cole sisters, daughters of A.R., not only sign their wares but write short messages on the bottoms. This is time-consuming and in the 1920s, 1930s, and 1940s, the potters had little time or money for this extra work.

Sometimes stamps were used, but they also might introduce uncertainty. There is the great Jugtown saga when the stamp in use in the 1960s was lost, so another was made from the mark on a finished piece. In the firing process there is a significant reduction in size of the wares (10 – 12%), and the stamp was also commensurately smaller and could be completely obscured by a quarter. This size disparity allowed dating of the Jugtown pieces for a period of time, but over a decade later the original stamp was found and put back into use. This created havoc with the dating process because Jugtown continued to use its traditional forms and glazes.

However, as soon as Vernon Owens, the owner and master potter, learned of the dilemma caused by the two stamps, he began to stamp and date the pieces as well as stamp them. Now the challenge is to differentiate a salt glazed piece by the late Ben Owen, master potter at Jugtown from 1921 to 1959, from a Vernon Owens traditional piece, circa 1960s. Ben's comparable pieces are heavier than Vernon's with the weight more evenly distributed in Vernon's, but we suspect there are those experts who believe they can tell by the patina, which with salt glaze, is sometimes a non sequitur. There is a definite patina of an early Jugtown piece as well as the wares of the Aumans and Cravens, but patina connotes age, not pottery identification.

One would hope that the clay would allow you to identify a piece of North Carolina pottery as opposed to that made in Virginia, Georgia, Kentucky or Pennsylvania. Certainly the most common appearance is that characteristic of the red/orange clay in the region south of Asheboro and Sanford. This would not be the expected appearance of the Catawba Valley wares or those made in the Asheville area. In fact, many Seagrove area potters used an almost white (Mitchfield) or white (Candor) clay when it was available. Thus, when you examine the undersurface for the identifying stamp or signature and find none, do not have preconceived notions about the clay. In fact, the color of the clay may be obscured by shellac applied to the bottom to seal it, soot from coal firing, or the glaze which has been allowed to run over the surface. J.B. Cole's shop often ran the glaze over the bottom and used a belt sander to remove it. Sometimes the sander may have missed the mark. The belt sander effect will be seen as continuous removal of glaze across the entire bottom of the piece, forming a smooth rim, whereas hand sanding will not be as uniform side to side.

Molten glaze on the base of pottery could cause pots to stick to the kiln shelf during firing. To keep the pottery from resting in a glaze puddle, several potteries employed stilts or ceramic tripods. When removed after the firing, the stilts left a distinctive, three-point mark on the bottom. This is most commonly seen from the J.B. Cole Pottery and if there are concomitant patterns from the belt sander, then these two correlative observations are compelling reasons for attribution. Early J.B. Cole pieces will not have these marks because stilts were not used and they had not yet acquired a belt sander, but they had an extensive catalog demonstrating their wares and several unique glazes which aid in their identification. Pisgah Forest Pottery did not use stilts, choosing instead to use small clay balls or pills to keep glazed ware from sticking to the kiln shelf (Leftwich).

A collector can quickly identify the turquoise blue and aubergine wine crackle glazes of Pisgah Forest. Frequently the blue was used on the shoulder above the wine, a distinctive combination for this pottery. Likewise, Pisgah's crystalline glazes with frost or starlike crystals make attribution to this pottery probable.

The use of glaze appearance for identification is a bit like "I can't describe it, but I know it when I see it." Obviously this is not very helpful, but there are certain generalizations that may help. When A.R. Cole made wares in his Rainbow Pottery (1926 – 1941), the color of his glazes were mellow, duplicating hues and shades of the rainbow. The Jugtown orange and "tobacco spit" glazes are also unique. Their orange has a clear, homogenous dark hue that truthfully evokes the colors of an orange. Their frogskin looks more like the epidermis of an amphibian than the attempts by any other pottery. It is difficult to articulate the subtle difference. The most famous glaze of Jugtown is Chinese blue which is the product of reduction firing resulting in an exotic Oriental pattern developed by Jacques Busbee.

No pottery achieved more dramatic results with multiple glazes than did C.C. Cole. There were the small jugs that were shipped to tourist areas in multi-thousand lots. However, large vases with intricate shapes and handles by other potters have a very distinct appearance. Some collectors find them beautiful while others see them as gaudy. A.R. Cole and Joe Owen used these multicolored glazes as well but never to the same extent as C.C. Cole.

One must use an assessment of shape, form, glaze, and clay to make a reasonable attribution to a particular pottery. Additionally, the provenance of a work, if known and documented, adds significant circumstantial evidence to the identification. For example, a 90-year-old collector told me of purchasing a large unglazed Seagrove vase in the early 1920s which she painted herself. The vase must have been by Auman Pottery as they were the operative potting establishment there during that time. To corroborate this, the vase with rather important handles conformed to one of their documented styles. Thus, time and place along with appearance can contribute to a very strong attribution.

This leads to another point in identification, the reference texts. Probably the most helpful would be copies of each pottery's catalogs. This is probably the best method for dating works. Also, the best method for identifying the actual potter is with an advertising catalog. They show a wide spectrum of wares, but all are out of print and copies are rare. Your best source will be a fellow collector or historian. Useful and informative are the exhibition catalogs from museums and auction catalogs by the Southern Folk Collectors Society, Harmer Rook, Leland Little, and Brunk Auctions. I would also recommend the texts *Turners and Burners* by Charles Zug and *The Traditional Potters of Seagrove* by Robert Lock.

Another great resource is the progeny of the potters, especially those working in the same potteries today. As with any acquisition endeavor, knowledge makes the collector more successful, but even more important, it enhances the pleasure of the process.

From the early decades of the twentieth century until recently, much of the North Carolina art pottery was unstamped and unsigned, and these wares were shipped and transported throughout the United States. Thus, the challenge of identification and acquisition may be of materials, style, decoration, and geography as well. I will discuss the stamps and other identifying features under specific considerations of a pottery or an individual potter later in this book. As with any type of analytical diagnostic process, the more one knows, the more fortunate one becomes in the accuracy of their decisions.

References: Arthur Baer, Mick Bailey, Steve Compton, Rodney Leftwich, M.L. Owens, Joe Wilkinson

Vase/urn, 14", salt glazed, decorated with sine wave incision and cobalt. Unusual footed form by James H. Owen (sometimes Owens), circa late 1910s or early 1920s. James Owen (1866 – 1923) apprenticed under Paschal Marable, established his own shop in 1910, and worked at Jugtown from 1918 – 1923. M.L. Owens Museum.

Alkaline glazed stoneware jar by George Donkel near Weaverville. Stamp impressed key, 12", crushed glass alkaline glaze. $375.00 – 525.00. St. James Place Museum collection.

The impressed key, signature of George Donkel, first quarter of the twentieth century. Asheville area, Zug collection. Farmer/James gift, Chapel Hill Museum.

J.D. "Dorris" Craven two-handled stoneware lidded butter churn. Craven (1827 – 1895) operated a large shop and employed several potters, but wares were stamped J.D. Craven. His son Daniel Z. made art pottery.

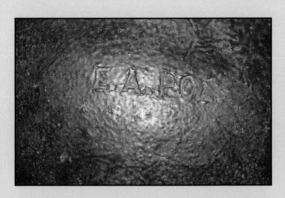

E.A. Poe stamp. Poe (1858 – 1934) owned a shop in Fayetteville, in Cumberland County. Also used stamp "Poe and Co."

Stamp of John R. Chrisco (1861 – 1916), "J.R. Crisco" (note missing h). Storage jar, salt glaze, circa 1880 – 1890s. *Farmer/James collection.*

Detail of strap handle of the J.D. Craven pottery school. Note thinness of the handle itself and simple insertion without significant thumb indentation. Craven was the most prolific of the Piedmont potters. Will Henry Hancock (who made this jug), William Henry Luck, and W.H. Crisco potted at Craven Pottery.

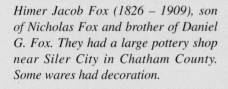

Himer Jacob Fox (1826 – 1909), son of Nicholas Fox and brother of Daniel G. Fox. They had a large pottery shop near Siler City in Chatham County. Some wares had decoration.

Jug by William Henry Hancock, 1845 – 1924. Apprenticed under J.D. Craven. Also worked for E.A. Poe Pottery in Fayetteville, circa 1890. Also used cogglewheel decoration.

Masonic emblem. Many of the potters were members of the all-male Masonic lodges and made this sign of square and compass, the symbol of Masonry, part of their signature. Himer Fox characteristically did this. It is extremely rare on art pottery.

Detail of Hancock jug with cogglewheel decoration. The graceful strap handle of the "Craven style" was adopted to some extent into the art pottery area, especially by these potters attempting to make the transition from utilitarian to decorative pottery.

Salt glaze jug stamped J.D. (Jacob Dorris) Craven. Most prolific of Seagrove utilitarian pottery shops. Impressed reed at the handle base. Stamped, cogglewheel design "2." The reed impression is thought to identify J.D. Craven as the specific potter.

James M. Hays stamp, near New Salem community, northern Randolph County. Hays (1832 – 1922) made salt glazed stoneware, sometimes using two sizes of band sets. Full jar photo is on facing page.

Stamp, W.T. Macon, Erect, NC., on jug below left. Macon was active in the late nineteenth century in Randolph County making salt glazed stoneware.

Signed jug by W.T. Macon, Randolph County, last quarter of the nineteenth century. Note wide strap handle. $450.00 – 600.00. Farmer/James collection.

Wide storage jar, 12", salt glaze by J.M. Hays. Salt glaze made its way to North Carolina as early as the 1770s. It worked well with the "tight bodied" clay found in Randolph, Chatham, Alamance, Moore, and Montgomery counties. $425.00 – 500.00 pristine; (rim defect $175.00 – 225.00).

Detail of Propst (S.A. Propst, 1882 – 1935) handle, incised bands, pottery located at Vale.

McGruder Bishop, Ronda. Bishop, circa 1925, worked in several shops as a journeyman potter. In the 1930s he operated his own shop in Ronda and later worked at the O'Henry pottery in Valdese. Very rare stamp.

Stamp, W.H. Hancock (1845 – 1924). William Henry Hancock, wonderful triangle decoration. Turning looks like Craven form which would be expected.

Stamp of James Broome (1869 – 1957). Alton Community, Union County. "Jug Jim" was the son of Nimrod Broome. St. James Place Museum.

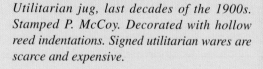

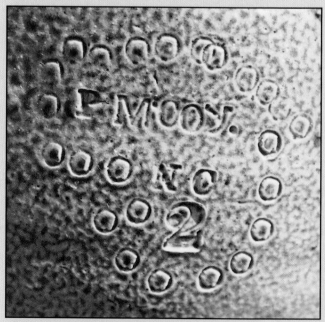

Utilitarian jug, last decades of the 1900s. Stamped P. McCoy. Decorated with hollow reed indentations. Signed utilitarian wares are scarce and expensive.

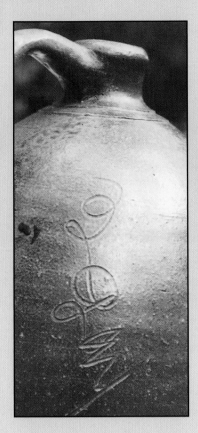

Three-gallon jug, Isaac Gay, Union County. Script signature, rare. St. James Place Museum collection.

Two-handled large churn, 26", stamped three times. Auman Pottery (round stamp Seagrove, NC), 1919 – 1936. Charlie and Ray Auman seldom stamped their wares.

Auman Pottery, Seagrove. Early stamp on large storage crock, salt glaze. Auman stamp is rare.

Vase, 10¾", Albany slip with heavy fly ash deposit from placement near firebox of kiln. Penland Pottery, Buncombe County. Stamp Penland Pottery. Stamp was used between 1910 – 1945, William Penland (1868 – 1945) and son Cash Penland were potters there. $325.00 – 375.00.

W.H. Hancock, two-gallon jug. Note J.D. Craven form and handle.

Detail of handle on Outen jug, stamp on bottom shown below left. The handle is thick and round with insertion at shoulder of jug.

Small one-handled jug, 4½", Outen Pottery. Examples of Outen Pottery are rare (see Zug, Turners and Burners). St. James Place Museum, Baynes gift.

Brown Pottery stamp on crock below.

R.F. (Rufus Frank) Outen, Matthews, active 1900 – 1930 in Mecklenberg County. Son of W.F. Outen and brother of Gordon Outen, both potters. Farmer/James collection.

Crock, Albany slip glaze, Brown Pottery.

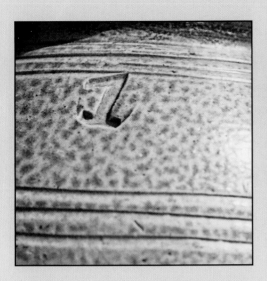

Unsigned storage jar, salt glaze. Note the incision rings and gallonage indication. Attributed to Paschal McCoy.

John Wesley Hilton Pottery stamp, rare. Danielson collection.

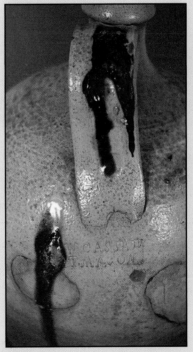

Pitcher, E.A. Hilton (1878 – 1948), Catawba Valley.

Randolph County, salt glazed stoneware jug, late nineteenth/early twentieth century. Note well-formed neck and handle. Drips on handle and body are from kiln bricks. Turned by W.T. Macon; stamp, Macon and Cassady; commercial contract. Cassady was not a potter. $450.00 – 500.00. Farmer/James collection.

Detail of handle and stamp on Cassady/Macon jug at left.

Initials "SLH" on top of lug handle. Sylvanus Leander Hartzog (or Hartsoe) was the most prolific of the traditional Catawba Valley potters. Hartzog often signed his wares. St. James Place Museum collection.

Two-handled storage vessel with incised ring decoration. Catawba Valley, alkaline glaze. In the early nineteenth century a green to brown glaze evolved that had a lustrous coating — this came to be known as an "alkaline" glaze. Alkaline refers to the flux which lowers the melting point. In the Catawba Valley the potters used lime or wood ashes to impart the surface "sheen" (or "shine"). They might also use quartz, feldspar, iron, cinders or glass which were ground to a uniform consistency in a stone mill. Farmer/James collection.

Two-handled large orifice vase, 7½", by J.B. Cole. Of the very few stamped pieces by this famous pottery, most are rather undistinguished forms. This example is an exception. $325.00 – 450.00. Farmer/James collection.

J.B. Cole stamp on vase at left.

White ovoid vase, 7½", by Nell Cole Graves. Very few wares were signed by Nell. This etching of her signature was, according to legend, at the insistence of Dot Auman, historian and potter at Seagrove Pottery.

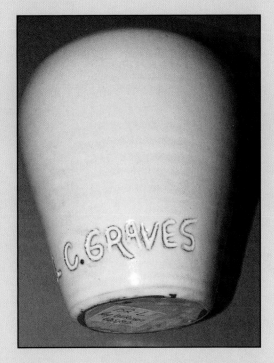

Detail of Nell C. Graves signature. Nell, daughter of Jacon B. Cole and wife of Philmore Graves, was North Carolina's first recognized woman potter and at her death, the oldest potter in the state. She was the winner of the North Carolina Heritage Award.

Signature mark of Virginia Shelton (1923 – 1991), daughter of Vellie Cole and Bascomb King. Potted at J.B. Cole Pottery until her death in 1991. Her works resemble those of Nell Cole Graves.

Two-handled wide mouth vase, J.B. Cole, circa 1930, stamped "Marion, Va." One would assume this was a contractual arrangement of which J.B. Cole had many. $175.00 – 225.00. Farmer/James collection.

Marion, Virginia stamp, rare, J.B. Cole ware.

Stamp of Sunset Mountain Pottery, from J.B. Cole Pottery. Sunset Mountain was located outside Asheville. J.B. Cole Pottery would turn wares and place your stamp on them in a contractual relationship.

Bowl with fancy handles, dark green glaze, stamped "Carolina Craft Hand Made". This is a rare stamp (pictured on page 170) on a desirable form. $175.00 – 210.00. Farmer/James collection.

Bottom of fancy handled bowl above, showing stamp "Carolina Craft Hand Made." This Cole stamp was used for a short period of time. Farmer/James collection.

Sunset Mountain stamp. One of the best known of the contractual arrangements with J.B. Cole Pottery. Sunset Mountain overlooks Asheville.

"Original" Jugtown label. For period 1923 – 1959, all pieces were stamped. From 1960 – 1977, most wares were stamped before Vernon Owens instituted dating by year as well.

Jugtown stamp on Chinese blue small ovoid vase, circa 1930s.

Undersurface of Pisgah Forest ware showing potter at wheel. No date, meaning 1920s.

Jugtown, first stamp (circa 1930 – 1940).

Jugtown stamp, first or original stamp.

Rainbow Pottery ink stamp of A.R. Cole, 1926 – 1941. There are many variations of A.R. Cole signatures, and at least five incised stamps are known.

Rare stamp, Rainbow Pottery, Sanford. A.R. Cole.

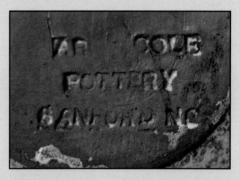

A.R. Cole, incised stamp, circa 1940s.

Small stamp of A.R. Cole, Sanford. Often used on small pieces.

A.R. Cole Pottery stamp.

Stamped two-handled vase of A.R. Cole. Stamped in ink, "Toxaway Falls". Lake Toxaway was a well-known tourist resort which flourished in the first half of the twentieth century. It was depicted by the artist WCA Frerichs in the 1850s.

Cup, Ben Owen, master potter. The low profile and warm brown/ochre glaze demonstrate technique and glazes used by Owen at Jugtown.

Underside of Ben Owen cup with stamp, "Ben Owen Master Potter." 1960s – early 1970s.

Vase, 8½", stamped Brown Pottery, Arden. Well-glazed earthenware, vase of common shape. $90.00 – 110.00. Ray Wilkinson collection.

Daniel Seagle stamp.

Seagrove Pottery (attributed to Dot Auman). Farmer/James collection, Chapel Hill Museum.

Stamp, Craven Pottery, Steeds.

Open vase, 11¼", Brown Pottery, EB initial etched. Decorative brown glaze.

Brown Pottery stamp on vase at left.

Royal Crown Pottery stamp (1939 – 1942). Part of their title was "and Porcelain Company." They never made porcelain, but some of their wares appear more highly vitrified than most from the Seagrove area.

Joe Owen stamp.

Owens signature, attributed to M.L. Owens. In the late 1940s M.L. Owens Pottery was listed at Steeds, but at Seagrove from 1952 forward. Daughter Nancy Owens Brewer also signs her work.

Label of Glenn Art Pottery on basket at right, paper coated with foil. Usually placed in full view, inviting removal.

Glenn Art basket, by Joe Owen, circa 1948 – 1952. Notice the paper and foil label. $175.00 – 250.00.

C.C. Cole Pottery stamp. Infrequently used stamp, 1940s – 1950.

Log Cabin Pottery. Jack and Bessie Hunter opened this pottery in 1922 – 1923, hiring several local potters from the traditional pottery families such as Clarence Cole, Jonah Owen, and Cecil Auman. They had the operation on Market Street, now an antique district in Greensboro. The production is rare and uneven in its quality. It only lasted from the early 1920s until 1932.

Teague signature. Although Teague Pottery dated from the 1930s, the signatures by B.D.'s daughter, Zedith, and her husband Hobart appear in the late 1960s or after. B.D. opened the shop in the 1960s. This appears to be Zedith Teague's signature.

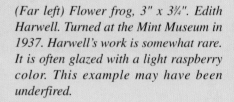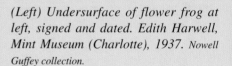

Teague signature. There are both signatures and pottery stamps. This was probably in the 1970s when the hazards of lead glazes became apparent.

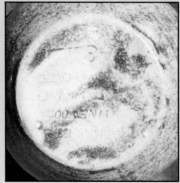

(Far left) Flower frog, 3" x 3¾". Edith Harwell. Turned at the Mint Museum in 1937. Harwell's work is somewhat rare. It is often glazed with a light raspberry color. This example may have been underfired.

(Left) Undersurface of flower frog at left, signed and dated. Edith Harwell, Mint Museum (Charlotte), 1937. Nowell Guffey collection.

Hilton by contract made pottery for a business in the resort town of Tryon. It was signed Melmar but made in the distinctive style and decoration of Hilton Pottery in Hickory.

To identify Hilton pottery, certain features must be shown as wares may not be stamped Hilton Pottery Company or signed F.W. Hilton, E.W. Hilton, or F and W Hilton. Someone signed this piece in script. *Guffey collection.*

Brown's Pottery, handmade, Arden.

Penland Pottery stamp, circa 1925. Cash Penland, William Marion Penland, and son operated a pottery in Buncombe County near Candler.

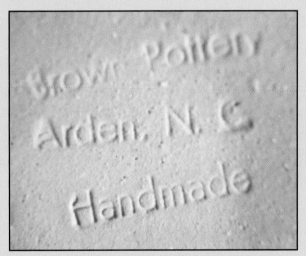

Stamp, Brown Pottery, Arden.

O'Henry Pottery, Valdese. *Farmer/James collection. Chapel Hill Museum.*

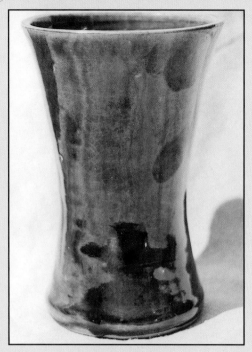

Small vase or wall pocket, uncommon form made by Brown Pottery, Arden, 5¾". $60.00 – 75.00.

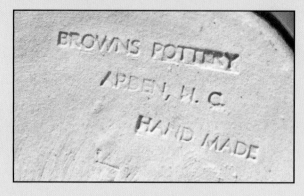

Stamp, Browns Pottery, Arden. Dates from the late 1950s. Father Davis Brown operated Davis Pottery. Sons Robert and Charlie operated it after the father retired in 1977.

Penland Pottery Shop. Asheville area. St. James Place Museum

Vase with two handles, 22½", made by Joe Owen. Joe, born in 1910, learned to turn from his father Rufus. Joe managed Glenn Art Pottery 1948 – 1968. The vase body has a shapely tapering, and the handles demonstrate his mastery in clay. $300.00 – 450.00.

Stamp, Joe Owen. Owen used several identification methods including a foil label at Glenn Art Pottery (1948 – 1952), a script stamp in the 1970s and 1980s, and a script signature.

Carolina Pottery label (stamp). The site and owner-ship of this pottery changed several times. As a small roadside pottery near Highway 220 by Joe Steed, most of the pottery was made by Wren Cole.

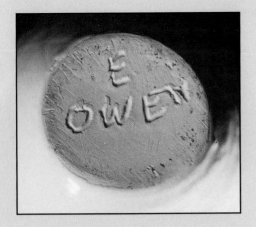

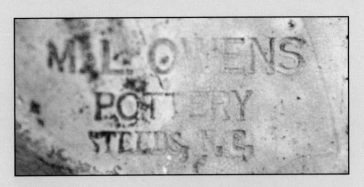

Elvin Owen's inscription. The youngest of J.H. Owen's sons, he turned at times for his father and brother M.L. Owens was also in the carpet business. Courtesy M.L. Owens.

M.L. Owens pottery. This stamp dates from the 1940s. M.L. (1917 –) took over his father's shop in the late 1930s. Owens Pottery is the Seagrove area shop that has been longest in continued operation.

North State (third stamp) used from the late 1930s until 1959 when W.N. Owen changed it to Pine State in accordance with the Palmers' testamentary request.

Two-handled vase, 9″, with buff underglaze and applied chrome red above. Excellent results from chrome red. Turned by Jonah Owen while working at North State Pottery (second stamp). George Viall collection.

Undersurface of Jonah Owen vase above right. North State Pottery (second stamp).

Undersurface of scalloped top vase at left with partial Goose Creek label. Rare label, among the many contractual relations of this famous pottery.

Blue lead glazed scalloped top vase. Earthenware, circa 1930s – 1940s, J.B. Cole for Goose Creek Resort in South Carolina. Turned by Philmore Graves. Deep upper glaze creates almost double glaze appearance. $135.00 – 165.00.

Bottom of Farrell Craven vase turned at Smithfield Pottery on Highway 301. The dusky gray of the bottom may have been due to the coal-fired kiln at Smithfield. This large operation had more than one kiln and hired a number of potters.

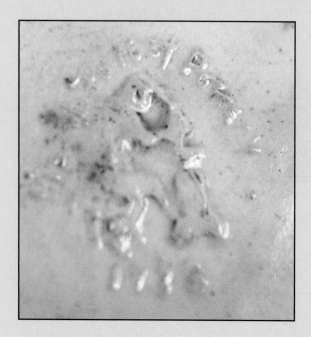

Pisgah Forest Stamp, potter at wheel.

Script signature of Louise Bigmeat Maney.

Brown Pottery, Arden. The "handmade" and the address "Arden, N.C." appear to have been made with separate stamps. St. James Place Museum collection.

Three-handled vase, 7¾" with lead clear glaze and decorated with manganese to produce vertical black/green runs. Unsigned. Clay and glaze suggest 1920s, but form usually is seen in later wares.

Light colored clay on three-handled vase at left. Attributed to C.R. Auman or Daniel Z. Craven. George Viall collection.

Detail of decoration on rim of early (1917 – 1920) Craven vase. Almost all wares produced at the shop have a warm orange hue, a product of the kiln's slight overheating and the clay recipe. (M.L. Owens)

Blue rim ware, Hilton Pottery. Decorated by Maude Hilton. Local clay, clear glass glaze, cobalt decoration. Danielson collection.

Early vase by C.R. Auman Pottery, circa 1920 – 1925. Buff color is due to clear lead glaze over clay from the Auman clay pit. Decorated with cobalt. $275.00 – 350.00. Farmer/James collection.

Rim of early art pottery vase, Auman Pottery, early 1920s. Note handles on Chinese or Oriental-inspired "hanging vase." These handles are susceptible to breaks because these were often fired at a lower temperature than the usual 2200 – 2400° F.

Tobacco Road wares, turned by Charlie Craven. Decorated by Ernestine Hilton Sigmon. Danielson collection.

Examples of Hilton wares with applied lines. Often alternated different glazes. Danielson collection.

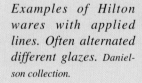

Figurines by Maude Hilton, probably made at Pleasant Garden Shop. Rare. Danielson collection.

Hilton "Catawba Indian Pottery," circa 1920s. These wares show particular attention to turning, and form is usually very good. Danielson collection.

Joe Owen floor vase, 20", multiglazed. Note characteristic cogglewheel decoration.

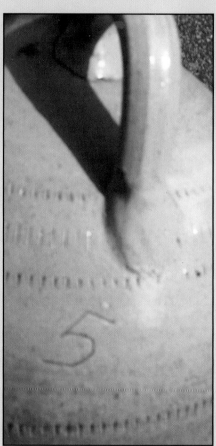

(Right) Two-handled jug (5 gallons) by Charles Craven. Craven had a long career as a potter and after a hiatus of several decades began turning traditional forms again in the 1970s. Note script gallonage and cogglewheel decoration. $275.00 – 450.00.

(Far right) Detail of handle of 5-gallon jug. Craven (1909 – 1990) was the son of Daniel Craven (1873 – 1949) and brother of Farrell, Grady, and Braxton, all potters.

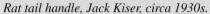

Rat tail handle, Jack Kiser, circa 1930s.

Pansy pot, burgundy glaze, 3¾", by Edith N. Harwell (1904 – 1988). This was made in the 1930s while she was at the Mint Museum Shop. $145.00 – 175.00.

Small pitcher with exquisite potting of rim and spout. This type of turning could be expected of wares made by Nell Cole Graves. Although she never made the heroic porch vases or other large wares, the delicate products of her artistry are very collectible as are Maude Hilton's painted wares. $110.00 – 125.00.

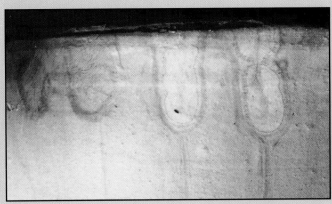

Fingerprints in glaze. After ware was dipped, potter did not smooth the glaze where he grasped the "pot" and after firing, the imprint remained. Farmer/James gift, Chapel Hill Museum.

Note thinning of the glaze at lip of bowl turned at Royal Crown Pottery, circa 1940. This may reflect the heating and vitrification process or glaze properties, but such thinning is frequently seen with Royal Crown wares.

Large strap center handle on low bowl, 14¾". Unsigned, bowls of this type were made in the 1930s and 1940s by A.R. Cole (Rainbow), J.B. Cole (note prominent turning grooves), and Duck Teague. $250.00 – 275.00. Farmer/James collection.

Low pot, glazed on the inside, partially glazed outside. Maker unknown, darker clay. More likely Catawba Valley than Seagrove transitional example. Howard Smith collection.

(Right) Porch vase, 14¼", gun-metal glaze with unusual handles, unsigned, maker unknown, but clay and form are consistent with Seagrove but is probably European.

(Far right) Handle view of previous pot. Sold as North Carolina pottery but is probably European. Note "3" at base.

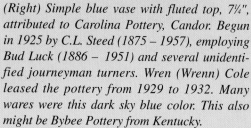

(Right) Simple blue vase with fluted top, 7¼", attributed to Carolina Pottery, Candor. Begun in 1925 by C.L. Steed (1875 – 1957), employing Bud Luck (1886 – 1951) and several unidentified journeyman turners. Wren (Wrenn) Cole leased the pottery from 1929 to 1932. Many wares were this dark sky blue color. This also might be Bybee Pottery from Kentucky.

Large, one-handled storage vessel. Cobalt stripe used by Hilton but gallon marker is unusual, possibly from Georgia pottery.

The Rare and Unusual in
North Carolina Art Pottery

The virtues of North Carolina art pottery are becoming increasingly appreciated through texts, catalogs, and exhibitions. Exhibitions and accompanying catalogs have provided the exposure for this particular genre while several reference texts have created a body of data suitable for independent scholarship by the individual collector. Dealers and auction houses have also disseminated this information.

North Carolina pottery as emphasized before is the symbol of a tradition that can trace its lineage seven or eight generations. These same families have been engaged in this activity beginning with the fashioning of utilitarian wares and participated in the transition to art pottery early in the twentieth century. These family potteries later engaged in such volume production to make many of these wares, in general, rather commonplace. The circumstance creates a ready availability of examples for the novice collector as well as the idea held by the general public that North Carolina art pottery is rather undistinguished.

Much that was produced was made in volume to appeal to rather pedestrian tastes, but a significant number of pieces reflect the potential artistry and imagination of these extraordinary potters.

Certain examples of North Carolina art pottery were clearly made to demonstrate the facility of their maker, and commercial considerations were secondary. They reflect the independent spirit and originality that allowed the traditional potters to adapt to consumer demands in the late teens and to endure the financial and physical hardships of the Great Depression. Unusual forms such as the "buzzard" vase and its variations demonstrate the potting abilities of families such as the Coles, both Waymon and A.R., representing two different potteries.

Multihandled vases were made in limited editions as were intricately stepped low bowls and wide mouth vases. These objects represent the very best of North Carolina art pottery and reflect the turning ability of these virtuoso potters.

Another area that reflects the skill and creativity in North Carolina art pottery is the glazes. Many owners of the potteries as well as the potters made contributions themselves. The most well-known glaze was Chinese blue developed by the founder of Jugtown Pottery, Jacques Busbee. Henry Cooper of North State used double dip methods extensively and worked with the chemists at North Carolina State University. The Aumans invited C.B. Masten, a ceramics engineer from the University of Indiana, to come and experiment with his glazing techniques using local clay (Mitchfield from the Auman clay pit). He produced some interesting and unique wares. These are rare and highly collectible. Legend has it that Masten worked in isolation and his methods were tightly held secrets.

Despite the fact that many potteries identified their wares, several of the famous did not. Thus, stamped pieces by J.B. Cole are very rare as are those made at the C.C. Cole Pottery. A.R. Cole founded Rainbow Pottery in 1926 and used an ink stamp to identify his wares. Many of these markings did not survive, making the identifiable stamps very desirable. The Glenn Art pottery used a paper label, making those identifiable pieces very rare.

The large planters and porch vases are elegant and impressive examples of North Carolina art pottery. Few have survived due to breakage, and this number represents a highly desirable group of wares. Some, because of their size, allowed the potter/glazer to exercise his abilities to the fullest.

Singular examples of North Carolina art pottery may be so designated by considerations of their shape and form, the glaze pattern, or uniqueness and rarity. As further scholarship is applied to this genre, rare collectible examples will be increasingly identified. Their value will increase as collectors become sufficiently informed to have a specific desire to acquire an example.

*Goose or elephant neck pitcher, solid agate, 7¾",
attributed to M.L. Owens, 1940. Unusual form
and glaze by the Dean of Seagrove potters.
Wilkinson collection (1994). $225.00 – 275.00.*
Farmer/James collection.

*Salt glaze, simple vase by North State Pottery, circa 1927 –
1929. North State evolved from the interest of Rebecca Palmer
Cooper who employed Jonah Owen (1924). Husband Henry, an
R.J. Reynolds employee, became expert in glazes. In 1926 North
State was incorporated and existed until 1959. The early salt
glaze wares are rare and quite collectible. $425.00 – 475.00.*

*Rebecca pitcher, 14¼", with multiglaze, stamped M.L.
Owens. This is a very unusual glaze for M.L. Owens whose
pottery has now been in the longest continued existence in
Seagrove. The thickness and skip areas suggest this was
overglazed. $225.00 – 300.00.*

Vase, double dipped glaze, 12", attributed to Joe Owen, 1950. Unusual colors. Wilkinson collection (1994). $275.00 – 300.00. Farmer/James collection.

Vase, 12" h, with decorative ring handles, cogglewheel decoration, and unusual application of second glaze, by Joe Owen. Probably turned at shop operated with brother Charlie Owen. $235.00 – 250.00.

Unusual, striking glaze. Similar glazes were seen, albeit rarely, from different potteries in the 1940s – 1950s. All are collectible on aesthetics alone. Apothecary jar on left (described on page 94) is by an unknown maker. Bowl is Jugtown with black ankle glaze.

Apothecary jar, 7¾", with glaze similar to Jugtown's black ankle glaze but unstamped. This jar is shown with Jugtown black ankle glaze bowl on previous page. May have been an experimental piece. The form and unusual glaze make this a very collectible piece of North Carolina art pottery.

Porch vase, Joe Owen, unusual "pink" glaze and green cogglewheel application area. $175.00 – 225.00. Chapel Hill Museum collection.

Pitcher, 12¾", with unusual rather primitive, thick handle. Early transitional form attributed to Teague Pottery. Shop was operated after John Wesley's death by sons Charlie (1901 – 1938), James (1906 – 1988), and Bryan "Duck" (1898 – 1987).

Elephant trunk pitcher, 16¾". These are usually in the 9" to 13" format and are very collectible. This unusual over-sized version is quite desirable. Collection of the North Carolina State University Gallery of Art and Design.

Detailed view of internal insertion of three handles on A.R. Cole vase at left.

Unusual, three-handled vase, 13½", by A.R. Cole. Note the unique combination of three handles with internal insertion and four incision rings on body of the vase. $350.00 – 450.00. St. James Place Museum.

Pitcher, "drooping" spout, an unusual form.

Refrigeration or refrigerator jar, J.B. Cole (circa 1930). Refrigeration jars, large porch vases, large apothecary vessels, and large baskets are all rare and valuable. $145.00 – 175.00. Farmer/James collection.

Wide based jug, unusual form, probably inspired by "buggy jug." J.B. Cole Pottery, circa 1930s, 7¼. $200.00 – 225.00. St. James Place Museum.

We believe that these identification factors are significant enough to warrant our presenting them from a slightly different perspective, repeating some of the factual material in preceding chapters.

Many of the present-day artisans can trace family involvement in this trade back seven and eight generations and did not necessarily sign their wares for local consumption. The Coles, for example, have documented ancestors who were potters in Staffordshire, England. J.B. Cole Pottery signed less than one percent of their production.

With the makers coming from the tradition of utilitarian pottery, there was even little precedent to identify the wares themselves except to indicate the capacity of a vessel. This was most often done in script on the crocks, jugs, and storage vessels. Some decoration might have been applied and, if so, the maker occasionally indicated their name. Most of the churns, storage jars, crocks, and pitchers were sold locally, often by the potters or their families, so who made the piece was not an issue.

Even after the production of art pottery, "fancy ware," became a thriving enterprise, most potteries did not have a stamp; those that did stamped only a part of their wares. Many of these cottage enterprises hired transient (journeyman) potters. Many of the finest potters were journeymen, and others hired out to more than one pottery, wishing neither to handle the business of a pottery or the mundane work of digging for clay and gathering material for the burn. The North Carolina potteries also had contractual arrangements with sellers that may have precluded the need or opportunity to identify the pottery. Thus, most of the art pottery made before the 1950s in North Carolina, with the exception of Jugtown and Pisgah Forest, was unsigned and unstamped. J.B. Cole, Hilton, Carolina Pottery, and C.C. Cole rarely marked their pieces. However, the marked pieces can be dated and the unsigned ones identified by careful attention to shape, form, glaze, study of archival records, and discussions with fellow collectors. Other sources can be knowledgeable dealers who now specialize in this art form, as well as "show and tell" with senior potters or at convivial gatherings of the various clubs, societies, and interest groups that have been formed such as the Pottery

Collectors Guild in Raleigh, North Carolina. These latter activities will greatly enhance the acquisition process.

The stamps and signs are interesting from a number of viewpoints. As noted in the previous chapter, Jugtown, except for the very earliest pieces, traditionally signed their wares, but the stamp they employed was not always the same. If you want to differentiate a Ben Owen Jugtown piece from one made with the same form and glaze in the 1960s, you might use other parameters. Either is a perfectly collectible piece; in general, the earlier Jugtown example will be more valuable. Given the circumstance, the acquirer will need to know something about the potter's styles. Ben Owen left substantial clay in the bottom of his pots while the weight in his younger relative's (Vernon's) ware is more evenly distributed. Just feel the balance, and the identification will become obvious.

J.B. Cole after turning for his father Evan, started his own pottery in the second decade of the twentieth century at Steeds, North Carolina. This pottery later sold wares made by his daughter Nell Cole Graves at Holly Hill Pottery until a few years ago. Except for the early years of operation when this was a fledgling business, J.B. Cole Pottery neither signed nor stamped almost all of their production. They were a volume manufacturer employing a number of potters and produced wares under contract. For example, those pieces stamped Sunset Mountain Pottery were made by J.B. Cole for the Sunset Mountain Craftshop in Asheville. The same arrangement was employed with Goose Creek in South Carolina. Another interesting stamp involving the J.B. Cole pottery was with Mr. Smith's in Virginia, circa 1930s, using an ink stamp.

For the majority of J.B. Cole pieces, of which there are many all over America, other forms of physical evidence can be used. Some time in the 1940s, J.B. Cole Company (which by that time was managed by son Waymon and daughter Nell) began using stilts in the kiln to raise the pots so they would not be sitting in a glaze puddle. They also acquired a belt sander (at considerable expense) to smooth the bottoms of their wares quickly and efficiently. Thus, with the identification of the telltale tripod residue and the sanding marks on the bottom and around the rim, one can feel relatively certain a piece was made by someone at the J.B. Cole Pottery.

This leads to another fascinating and more productive exercise in identifying J.B. Cole pottery and even determining the individual potter. In the Cole catalog (circa 1932) pieces made by Bascomb King, Philmore Graves, Waymon Cole, and Nell Cole Graves are pictured and identified. Thus, a form may tell you that Philmore made that piece or the handle will identify a piece by the hand of Bascomb. This does not always obviate your handling the object because the thin, delicate edges to the rims of the smaller pieces will tell you Nell was the potter or with deep grooves on the inside, the pot was most likely turned by Waymon.

This attention to form is never absolute because different potters worked in different potteries. Many of the potters also were related by birth, marriage, and common interests and were all trying to interpret European and Oriental forms, and much information was shared among them. Royal Crown, C.C. Cole, North State, Pisgah Forest, and A.R. Cole also had catalogs or shopbooks, all of which are out of print and difficult but not impossible to acquire. Unquestionably, shape and form can lead to an almost certain attribution; but the collector should remember that all the Rebecca pitchers were not made by Joe Owen and if they have a narrow base and bulbous middle were likely turned by either M.L. Owens or A.R. Cole.

Because of their desirable form, almost every Seagrove area pottery made apothecary or medicine jars, but the split handles of A.R. Cole are identifiable. His treatment of the multiple indentations of the lower handle insertion to our knowledge was not the style of any other potter. A.R. Cole was an outstanding turner and developed many desirable glazes as well. Particularly compelling are the hues and colors of the rainbow which he used from 1926 to 1940 which will identify Rainbow Pottery wares even with absence of the ink stamp, lost through use.

Glazes as noted previously can be very important in the identification process, but in general should not be considered absolutes. Glazes as well as forms were shared, especially among families. Recall also that potters did move around or after a career as an itinerant potter would start their own shop. Whatever "secrets" they had previously acquired could be put to good use. There are certain glazes like Chinese blue of Jugtown that have not been successfully reproduced, but most could be with some experimentation. For some reason, a few appear unique to a certain pottery. Jacques Busbee, a creative man in several artistic areas, never revealed the combination of ingredients and firing times that would produce an appearance so treasured by collectors. Certain of Henry Cooper's "double dipped" glazes at North State Pottery have a clearly identifiable appearance. The covering or second glaze can have such a three-dimensional quality as to appear molten.

Attribution can sometimes be made by elimination. For example, confronted with a complex, multi-patterned glaze of many colors, one should think first of C.C. Cole Pottery. A.R. Cole certainly used similar glazes, but C.C. Cole's base white gives a more clearly identifiable mixed appearance. Dorothy Cole Auman, C.C.'s daughter, made a few examples like this at Seagrove Pottery, but most of her wares had a matte finish. Jugtown, North State, Smithfield, and Carolina Potteries quite rarely used matte type glaze. Joe Owen's colors appear more splotched than the runs of C.C. Cole, and he also used cogglewheel decoration. C.C. Cole's multicolors are light in shade and include yellow, aqua, tan, and pink, most commonly a blue, and burgundy occasionally. The horizontal bands of color will vary in sequence. While it would be desirable for these signs to be absolute, they are not; but neither is the authentication of an unsigned Cezanne.

Matching potters with particular forms is a pleasurable exercise, especially if you have a catalog published at the time of the potter's activity. This will more precisely serve as a way to identify the pottery. If a piece is signed W.N. Owen, then it was turned at North State Pottery or later, when Walter inherited the pottery, Pine State. Since most Carolina Pottery wares are not stamped, identification of Wren Cole's characteristic shoulder and blue glaze might be as well as one can do in an attribution. Is a Jack Kiser rat tail handle or a J.B. Cole drooping spout or an A.R. Cole duck bill pitcher specific? They are until future evidence disproves this line of reasoning.

While the attribution process in identifying unsigned North Carolina art pottery is frustrating, it is both interesting and rewarding. To uncover a

Rainbow Pottery piece turned by A.R. Cole in the 1930s or a heroic porch vase by Waymon Cole or Joe Owen is an exciting event that will long be remembered by the acquirer and a moment cherished in perpetuity by the true collector. The value of signed and stamped pieces of this genre has increased substantially in recent years; heightened awareness of the aesthetic and monetary value seems now to be increasing the acquisition costs further, making it a prudent investment of time and scholarship for the intended collector to learn the shapes, signs, and symbols to attribute, with some degree of confidence, those unsigned and unstamped pieces of North Carolina art pottery.

J.H. Owen stamp, 1910 – 1923. J.H. worked at Jugtown from 1918 – 1923 and was a leader in the art pottery transition 1915 – 1920.

Owen stamp on two-handled vase. Circa 1920s.

Carolina Pottery stamp, Candor. Much of the production of this small pottery was undistinguished, but certain examples are very collectible.

Stamp #1 – 1924-1926
Stamp #2 – 1926-1938
Stamp #3 – 1939-1959
Pine State Stamp – 1960-1965

NORTH STATE POTTERY CO.
HAND MADE
SANFORD, N. C.

North State Pottery Co
Hand Made
Sanford-N.C.

HANDMADE
by
NORTH/STATE
POTTERY
SANFORD, N.CAROLINA

HANDMADE
PINE STATE
POTTERY
SANFORD, N. CAROLINA

W.N.
OWEN
HAND MADE

WM
OWEN

Adapted from Southern Folk Pottery Collection Association. Billy Ray and Susan Hussey.

Melvin Owens, 1950s, stamped "Pinehurst Craft." J. Wilkinson collection.

Pottery stamp, "Carolina Craft American Handmade." J. Wilkinson collection.

Masten, C. at C.R. Auman Pottery, 1925 – 1932, cobalt/salt vase, stamped "I-33." J. Wilkinson collection.

More Identification Clues From the Undersurface

Knowledgeable collectors and dealers depend greatly upon the appearance of the undersurface of wares in the identification process. First, one can reassure themselves as to whether the example is one of stoneware or earthenware. The color of the clay, if unadulterated, may very well identify the area of origin in older pieces, and almost always one can identify North Carolina clay from that of other states. With the commercial clays now in common use, this differential feature is eliminated, but most contemporary potters either sign or stamp their wares, making this differentiation moot.

Mitchfield (sometimes spelled Michfield) clay, also referred to by its source, the Auman clay pit, is a large vein of primary clay that when fired to approximately 1400 degrees F. and above would provide a relatively tight vessel and, due to its plasticity, a base material with good turning characteristics (Owens). The turning capabilities might, for certain purposes, be improved by adding other regional sedimentary clays. Mitchfield clay will be expressed as a white or very light tan bottom whereas other regional clays have a very light orange appearance (Teague). Catawba Valley clay is a dull brown/gray when fired. This can be seen both in the early art pottery by Daniel Z. Craven and C.R. Auman potteries, but since the clay pit still exists, even to this day one might potentially encounter a specially made example.

The locus of the Mitchfield clay was excavated extensively by the Department of the Army but enough was left that several years ago M.L. Owens leased the land where the remnants of this vast accumulation once resided (Owens). In the Catawba Valley the Rhodes clay pit (or hole) in Lincoln County on the west bank of the South Fork River has provided clay for generations of potters in this area. When burned, it has a dull brown/gray appearance.

Each pottery had its own defined technique in preparing and finishing the undersurface of their wares. In some early pieces, the glaze was simply sanded off. If this was done by hand, the abrasion to the glaze will not be uniform and will most characteristically be located centrally. The removal of the glaze from the central area will be fairly complete, depending upon the potter's resolve and tenacity.

Some potteries used ceramics stilts, often arranged in a tripod-like fashion to support the vessel in the kiln during the firing process. These stilts might be very adherent to the undersurface of the ware and upon removal will leave the telltale sign of their use as dimples in the undersurface glaze. Several potting operations employed these stilts, but they were used from the late 1930s and beyond quite extensively by the J.B. Cole Pottery. Since this was the largest North Carolina pottery, you may encounter these on quite a number of pieces.

Another manifestation of the glazing process was the innovation of the belt sander. One was purchased by the Coles in the early 1940s at considerable expense. Nell once confessed that she and brother Waymon entertained doubts they would live long enough to recoup their investment. The sander allowed the bottom to be smoothed very rapidly by pressing the undersurface of the pot against the moving flat surface of the belt sander. This will give the appearance of peripheral smoothing with some glaze remaining on the central area of the ware. This is in contradistinction to the slower process of hand sanding in which the diligence of the potter determined the area covered and the amount of glaze removed.

The intent of each method was to achieve a smooth bottom free of abrasive debris. One might imagine the reaction of the Lady of the House (or the Lord of the Manor) if the bottom of their Han Dynasty-inspired Chinese blue vase scratched the surface of their Newport card table attributed to Townsend. A more local scenario might be a Thomas Day server, but the message remains that having a smooth bottom on North Carolina art pottery was mandatory.

The undersurface of ware can provide much information regarding the turning process and while the differences are quite subtle in most circumstances, in a few they are very informative. There is the apocryphal tale of Burlon Craig showing the unglazed undersurface of his swirl ware to a younger potter and incurring the ire of his contemporaries who wanted to keep their technique for fashioning this popular appearance secret.

The undersurface of North Carolina pottery can assist greatly in the determination of age as can the patina of the glazed surface which has been compared to evaluation of the age of a painting by the varnish reflection or the mellow tonalities apparent in the visual image of late eighteenth and early nineteenth century furniture. The undersurface would be equivalent to the appearance of the edges of the canvas or the construction and underside of drawers of a vintage chest.

In order to properly assess any collectible, certain basic observations need to be mastered, and North Carolina art pottery is no different. It is a challenge but so is discriminating between a watercolor, a gouache, or a print or identifying secondary wood. All of the surface contains interpretative data, and a careful examination of the undersurface will provide the potential acquirer significant information. For this reason, we have included many illustrations of the undersurfaces in this text.

I am especially indebted to Steve Compton, Mick Bailey, Arthur Baer, Joe Wilkinson, and Charles Zug for their insights into the identification process.

References: M.L. Owens, Archie Teague

Undersurface of D.Z. Craven two-handled vase. Slightly more orange or brick color than wares from C.R. Auman Pottery.

Undersurface of vase. The light yellow clay can be found in a number of areas in North Carolina, if you know where to look. This vase is from J.B. Cole and Company.

Undersurface of two bowls made for tourist shop in Tryon, North Carolina (stamped Melmar) by Hilton Pottery of Hickory. Note difference in color of clay; on right is color typical of clay from Rhodes clay pit from the west bank of South Fork River in Lincoln County.

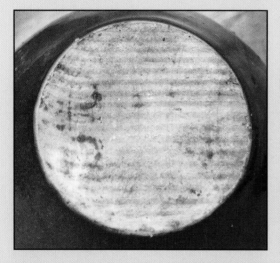

Photo shows marks left by cleaning undersurface of glaze using a metallic wire device. As drawn across the bottom, a curved pattern will be formed and appears, almost like a large finger-print. Certain potteries used ceramic stilts.

Undersurface shows failure to clear glaze and the subsequent accumulation of debris from resting in kiln. Some trace of sanding attempt which was not completed.

With experimental pieces, potteries kept their records in numerical fashion.

To date, very little is known about pottery made by Native Americans in western North Carolina. The tradition is likely hundreds of years old when the Cherokee and Catawba were powerful cultures and pottery was made for both utilitarian and ceremonial purposes. Only a few individuals collect this pottery avidly, and they are generally from the region of production.

The few comments made here should be taken as rudimentary and fragmented. They are mainly from discussions with collectors L.A. Rhyne and Nowell Guffey and from the material of Charles Zug and Rodney Leftwich.

The character of the wares suggests that they may be fired in several manners, including in an open pit. They might be bisque fired in a conventional oven and then over a flame fire fueled with wood (Rhyne). There are oral accounts of later firing in shallow pits in the earth, using the ground as a barrier to contain the heat. This would mean that the unglazed ware might be fragile and subject to breakage. For this reason, many of the tourist pieces might well be in very simple shapes and sizes. This also contributes to the difficulty of distinguishing from the wares of the Cherokee and the Catawba. Additionally, the Catawba Indians attend Cherokee schools where designs specific to either tribe certainly began to be combined. (Rhyne).

Recently, more elaborate forms and exotic decorations have been seen and attributed to specific potters, such as Maude Welch or Ethel Bigmeat, who died in 1939. The decorations of snakes and faces done by Maude Welch demonstrate a high degree of sophistication and are expertly formed.

At present one may encounter the work of Louise Bigmeat Maney and other members of the Bigmeat family. These are simple, small forms usually signed in script and decorated. These are often decorated, unglazed vases with multiple impressed decorations (Hussey) and are always low fired. Sometimes these and the wares of Ethel Bigmeat have barked, scratched incisions in the unglazed clay.

While this is an incomplete statement regarding the North Carolina art pottery by Native Americans, a powerful message resides in these forms, inviting further enjoyment and investigation.

References: Nowell Guffey, Billy Ray Hussey, Rodney Leftwich, L.A. Rhyne, Charles Zug

Small vase, 3", unglazed with scalloped top. Geometric coggle-style impressed design, ca. 1950s, signed Bigmeat, Cherokee, N.C. in script. Those wares signed only with the family name could have been done by any member. $110.00 – 125.00.
Farmer/James gift, Chapel Hill Museum collection.

Unglazed decorated vase, 3¾", satin black gloss, low fired. Signed L. Bigmeat Maney. Multiple impressed decorations; a time-consuming process and rarely seen. Attributed to Louise Bigmeat Maney. Farmer/James gift, Chapel Hill Museum collection.

Wedding jug, c. 1960, Cherokee (coil method), by Rebecca Youngbird.

Swan, sculptured, 2¾" x 5½". Note the graceful side walls of this decorative example. Low fired, these Native American pieces are fragile. Nowell Guffey collection.

Two-headed vase by Maude Welch, Cherokee. Native American pottery does not appear to be influenced by any traditional Oriental or European aesthetic. Nowell Guffey collection.

Vase, 6¾" x 6¾", with sophisticated decoration and snake handles. Maude Welch, Cherokee. Rare and valuable. Nowell Guffey collection.

Snake-handled vessel by Maude Welch. This represents an unrecognized genre of North Carolina art pottery. Native Americans of the Cherokee tribe have been making pottery for centuries.

Corn pot, Cherokee. Rodney Leftwich collection.

Pots and effigy bowl. Philip Leftwich collection.

Low-fired pottery, Cherokee, by Maude Welch.

Peacepipe (Bigmeat); Cherokee corn-pot design (Cora Wahnetah); ancient effigy bowl.

Cherokee weaver and potter.
Leftwich archives.

The settlement of western North Carolina in the eighteenth century was impeded by the Catawba River and the Indian tribes who roamed the valley for game, as this was their hunting ground. Welshman Adam Sherrill crossed the river in 1747. However, another 70 years passed before a definitive pottery-making tradition emerged in this region. This would be a utilitarian enterprise born of necessity. The transition to art pottery from these origins was a slow process and different from that of the other two major pottery areas in North Carolina.

Food storage vessels were critical to survival in the eighteenth and nineteenth centuries throughout North Carolina, but the utilitarian pottery that evolved in the Catawba Valley was different in shape, form, and glaze from that in the eastern part of the state. A few surviving vessels from this period indicate that earthenware was made by these early Catawba Valley potters who had a different ethnic origin from their neighbors of English descent in the Seagrove area.

The Catawba River valley was settled predominantly by German immigrants who followed the Great Wagon Road from the North through the Shenandoah Valley of Virginia. They crossed the Catawba River and later found good clay on the banks of its South Fork, clay that would withstand the high temperatures required to make stoneware with enough plasticity to support the thin but sturdy walls of the large vessels turned there.

Potters of Germanic descent used an alkaline glaze, which was an adaptation of that previously known in the Far East. Scholars continue to explore the passage of this glaze to the Catawba Valley, and conclusive evidence remains elusive (Huffman). However, speculation has the knowledge of salt glaze arriving in the American South through the port of Charleston, possibly with a potter named A. Duche. By about 1820 the Edgefield District of South Carolina had developed a pottery industry producing alkaline-glazed stoneware, yielding vessels that were far stronger and safer than lead-glazed earthenware. Alkaline-glazed stoneware was present in the Catawba Valley by the early 1830s. (Huffman)

As noted, pottery food storage vessels were an essential part of survival for early settlers. Food harvested in the growing season had to be preserved in quantity to feed the settlers during the winter months. Not only fruits and vegetables, but also meat, vinegar, and molasses preservation required jars and jugs in a variety of sizes. Corn, however, could be brought to market in the liquid form of corn whiskey in jugs. These jugs ranged in size from less than a gallon to huge multigallon vessels. Because of the demand for these wares, over the next century and a half, more than 100 potters-farmers worked in the Catawba Valley area to provide these vessels, mainly for local needs. (Danielson)

The pottery that evolved in the Catawba Valley differed from the pottery made in the eastern part of the state in several ways due to physical differences in the materials employed; the clay from the Valley very strongly defined the pottery that emerged. It contained titanium oxide, which will produce flecks of blue on the surface, and appears more red/brown in color than the clay from the Piedmont and is distinctly different from Mitchfield (Michfield) clay, which turned white when fired at the usual kiln temperatures. (Wilkinson)

The alkaline glaze ranges in color from clear to celadon green as well as much darker hues of green and brown to almost black. Iron slag from Lincoln County iron furnaces often was ground and added to the glaze, sometimes creating dark runs on the pots. Shapes were derived from the Germanic heritage of the makers, the earliest strongly reflecting the rounded vessels of the seventeenth through nineteenth centuries in Germany. (Huffman)

The groundhog kilns of the Catawba Valley that fired the vessels to the hardened form were dug into the ground to help insulate the kiln and attain the high temperatures necessary for stoneware. In the end, the pots looked quite different in both color and form from the nineteenth century vessels from Moore and Randolph counties.

The pottery industry developed in the southwestern section of the Catawba region as well as the adjoining areas of Lincoln County due to location of the clay and the prevailing road system. In more recent times, the defining northern limit has been Highway 10, encompassing the pottery areas of Vale and Cat Square to the south, and to the intersection of Highway 10 and NC 127 in the east. The physical journey from these areas of utilitarian production to the location of the Hilton potteries where art pottery was to be fashioned was not as long as the philosophic distance.

Daniel Seagle, born c. 1805, was truly a giant in the manufacture of utilitarian pottery, not only for his own production but also for the style he inspired. Seagle is listed on the 1842 census as a potter. Included in his household or employ were among others, a son, James Franklin Seagle, Isaac Lefevers, and John Goodman. These men would also become well known in their own right as potters. The initials DS, JFS, IL, and JG on utilitarian wares are eagerly sought by collectors.

Also listed in the same census are Thomas Ritchie, David Hartzog, and Jeremiah Clemer. Their wares are identified by letter initials impressed on the handle or shoulder of the vessel which identify the maker and define one of the parameters, along with condition, to judge the most collectible vessels by this group for those collectors interested in utilitarian forms.

The Hartzog/Hartsoe family, another familiar Catawba Valley potter name, made pottery continuously from 1850 through 1956. David Hartzog, who is listed in the 1850 census, signed his early pottery "David Hartzog His Make." Either he and/or his son, Daniel Hartsoe, used a DH stamp.

David's other son, Sylvanus Leander Hartsoe, stamped "SLH," made pottery that had a high content of natural rutile. This was contained in the clay from their source, giving an almost sky blue appearance. Hartsoe passed his skill on to his son, Poley Carp, who made pottery until 1956. Poley Carp did not use a stamp, but he uncommonly signed a few pieces. During the century this family worked, very little changed in the production techniques used.

The Reinhardt family who would become early contributors to the art pottery movement arrived in the Catawba Valley in the third quarter of the nineteenth century. Ambrose Reinhardt signed his wares AR (Huffman). His sons, Jim and Pinckney, also made pottery, and Pinckney's two sons, Enoch and Harvey, continued the tradition and were important in the Catawba Valley art pottery movement into the 1930s.

Enoch and Harvey worked together to build two kilns in the Henry area of Lincoln County. They signed the pottery they made together REINHARDT BROS. POTTERY. After they dissolved the partnership, their pottery was marked E.W. REINHARDT or H.F. REINHARDT. Enoch became renowned for his

early swirl ware, and Harvey's face jugs, an important form of the folk pottery tradition, are sought after today.

The Reinhardt brothers made utilitarian ware and also fancy ware for tourists and sometimes for individual customers whose taste had been influenced by art pottery from other regions.

Sam Propst, who learned the craft from his father Jacob, is credited with making the first swirl ware in the Catawba Valley. Using two clays, a light, near-white clay and the darker local clay, he pulled the two up on the wheel to form what he thought was an interesting pattern. This ware was then glazed with a clear glaze to allow the clay colors to provide a vivid contrasting pattern. We will include the story of Propst's alleged "discovery" later in this chapter and a description of their stamps. Sam's son Floyd also made swirl or striped ware.

Enoch Reinhardt is considered by most scholars of Catawba Valley lore to have improved the technique in fashioning this design. His swirl was more delineated, with less blurring between the light and dark clay. (Rhyne)

A large number of Ritchie family members made utilitarian pottery, but apparently only Thomas and his son, Luther Seth, commonly signed their work (Rhyne). The vast majority of pottery made in the Catawba Valley was not signed by the maker. The utilitarian value, i.e., would the vessel conform to function, was paramount and identification of the maker of little importance. The early potter received no greater financial reward for added decoration, for the beauty of his glazes, or for the gracefulness of his shapes. Only a few saw a value in marking their works. These were practical considerations and not aesthetic, yet the beauty of the forms of these bulbous storage vessels is undeniable.

Members of the Helton/Hilton family were making pottery in the area south of Hickory by 1890. John Wesley Helton, a veteran of the Civil War, his brother, Robert Jehu, and a number of their descendants were active in the craft. Although early family members made traditional storage vessels, their progeny later made the most important contributions in art pottery by moving into the decorative arena created by changing times.

After the turn of the century with the advent of canning jars, refrigeration, canned foods, and cheap, commercial stoneware, the demand for food storage vessels decreased, and many potters had to seek employment in other industries. Potters had to conform to the marketplace to survive in their chosen trade. The other choices were farming or the local furniture factories and textile mills.

Two factors made that survival possible for potters who could innovate. An important one was the development of tourism as visitors to the North Carolina Mountains passed through the Catawba Valley area on Highway 10. Equally important to the aesthetics was the influence of the Arts and Crafts movement upon the decoration values of the public, creating a demand for more artistic tableware and later, objects acquired for purely aesthetic consideration.

Members of the Hilton family, along with Sam and Floyd Propst, and Enoch and Harvey Reinhardt, were the leaders in the move toward art pottery. John Wesley Hilton's homesite, nine miles west of Newton, was probably the first pottery site in the area. His sons Ernest Auburn "Auby" (1878 – 1948), Shuford "Shuff" (1875 – 1947), and Claude (1880 – 1969) began their careers working for their father making food storage vessels. They utilized two glazes: the thick, dark brown glaze made from ground iron slag cinders, ashes, and clay slip, and a clear glaze made from ground glass, ashes, and clay slip. A few pieces with the initials JWH have survived from this early pottery. (Huffman)

Just after the turn of the century, George Robert Hilton, son of Robert Jehu, and Luther Seth Ritchie, son-in-law of John Wesley, established a pottery near Harmony (Iredell County). Other family members worked there as needed until the pottery closed around 1909.

Brothers Auby, Shuff, and Claude Hilton established a pottery near Propst Crossroads on Highway 10 in 1917 or 1918. From there the Hiltons began producing wares that responded to the evolving market for art pottery. They developed a line of wares they described as "Catawba Indian Pottery" and a catalog showing 69 examples of Catawba Indian Pottery that could be ordered. The catalog was included in the Mint Museum Exhibit catalog by Stuart Schwartz and Daisy Wade Bridges. The name was an advertising ploy having little or nothing to do with Native Americans. Apparently, unglazed ware was in demand for ladies to hand paint with scenes and motifs as a pastime. A number of painted pieces have been found that are quite extraordinary. (Huffman)

The events described here set the stage for the entry of the Catawba Valley into the uncharted world of North Carolina art pottery production. Some of the material might bear repetition for understanding of these developments in context.

The tradition of fashioning utilitarian stoneware in this region dates back several hundred years and this was largely unheralded until several important and related events, starting approximately 20 years ago. Exhibits were held at the Mint Museum in Charlotte (1980) organized by scholar and collector Daisy Wade Bridges. The catalog at that time provided almost the only national exposure of the efforts of these Catawba Valley potters.

Under the leadership of Charles G. (Terry) Zug III, professor of folklore at the University of North Carolina at Chapel Hill, the school organized an exhibit at UNC's Ackland Art Museum. Dr. Zug also published the seminal work on North Carolina folk pottery, *Turners and Burners* through UNC Press in 1984. The Catawba Valley potters, especially Burlon B. Craig, were well documented and their contribution to the folk pottery movement elucidated. More germaine to the considerations in this text, some discussion was devoted to the art pottery contributions of the Reinhardt and Hilton families regarding swirl and other decorative pottery.

In 1987 an exhibit of Catawba Valley pottery was held at the Hickory Museum of Art with Dr. Allen W. Huffman, collector, as guest curator. This exhibit featured 491 examples of Catawba Valley art pottery. Many examples were seen there by the public for the first time.

In 1999 the Lincoln County Historical Association had a very successful exhibit, "Two Centuries of Potters: A Catawba Valley Tradition." The exhibit of 515 examples and catalog rekindled and re-created interest in Catawba Valley art pottery. Collectors may have been cognizant of the beauty and spectrum of the regional contribution of the North Carolina art pottery for the first time. The exhibit also featured examples of contemporary Catawba Valley art pottery. The essay by Professor Leon Danielson became the definitive statement on the contribution of the Hilton family.

These and other events have led to further consideration, understanding, and appreciation of that Catawba Valley art pottery that grew in the 1930s and 1940s out of the utilitarian tradition.

Three families dominate the art pottery movement in the Catawba Valley; the Propsts, the Reinhardts, and the Hiltons (Heltons).

If one is to accept oral history, the Propsts' "discovery" of swirl was literally by chance. Samuel (1882 – 1935), the family patriarch who made pottery with his son Floyd (1914 – 1983), once received a white clay from the nearby Mt. Holly region. The turning properties of this light clay were substandard compared to others in the area. Samuel mixed some of their darker clay from the Rhodes pit (or hole) from the South Fork of the Catawba River with the Mt. Holly clay. The Rhodes clay was a much darker brown and had more desirable properties (plasticity) for turning. Allegedly, Propst noted that the body of the vessel demonstrated an alternating pattern of light and dark stripes which was later called swirl. The potter could control the demonstration of the borders which at first were irregularly defined but have become very well delineated by contemporary potters such as Charles Lisk, a pupil of B.B. Craig.

The Propsts found that they could substitute the usual clear glass glaze with one created by mixing an alkaline glaze with Albany slip (a clay slip from Albany, New York, often used with utilitarian ware). This glaze was darker and would impart warm tonalities to the swirlware. The swirl pitchers, larger vases, and unusual forms by the Propst family are avidly collected.

Much of the production of Propst pottery was sold in gift shops in the tourist areas of western Carolina. They were sometimes stamped "North Carolina" and later "Propst Pottery, Vale, N.C." This was chiefly at the insistence of the shop owners so the tourists would be aware that they were acquiring a manifestation of North Carolina craftsmanship and not some imported trinket. The Propst pottery closed in 1937.

In 1932 Harvey and brother Enoch Reinhardt started a pottery company in Vale, North Carolina. They were the sons of Pinckney A. and Mary Baker Reinhardt and had learned their trade from their father and Jim Lynn, a neighbor.

Harvey and Enoch were seventh generation German-Americans, descended from Ambrose Alexander Reinhardt (1831 – 1914), the first documented potter from their lineage. The "Reinhardt Bros." as their stamp was configured, made traditional wares and swirl. Harvey (1912 – 1960) is thought to have made most of the traditional Catawba Valley utilitarian wares while Enoch (1903 – 1973) turned most of the swirl and items that would generally be termed tourist pieces. In 1937 the brothers divided their operation and

went into business separately. Harvey constructed a new kiln and began stamping his wares "H.F. Reinhardt, Vale, NC." Enoch continued to operate his pottery at their previous location and stamped his goods "E.W. Reinhardt, Vale, No. Car." He made baskets, birdhouses, flower/frog vases, and very collectible swirlware. For a visual spectrum of the Reinhardts' production, we refer the reader to the images of the Springs, Cline, Koscheski, and Rhyne collections in *Two Centuries of Potters: A Catawba Valley Tradition.*

When considering the art pottery movement in North Carolina, one must recognize that this development has come late to this region and did not have some of the attendant stimuli of the Seagrove area or even the Western art pottery movement. The main arteries for transportation of humans North and South along Highways 1 or 301 were not existent or even approximately in the Catawba Valley. Although somewhat on the path to the western North Carolina tourist areas where there were well-known resorts such as Asheville, Hendersonville, Tryon, and Pisgah National Forest, the resorts were principally in the west.

From the human side, the inspirations were also different, and innovators such as Jacques and Juliana Busbee, the Coopers, Victor Obler, and Mrs. Bessie Hunter provided inspiration and new ideas in the Seagrove area. The wealthy patrons from nearby Pinehurst often brought drawings and even fine art objects to be reproduced by the potters in nearby Seagrove. The Aumans brought C.B. Masten to their pottery to introduce glazes that were unique to the region and Henry Cooper worked with scientists at North Carolina State College (now University) in Raleigh. The Catawba Valley was much more insular and conservative.

In the Catawba Valley the need for vessels for food preparation and preservation as well as jugs extended well into the twentieth century. This labor intensive cottage industry of pottery production also had to compete with the very successful furniture mills in the area. One's wages in this employ were regular and predictable as were the hours of labor. The outside factors were different in the Catawba Valley from the other two areas of pottery production. However, this does not in any way make apology for the art pottery expression in the Catawba Valley.

The family most responsible for the Catawba art pottery movement was the Hiltons (or Heltons). John Wesley Hilton (1846 – 1923) was an accomplished utilitarian potter. His three sons Shuford Daniel (1875

– 1947), Ernest Auburn "Auby" (1878 – 1948), and Claude Watson (1880 – 1969) were all potters. John Wesley, who opened his pottery upon his return from the Civil War, also had three daughters who were married to potters.

The Hiltons dug their clay from Lincoln County, the Rhodes clay hole, and used alkaline, cinder and glass glazes. The ground glass used to produce a clear glaze was from crushed and ground bottles. In approximately 1917, the three brothers founded the Hilton Pottery Company on land owned by Claude. This was on Highway 10 near Propst's Crossroads. Additional potters included Claude's son, Floyd Hilton (1905 – 1979) and occasionally the family patriarch, John Wesley, who was by that time in declining health.

While operating under the Hilton Brothers' label, Clara Maude Hilton (1885 – 1969), wife of Auby, a truly creative woman, began using the cobalt edging to decorate entire sets of tableware. These were quite popular and very collectible today, especially if full sets can be acquired in good condition, a rare find indeed. Very desirable are the Hilton coffee and tea pots with highlights of the blue decoration at the edges contrasted against the somewhat light gray/brown hue clay from local sources and covered with a clear glaze chiefly from ground glass.

In approximately 1928 the brothers' shop closed, and Auby and Maude moved their potting operation to a small village, Oyama, east of present-day Hickory, along Highway 70, the main east-west route.

Floyd and his wife Annie Mae Ritchie worked in Seagrove. Floyd worked for the C.R. Auman Pottery in the late 1920s and into the 1930s. This was at the same time that C.B. Masten was working for the Aumans. There they also would have seen the effects of the Mitchfield (Lock) or Michfield (Zug) clay and how it responded to the clear lead glazes and cobalt decorations. When they returned to the Catawba Valley region, these experiences undoubtedly were translated into some of the images representing the arts pottery movement there.

According to Hilton scholar Leon Danielson, Annie Mae may have painted underglazed decorations. Certainly there was a growing fashion in the Seagrove area to leave wares with an unglazed exterior and have amateur and would-be artists paint whatever they wished to decorate the outside. These are seen as examples with an overall exterior paint and decorated with flowers and birds. These pieces were often not glazed, so the decoration would deteriorate with time. Whether Annie gained her inspiration from observing this practice, or she was directly influenced by Maude Hilton is not known.

Shuford Hilton also worked for C.R. Auman. (Rhyne) Later, Auby sold his pottery to Weir Jarrett who, according to Barry and Allen Huffman, was not a potter but hired George Baker and Shuford Hilton to turn wares at the Oyama site.

Earlier in the 1920s, the Hiltons had published a small catalog of their wares. One of the more interesting lines they offered for sale were the so-called "Catawba Indian" wares. These did not represent either the output or inspiration of the early tribe for which the region was named, but more likely a marketing ploy to gain the attention of the tourists traveling in the area. These typically were vessels glazed internally but unglazed on the exterior. The clay would be rough, even abrasive to touch, and sometimes contained visible debris including quartz crystals. Many of the utilitarian shapes and forms were duplicated in the Catawba Indian wares. They have become collectible as oddities because of the varied sizes of the vases and the more traditional appearance than some of today's form and glaze combination.

At Oyama, Auby Hilton hired several potters to turn ware. Among those were the well-traveled Bill Gordy who had also worked with Jack Kiser, the Coles, and Farrell Craven at the large operation in Smithfield. At Smithfield they had a large bottle kiln as well as a wood-fired one. Located on U.S. Highway 301, Gordy would also have been exposed to the suggestions of the tourists traveling North and South.

Floyd Hilton had traveled through the Seagrove area gaining knowledge regarding the glazes and glazing techniques practiced there. One can sometimes see these influences in art pottery pieces turned by him when he came back to the Catawba Valley. In addition Auby hired Archie Killian and Willard Huffman, but little is known about their specific contributions.

While at the Oyama operation, Auby and Maude moved more and more into the direction of pure art pottery. While the tableware was somewhat elevated to an art form with Maude's decoration, their pieces were now fashioned from a purely aesthetic premise and intent. Maude decorated small jugs and other wares with multiple circular bands on the upper body of the ware, often in contrasting cobalt blue and a white glaze but sometimes with a third brown oxide as well. The bands provided contrast to the alkaline overall glaze and were very decorative.

In 1934 the Hiltons closed the Oyama pottery operation and moved to the area of Pleasant Gardens in McDowell County, four miles west of the textile town of Marion. According to Danielson, it was there that they made the almost complete commitment to art pottery. Clara Maude painted wares with oxides in underglaze slip and dogwood flower designs which might be flat on the surface but were often done with applied clay.

Around 1937 Maude began making figurines for which she is also widely known. At approximately the same time (1936 – 1939) they made pottery under contract for the tourist resort of Tryon and stamped this "Melmar Pottery" and "Hilton Pottery" as well (Guffey). Tryon has a flourishing art colony and a number of nationally recognized artists including Lawrence Mazzanovich, Rudolph Ingerle, J.S. Brown, and George Aid lived and visited there. These artists' frequenting of the area is documented in Michael McCue's book *The Tryon Painters.* America's "people's poet" Carl Sandburg lived in nearby Flat Rock, and his friend the famed photographer Edward Steichen visited often. These individuals created an atmosphere to appreciate art pottery. These Melmar wares consisted of lidded jars and small vases that tourists might take home from their journeys to show their friends, a natural marketing device also important for western North Carolina pottery.

Auby and Maude Hilton had five children including Ernestine Sigmon who later decorated wares turned by Charlie Craven for Tobacco Roads Pottery in Wake County, in the 1970s – 1980s. Other children were Hunter (1910 –), Mozell (1913 – 1986), Mildred, called "Tommie" (1915 –), and Lera. Ernestine, Lera, and Tommie assisted their mother with decorating the pottery.

Many of the figurines were sold to a shop in Asheville operated by Clementine Douglas. It is estimated that there were only about 100 figurines produced, but this has not been currently documented.

Another innovation of the Hiltons was the pinecone candlesticks, routinely designed by Maude. This consisted of an upturned pinecone with the orifice for the candle at the tip of the pinecone. The leaves of the cone are individually shaped.

The collector will discover that decorative ware by Hilton is often still located in the region of orgin. The production was small in comparison to Seagrove (especially operations like J.B. Cole) or Pisgah Forest Pottery in the west. For this reason it may be inexpensive or very dear, the latter being the more likely circumstance.

Underglaze painted scenes featuring local landmarks of houses and grist mills are not always from the potters. Many are obviously done by an untrained but talented hand, often compared with Grandma Moses, but no primitive painter of these rural scenes has been identified. Applied dogwood blooms with branches and leaves under a clear glaze are often seen. Sometimes branches, leaves, and grape clusters under a light green glaze provide variety as do the ware glazed with a thin layer of cobalt over the entire vessel surface. When fired, these pieces may end up a translucent to dark blue-green but if not signed are difficult to identify upon form alone. (Huffman)

The flower frog is a fairly ubiquitous form, but knowing certain characteristics of Hilton "frogs" may be helpful. They are often glazed with cobalt highlights around the individual holes crafted with raised edges for stem insertion. You can also see them from Randolph, Chatham, and Moore County potteries but without these distinctions.

Hilton wall pockets will usually be in Catawba Indian style and have flattened backsides and tooled notches at the rims. Whether one considers these collectible is an individual decision, and they are fairly rare.

The Hiltons made "face pitchers" and some with blue edges. They are interesting, but again whether this is truly North Carolina "art" pottery depends upon what the collector determines is the aesthetic premise. That they are important "folk pottery" is undeniable (Zug, *Turners and Burners*).

Turned cylinders combined to form the image of a tree trunk with applied branches and figural birds and pottery dolls were made by the Hiltons. We would apply the same criteria to these as to other collectibles. They are unquestionably an art form and are collectible, but do they represent the genre of North Carolina art pottery?

E.A. Auby Hilton died in 1948, but the pottery stayed open until 1953. Lera's husband, Ed Whitson, helped run the operation as did Bill Hendley, Tommie's son. Since that time there was a marked decline in interest in the Catawba Valley potters until definitive arts events occurred in the 1980s.

A number of new potters currently reside in the area, chiefly, in proximity to the late icon of North

Carolina folk pottery, Burlon B. Craig of Henry, who died in 2002.

Highway 40 and the international reputation of Hickory-made furniture have increased the number and geographic distribution of individuals exposed to this genre. Hickory itself has an excellent museum of art, Hickory Museum of Art, where exhibitions can be held. There is also the annual Catawba Valley Pottery Festival which combines the expression of the contemporary with the traditional wares. Auctions in the region including the Hollifield auction in Marion have Catawba Valley wares, and malls in the resort areas of Blowing Rock and Asheville sometimes have examples.

Catawba Valley pottery is different from that of Seagrove and that produced in western North Carolina. It tends to be more conservative, and one can trace the forms and glazes to more traditional ones. This 1930s – 1950s interpretation by the Catawba Valley potter has an inherent beauty and quality that appeals to contemporary sensibilities.

Although noted in the Acknowledgments, I would like to specifically cite the contributions of Leon Danielson, Barry and Allen Huffman, Nowell Guffey, L.A. Rhyne, and Joe Wilkinson to this chapter.

Flower frog/vase, 8¼" x 8½", cobalt glaze, closed vase form, multiple stem holes, attributed to Hilton, circa 1930. Rhyne collection.

Swirl teapot, 8½" x 10¾", clear glass glaze, brown handle, swirl spout, incised decoration. Stamp "E.W. Reinhardt's, Vale, No. Car." Circa 1940. Rhyne collection.

Floor vase, 18¼", cobalt glaze, two strap handles, clear glaze interior, attributed to Hilton, circa 1930. Rhyne collection.

Single chamber "monkey jug," 7¾" x 9⅝", swirl, pinched form, stamped "E.W. Reinhardt's Pottery Vale, No. Car." Circa 1940. Rhyne collection.

Swirl teapot, 6⅜" x 11¼", swirl handle and spout, interior lid ridge, clear glass glaze, stamped "Propst Pottery. Vale, North Carolina." Circa 1935. Rhyne collection.

Daniel Seagle jug, 4-gallon, alkaline glaze, stamped "DS." Large Seagle examples are quite valuable. $6,000.00 – 7,500.00. Farmer/James collection.

Jug, 2-gallon, alkaline glaze, stamped "JWH," John Wesley Hilton. Danielson collection.

Teapot, 4" x 4⅝", cobalt glaze, stamped "Reinhardt Bros Vale, N.C." Circa 1935. Rhyne collection.

113

Note pooling of glaze inside blue rim of cobalt decorated bowl shown at left in photo below.

Pitcher, 7", decorated with painted glazes under clear gloss glaze. Painted by Annie Mae Hilton, wife of potter Floyd Hilton. Danielson collection.

Hilton pottery, three examples of "banded" decoration. Note bowl in foreground has fluted rim while bowl on left has rim decorated with cobalt. Bands are multicolored according to glaze. Danielson collection.

Hilton pottery, series of frogs (pansy bowls). All seem to have raised edges for the holes. The turning excellence is best demonstrated on the unglazed bowl in the center. Danielson collection.

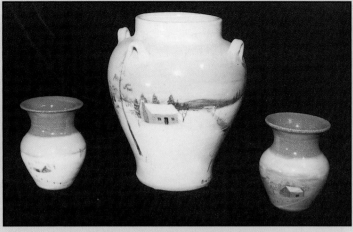

Hilton "Catawba Indian" pottery, unglazed exterior. Two vases with exquisite turning. These unglazed examples demonstrate the pieces' forms quite well. Danielson collection.

Tobacco Road pottery, turned by Charlie Craven and decorated by Ernestine Hilton Sigmon, daughter of Maude Hilton. Danielson collection.

Hilton Pottery teapot. This represents the signature piece for the blue rim tableware sets. The handles may vary in style, but these forms are all very collectible. Danielson collection.

Detail of Hilton blue rim teapot. Note the unusual posterior lip which holds the lid.

Wide low vase, 4¾", with unusual glaze and appearance not unlike frogskin. However, appearance of clay and provenance suggest Hilton Pottery. Without markings, attributions are often quite intriguing. Might this be Floyd Hilton upon his return from Seagrove?

Hilton blue rim tableware, probably turned and decorated with cobalt at the Oyama site, four miles east of Hickory. Danielson collection.

Hilton tableware, cream and sugar set of blue rim pattern. Danielson collection.

Figurines by Clara Maude Hilton. It is estimated by her daughter that fewer than 100 sets or examples still exist. Danielson collection.

Figurines by Ernestine Hilton Sigmon, daughter of Clara Maude Hilton. Danielson collection.

Vases, 3¼" (L) and 3¾" (R), decorated by Clara Maude Hilton. Vase on right is a molded piece with an unusual hummingbird decoration. Danielson collection.

Teapot with raised dogwoods underglaze decoration by Clara Maude Hilton. Pitchers, vases, and teapots of this genre are eagerly collected. Danielson collection.

Hilton pottery, dogwood decoration, small bowl and plate, cup and saucer. If one can obtain an entire tableware setting, these are very desirable. Danielson collection.

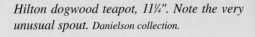

Hilton dogwood teapot, 11¼". Note the very unusual spout. Danielson collection.

Rural scene, 10" x 12" by Ernestine Hilton Sigmon. Danielson collection.

Hilton frog (pencil holder), large format, 8¾" x 11½" (approx.), Note decoration is cobalt wash. Holes without raised rims. Danielson collection.

"Melmar" pottery made by Hilton. Typical cobalt edging of rims. Clara Maude Hilton's pottery was called by collectors "blue edge." All four examples are stamped: covered bowl, 4" x 4", pitcher (large), 4¾" x 3¾", pitcher (miniature), 2" x 2½", covered bowl, 3½" x 3½". Nowell Guffey collection.

Pitcher, three-gallon, 16" x 10½", by the late Burlon B. Craig, the dean of Catawba Valley potters. Decorated by wife Irene. Nowell Guffey collection.

Three decorated examples by F.W. Hilton, Hickory. Creamer, 2¾" x 2¾", sugar, 2" x 2¾". Clear glass glaze, vase, 4¾" x 4¾". North Carolina is known as the "Land of the Long Leaf Pine." The grape decoration is also common. Signed Nowell Guffey collection.

Vase, 4⅞" x 5¼", with painted house in landscape, Lincoln County clay. Clear glaze, underglaze scene. After E.A. Hilton moved the pottery from Oyama to Pleasant Gardens in McDowell County, Maude made a complete transition to art pottery.

Hilton dogwood, signed: Hilton. Large 9" x 7¾" pitcher with painted, raised dogwoods. The dogwood is the North Carolina state flower, and many would-be artists in the Tarheel State painted dogwoods on unglazed pottery. In the Hilton pieces the flowers are under glaze and often raised. Huffman collection.

Bowl, 3⅜" x 6¾" with underglaze decoration of morning glory flowers and leaves. Clear glass glaze. Though unsigned, the bowl has Hilton form and decorative technique.

Detail of bowl with morning glory decoration. The choice of this flowering plant is unusual if not rare.

Small jugs, 4" x 4⅝" and 4¼" x 4½". Single strap handle, decorated with multiple circular bands, unsigned, attributed to Hilton Pottery. Maude usually decorated wares with blue, white, and sometimes brown concentric bands around the body. Nowell Guffey collection.

Vase with blue bands, 9⅝" x 5⅛". The blue banding was made famous by the Hilton dinnerware. Maude decorated rims and edges with blue cobalt decoration. *Nowell Guffey collection.*

Decorated pitcher, 4⅝" x 4⅝", by Hilton Pottery, circa 1930, single strap handle, two applied geese. Exhibited at Catawba Valley Tradition, 1999. *Provenance, Tony and Marie Shank, Nowell Guffey collection.*

Pine cone candleholder, 4½" x 4½", glazed with glass, probably from crushed bottles. Buff colored clay mix, unsigned, attributed on form to Hilton Pottery, probably at Oyama site. Auby (E.A.) Hilton employed a number of potters, including Bill Gordy, who had worked in Seagrove.

Painted scene underglaze. Milk pitcher and jar. Pitcher, 9½" x 7", clear glass glaze, 6⅝" x 5½" jar. Both signed Hilton. Painted by Clara Maude Hilton, mother of Ernestine, Lera, and Tommie. *Nowell Guffey collection.*

Unsigned vase with unusual handles, attributed to Floyd Hilton, possibly influenced by Jonah Owen.

Unglazed two-ring large vases by E.A. Hilton Company. Application of sealant material. Grounds decoration at St. James Place Museum. $175.00 – 200.00 (pair)

Figurines, mother and child, 5" x 2⅝", man with lambs, 7¼" x 4¾". The figurines were among the most important examples of Clara Maude Hilton's artistry, wife of E.A. Hilton and mother of Ernestine. The figurines were made after she produced the decorated tableware. Maude raised the Hilton Pottery wares to true art pottery with her dogwood vases, underglazed painting, and figurines made in the 1930s and 1940s. Nowell Guffey collection.

Large 18" deep bowl, central Piedmont, circa 1900. Inside glaze but no exterior glaze. Probably Alamance County, Snow Camp area. Sometimes confused with "Catawba Indian" pottery. Chapel Hill Museum.

Porch vase, 21½", Hilton "Catawba Indian Pottery," unglazed exterior, glazed interior. $225.00 – 250.00. Chapel Hill Museum.

Interior glazing of wall pocket at left. Not to be confused with Hilton Pottery. This combination of glazing was used in the Seagrove area as well.

Wall pocket earthenware, Randolph/Moore County, circa 1890 – 1920, unsigned, desirable greenish tint, hint of orange spotting and ribbed banded rim. See Country Living magazine, 3/87. Farmer/James gift, Chapel Hill Museum.

Left, basket 12", stamped North Carolina. Right, pitcher, 8", stamped E.W. Reinhardt.

Spittoon, 12¼", attributed to Hilton Pottery, circa 1935 – 1940, unglazed exterior, glazed interior with what may be Albany slip. Chapel Hill Museum.

Left, frog, 4", chromium; center, vase, 4", clear glaze interior; right, frog, 4". Pieces are unsigned. Huffman collection.

Hilton wall pockets, unsigned. Left, 8" with cobalt decoration; Right, 7", with cobalt decorated "knobs". Huffman collection.

Vase with landscape 9". By Maude Hilton, signed: Hilton. Huffman collection.

Center, bowl with white flowers. Left, decorated vase 5", stamped F.W. Hilton Hickory, North Carolina. All signed Mrs. F.W. Hilton.

Left, large decorated wall pocket, chromium glaze, signed A.M. Hilton, 1936. Right, lidded pitcher, 7", stamped F.W. Hilton. Huffman collection.

Left, pitcher, 3", with painted flowers. Center, vase, 4", with landscape, probably Maude Hilton. Right, vase with painted flowers, 4", stamped Hilton. Huffman collection.

Catawba Valley Swirl, unsigned. Left, swirl pitcher 8". Center, swirl vase 8". Right, swirl vase 10". Huffman collection.

The late Burlon Craig, Vale, NC, unloading kiln, 1978, Catawba Valley. Huffman photo.

Hilton Pottery. Left to right: Vase, 3" with cobalt decoration, unsigned; 4½" single handled vase, cobalt stripes, unsigned; vase, 3", with stamped decoration; frog, 3", cobalt decoration, unsigned. Huffman collection.

Hilton Pottery, unsigned. Left, vase, 4", with cobalt decoration. Center, vase, 9", cobalt decoration. Right, mug, 5", cobalt, cobalt striping. Huffman collection.

Mountain Pottery of Western North Carolina

by Rodney Leftwich

The principal area of pottery production in western North Carolina centered around Asheville in Buncombe County. A few folk potters operated in surrounding Yancey and Henderson counties, but the rich clay deposits, temperate climate, and prospect of little competition prompted most potters to settle in Buncombe County. Ties of kinship and friendship also were evident factors behind the establishment of many potteries.

The mountainous region of western North Carolina was the last area in the state to be settled and consequently the last region for potteries to develop. Since fewer potteries were established here, the area has been described as having a lesser tradition. Several aspects, however, show this region to be rich in pottery variety and a producer of wares equal to any in the state.

Other areas of pottery production in North Carolina evolved primarily from singular influences. The eastern Piedmont was settled by English potters while potters in the western Piedmont or Catawba Valley were mostly of Germanic origin. Around Salem, the potters were Moravian. Each of these regions developed distinctive wares and methods of production based on the origins and traditions of their founders.

The potters who moved into the mountain valleys of Buncombe County came from numerous other states and areas of North Carolina. Potters from the Edgefield District of South Carolina were the first to arrive, soon followed by potters from the Catawba Valley in North Carolina. These were followed by folk potters from the Atlanta, Georgia, region and journeymen potters from the North. Arts and Crafts pottery was introduced from Tennessee and elsewhere. Each immigrant to the area brought his unique skills, forms, glazes, and technology. Although craftsmen initially settled in different areas of the county, mutual need and interest led to the exchange of both workers and ideas.

Throughout much of the nineteenth century, utilitarian folk potters supplied crocks, jugs, and churns to the mountain populace. Predominantly, they manufactured stoneware, though some supplemented their production with low-fired earthenwares such as flower pots. Their alkaline glazes were created from various combinations of clay, wood ashes, crushed glass, or iron ore. Albany slip, a fine clay suitable for glazing, was shipped into the Asheville area by the turn of the century. Salt glazing was not done in the North Carolina mountains as the distance from the sea made salt a rare and expensive item.

Art pottery was produced in both stoneware and porcelain. The transitional art wares created by utilitarian potteries seeking new sales outlets were glazed with traditional alkaline or Albany slip glazes. Potters who came to the region from an Arts and Crafts background rather than a utilitarian one formulated their glazes. Initially matte green or brown glazes were popular, but these were gradually replaced by a rainbow of bright, glossy glazes.

Firing or burning of the pottery wares was done in a variety of kilns. Most utilitarian potters chose some form of long, low wood-fired groundhog kiln. A few, however, experimented with round dome-shaped kilns fired with wood or coal. Art potters preferred round bottle-shaped kilns, though most experimented with various forms of furnaces.

The mountain region remained a good market for functional wares until the early twentieth century. When the need for churns, jugs, and storage crocks diminished, most utilitarian potteries closed, but a few survived well into the twentieth century by making the transition to art wares. Long a destination for tourists, the mountains enjoyed considerable souvenir trade, and craft shops eagerly sought pottery to supply the demand.

Three separate pottery communities developed in Buncombe County. The earliest began near Candler, west of Asheville, in the 1840s. Another area developed north of Asheville around Weaverville during the late 1800s. The last to develop began in the 1920s, south of Asheville in Arden. The traditions, wares, and potters of each are described separately.

Candler Area

Penland-Stone Pottery

Present knowledge of the folk pottery tradition in Buncombe County began about 1844 when William W. Penland, a farmer near Candler, established a pottery on his property in Hominy Creek township. Family tradition and historical documents do not agree as to whether William Penland was a potter, but it is known that he hired turners from the Edgefield District of South Carolina. One account named the first potter as Mr. Matthews, most likely Isaac R. Matthews, a 44-year-old laborer from South Carolina, who was a neighbor of the Penlands in 1850.

The second potter from South Carolina was Edward Whitfield Stone, who was born in western Virginia, now Kentucky. Likely Edward received his introduction to pottery from his grandfather, James or Whitfield Stone, who learned the pottery trade in Blackpool, England, before emigrating to America.

At the age of 18, Edward moved to South Carolina to work for Edgefield District potter, Thomas Chandler. By 1845 Stone had moved to Buncombe County, North Carolina, to turn wares for William Penland. Other potters came from Edgefield including Francis Devilin, William Devore, and several Rhodeses, probably related to Edgefield potter Collin Rhodes. Soon the area around the pottery became known as Jugtown.

The Edgefield training of these potters is evident in their bulbous jars and double-collared jugs with handles attached to the shoulder instead of the neck. Their alkaline glazes, pale green to tan or brown from added iron rock, can easily be mistaken for Edgefield glazes.

One small jug attributed to the Penland-Stone Pottery shows a decorative application of iron slip dabbed over a pale alkaline glaze. Although blurred in the firing, it evidently was an attempt at floral decoration. Iron slips, as well as white kaolin slips, were used by Edgefield potters Collin Rhodes and Thomas Chandler to decorate ware with loops, swags, tulips, or rare birds, snakes, slaves, or ladies in hoop skirts.

It is not clear whether Edward Stone formed a legal partnership with William Penland, but he did stay with the pottery, teaching the trade to his own son James Henry and to members of the Penland family. Two of William Penland's sons, John H. and Charles J., are known to have worked at the pottery.

John Penland's son, Joseph Sylvester, learned the trade and was the first member of the Penland family listed in the census as a potter. As a master potter, J.S. Penland produced some of the most skillfully turned and beautifully glazed ware at the pottery. Blindness forced him to discontinue potting by 1890, and family tradition holds that his eyes were damaged by the searing light of the kiln firings.

James Henry Stone turned ware along with Joseph and Joseph's son, William Marion. In the 1890s Marion married Henry Stone's daughter, Susan Luemma, officially uniting the potting families. Henry Stone left to seek employment with the railroad and by 1910 was working for a Weaverville pottery.

Marion continued to operate the pottery with the assistance of his sons, Hobart, Lewis, and Cash. All turned some wares but helped primarily by digging and hauling clay, grinding glazes, glazing ware, and burning it in the groundhog kiln. Marion's daughters also assisted with the family business but probably did not make pottery on a regular basis. A 1926 newspaper article, however, states, "It is a business that has not been confined to the menfolk in the family. The women make as artistic potters as the men, and there is no tradition against the women turning at the wheel."

With a dwindling market for functional wares, Marion's sons sought other employment. During the late 1930s, Marion's health began to fail, wood was hard to obtain, and he had little help. The pottery was out of operation for long periods of time. With Marion's death in 1945, one hundred years of pottery making at Jugtown came to a close.

Benjamin Trull Pottery

The success of the Penland-Stone factory encouraged others to open potteries. Benjamin Trull, a neighbor of the Penlands, established his own pottery in nearby Big Cove by 1885. Most likely he learned the trade from the Penlands and Stones, as his forms and glazes closely resemble those from the Jugtown pottery. Apparently, Trull experimented with glazes because pot shards found at the site vary greatly. Alkaline glaze colors include pale greens, tans, rust, and dark browns both in matte and gloss finish. Albany slip was employed as well as an unusual purple to iron-red local slip.

Although it is not clear which of Benjamin's sons (John, Bill, Tom, George, or Jim) learned to turn, both Jim and John turned ware at the Rutherford Pottery. Scribbled on a notepad dated 1900 is the following: "One load by Tom-251 gal., one load by George-204 gal., by Tom-90, by B.R. Trull-47, by B.R. Trull-25." This could refer to ware turned, hauled, or sold.

Albert Ernest Fulbright, a potter from South Carolina, was working at the Trull Pottery by 1904. He may have operated a kiln on his own property next to the Trulls, as he is listed as a "potter working on own account" in the 1910 census. Fulbright is also known to have turned ware at the nearby Penland, Rutherford, Throckmorton, and Brown potteries as well as for potteries in South Carolina.

Benjamin probably hauled ware further than any other North Carolina potter of his day. During the Civil War, he had joined the Union Army in Tennessee and in later years continued to be away from home for long periods of time. He obtained an alleged cure for skin cancer from the Cherokee and made several trips to Texas to sell both the cure and his wares. Family tradition holds that Benjamin had a second family in Texas. While returning from Texas in 1905, he developed chills and fever and nearly died. His health was never good again and within a year or so, the pottery closed.

J.D. Rutherford Pottery

James Devrick Rutherford, owner of several sawmills and a neighbor of the Trulls in Big Cove, established a pottery around 1907 after the Trull shop closed. Never one to go into anything halfway, he built a large 40 x 100-foot two-story wood-frame shop with a 20-foot waterwheel at one end to power the equipment. A long wooden race channeled water from a nearby creek toward the power wheel. As he planned to operate year-round, Rutherford insulated the shop with dried sand poured between the inner and outer walls and piped heat from a furnace throughout the structure. Next to the shop, he constructed a large, brick, rectangular groundhog kiln, large enough to stand in. Three five-gallon jars could be stacked on top of each other in the center.

Craftsmen were hired to turn the wares, among them James Otis Trull, John Trull, Oscar L. Bachelder, Albert Fulbright, James Henry Stone, and Marion Penland. Most of the traditional wheel-turned utilitarian wares were glazed with Albany slip. Some small figurines of dogs, frogs, and monkeys were also produced from commercial molds and glazed with Albany slip or white Bristol glaze with cobalt blue decoration.

Rutherford had difficulty keeping turners and did not make the quick profits he had anticipated. The market for pottery churns, jars, jugs, and canning jars was quickly declining, so he closed the factory in 1914.

O.L. Bachelder Pottery

Oscar L. Bachelder, in partnership with a friend Bob Gudger, established a pottery at Luther and by 1916 was producing wares. For over 40 years Bachelder had worked as an itinerant potter, wandering through 28 states and territories east of the Rockies. He took pride in his ability to produce large pieces of pottery in great quantities. In recounting his work experience he stated, "My energy was greedily used by one boss after another, each urging me to greater effort until my heart would grow sick, and I would suddenly leave the place, only to seek another soon." At Luther, Bachelder at last was happy with the beauty of the mountains and his new-found independence.

First, a small groundhog kiln was built and later a round downdraft. Clays were dug locally in the creek bottom adjacent to the site. Later as Bachelder's interest turned increasingly to art wares, he ordered ingredients from other states to blend with the local deposits. Initially, utility ware was produced, some with straight sides so it could be nested for easier hauling. Bob Gudger hauled the wares by wagon until family and farm responsibilities caused him to dissolve their partnership.

By 1916 Bachelder had named his pottery Omar Khayyam, after the popular Persian poet. Jacques and Juliana Busbee, founders of the well-known Jugtown Pottery in Moore County in the early 1920s, visited Bachelder in 1916 and were influenced by his work. Mrs. Busbee wrote, "He is a most interesting man, and his feeling for form is remarkable."

Gradually Bachelder's efforts turned almost entirely to the production of artistic pottery. Vases of beautiful form and proportion were glazed with rich blacks, browns, yellows, greens, and blues. Occasionally he sprinkled the pottery surfaces with wood ashes, cobalt or manganese for decorative effect. In collaboration with Walter Stephen of Pisgah Forest Pottery, Bachelder achieved exceptional copper red reduction glaze. Unglazed ware, incised with lines to resemble wood, was called rusticated or cane ware. Bachelder's wife Agnes or "Pink" helped her husband at the shop and made some pottery which she marked with "AB." Other helpers who worked at the pottery included Ray Welch, Eugene Mintz, Ned Williams, and Morris Gudger of Buncombe County. Bachelder's work drew the attention of other potters — Paul St. Gaudens of New Hampshire, Walter

Stephen from Pisgah Forest Pottery, Edith and Converse Harwell of Alabama, and William Soini of Finland and New York.

Bachelder's art pottery was exhibited in Chicago, Boston, and Omaha, winning several awards. In 1935 Bachelder died, and in 1937 the property was sold to Bob Gudger's daughter Christine and her husband. They made a few pieces of pottery, one of which is incised "C. Bates Omar Khayyam Pottery, 1938."

Throckmorton Pottery

In 1940, the Bates sold the Bachelder Pottery to Mr. and Mrs. Thomas Throckmorton, who reopened it in 1941. Throckmorton, a native of South Dakota, had spent most of his life traveling and studying art. Accomplished at illustration, sculpture, and pottery, he had worked in Chicago, New York, New Orleans, Buenos Aires, and at Shearwater Pottery in Mississippi before coming to Candler.

Small vases and novelty items were formed from molds, although some pieces were turned by Albert Fulbright. Ray Penland and Roy Stamey assisted in the production of molded wares, and Mrs. Throckmorton, also an artist, assisted in decorating and signing the finished pieces.

With the outbreak of World War II and a depressed economy, the Throckmortons probably had difficulty selling art wares. In 1943 they suddenly left for New York, leaving most of their property behind. Tradition holds the Throckmortons had strong German accents, were mistrusted by the local population, and feared for their lives. While the Throckmortons retained ownership of the property, they never returned to North Carolina.

Weaverville Area

The earliest report of a pottery in western North Carolina was near Weaverville in Buncombe County. Matthew Cole had produced earthenware in Randolph County in 1790 before moving to Reems Creek in Buncombe County in 1797. According to tradition, he made pottery with the Penland family. This is unlikely as the Penlands of the Candler area established their pottery 50 years after this date.

The 1870 census lists Jammie Bassett, 20-year-old son of William P. Bassett, as a crock maker in the Flint Hill Community east of Jupiter in the Flat Creek township. It is unknown where Bassett received his training.

His site has not been located, and no signed wares attributable to this pottery are known.

Yoder-McClure Pottery

During the last quarter of the nineteenth century, a pottery known as the Yoder-McClure Jug Factory was established on the north side of Cherry Street (now Church Street) in Weaverville. Although the exact date of establishment is not known, the county court minutes of 1893 – 1894 recorded a complaint and ordinance filed ordering the pottery shop owners to "fill in the ditch adjacent to their operation," which had become a public nuisance or hazard.

Most likely Sheree Wheaton McClure financed the venture and was not a potter. He hired a skillful Catawba Valley potter, S. Leverick Yoder, to turn, glaze, and fire the utilitarian wares. All pottery produced was glazed with pale to dark green glass alkaline glaze. Some examples from this pottery show areas of bluish color fringed with milky white, a result of naturally occurring rutile in the local clays. Banding, or less frequently scalloping, decorated the shoulders and necks of some vessels. This was a common decorative techniques used by potters in the Catawba Valley region where Yoder originated.

Other workers at the Yoder-McClure Jug Factory include George and David Donkel and Joseph and Jeter Lankford. By 1905, the Jug factory closed, and Leverick Yoder moved back to the Catawba Valley.

J.R. Cheek Pottery

During the late 1890s, James R. Cheek, a teamster, built a pottery shop near Clarks Chapel Road northwest of Weaverville. Clay was hauled from nearby Flat Creek and a kiln constructed. For turners he hired his brother-in-law, Joseph Lankford, and son-in-law, Jedder (Jeter) Lankford. Some of James Cheek's sons were old enough to work at the pottery, and family descendants say that several turned ware. The Lankfords departed to set up their own shop, and in 1910 Henry Stone moved to Weaverville and turned for Cheek.

Glazes varied from gray green to tan glass alkaline formulas to dark brown alkaline with added-in iron rock. Inconclusive archaeological exploration suggests the kiln may have been circular instead of the more commonly used groundhog style.

William Cheek hauled the pottery to neighboring counties along with honey, wax, and tannery products. Faced with decreasing markets, the shop closed by 1912.

Lankford Pottery

By 1910 Joseph and Jeter Lankford established a pottery in the Stockville community north of Weaverville. Although a variety of utilitarian forms was produced, double-strap handled molasses jars were popular items made at the site. Glazes were predominantly a medium to dark green brown alkaline or a speckled iron red slip. This shop closed in 1915 when the property was sold.

Donkel Pottery

Potters George B. and David M. Donkel came to Weaverville from the Catawba Valley region where they had known and worked with members of the Yoder family. At first they worked with Leverick Yoder at the Jug factory in Weaverville. Good clay and a vacant cabin were located on the north side of Reems Creek Road, and in 1897 they leased this property to establish their own shop. Their stamp,, "D. & D./THE BEST," was probably the least modest in North Carolina.

About 1899 David Donkel married and gave up making ware to become a farmer. George continued to operate the pottery as well as a small store. Around 1907 he gave up the store and built a house, barn, log pottery shop, and brick kiln on newly acquired property a mile south. Here he operated until between 1930 and 1932 when he moved his shop back to his original property.

While most regional potters were producing thick, straight-walled utilitarian wares glazed with Albany slip, George Donkel's jars and churns retained the graceful bulbous forms of an earlier age. He preferred the glass alkaline glazes over the Albany slip that had become popular after the turn of the century. To some of his glaze he added iron rock, creating a gray to black ware.

Little decoration was applied to Donkel's pottery. One molasses jug is known to have a single wavy line. George, a traditional potter to the end, was reluctant to make the transition to "art forms." His nephew by marriage, Talmon K. Cole, worked around the shop and turned small tourist ware. It was probably his encouragement that led Donkel to create a few elaborately decorated terra cotta urns in the 1930s. These had ring-shaped handles, molded Indian heads, and hand-built reliefs of laurel, wild rose, and other mountain flowers.

George's family origins had been in Pennsylvania, the Keystone State. It has been hypothesized this is the reason he used an impressed key for his stamp. With sales declining during World War II, George closed his pottery shop during the early 1940s.

Arden Area

Lee Smith Pottery

During the early 1890s, a pottery was established in the Hillgirt community of Henderson County near the Buncombe County line. Owned by Lee Roy Smith, a prominent land owner, the pottery produced red-brown slip-glazed utilitarian ware. Marked ware was stamped with "LEE SMITH/HILLGIRT, N.C."

While the turner at this pottery has not been identified, it is interesting that a potter, Mark Shuford, was living nearby in the Limestone section of Buncombe County. An "M. Shuford" was listed as running a pottery works at Weaverville during the 1890s in a Board of Agriculture publication *North Carolina*. As Shuford was living some distance from Weaverville and has never been connected with a pottery there, it is likely he is the Lee Smith potter.

Ware from this pottery was skillfully turned and closely resembles some Northern pottery. In addition to churns, canning jars, and pitchers, small items such as vases and cone-shaped inkwells with handles were made. Incising on several pieces includes, "Daisey Smith, Sept. 5, 1893" and "W.F. Willard." It is not known when the pottery closed.

Brown Pottery

Davis Pennington Brown and Evan Javan Brown, two brothers from Atlanta, moved to Arden in 1924, and in 1925 opened Brown Brothers Pottery in a building that had been used as a blacksmith shop. They built a groundhog kiln, dug native clay, and formed ware which they glazed with Albany slip or formulated from commercial ingredients. Only for a short period during the Depression did they use the "sand and ash" alkaline glaze they had used in Georgia.

Wishing to advertise their skills and attract customers, the brothers made a huge vase in 1925. Standing 6 feet 2 inches and weighing about 500 pounds, the vase was displayed in their shop. Too large for the kiln, the vase was never fired.

Ware was stamped "BROWN BROS." until Javan left the partnership in 1930. After this date, several different stamps worded "Brown Pottery" were used. Other members of the Brown family including Otto, Bobby, Rufus, and Willie came from Georgia to work at the pottery, and in 1929 Brown Pottery employed six men, the largest number of any western North Carolina pottery. Davis's son, Louis, worked at the pottery along with grandsons Robert and Charles.

About 1930 the shop was moved to a house across the highway, just south of the first building. Pottery for sale was displayed on the long front porch of the house. During 1939 and 1940 a larger 110 x 45-foot building was constructed on this site. The round kiln outside was torn down, and a new large downdraft kiln was built inside the shop. For years a 1925 International truck (with a 3-inch devil face jug made by Davis decorating its radiator cap) was used to haul clay and peddle ware to hardware stores.

The Browns adapted to changing tastes and demands, successfully weathering the decline in the folk tradition. A major change came to the operation in the 1930s when a New York distributor contracted Brown Pottery to produce valor ware, a jiggered earthenware French-style cookware. This became their chief product during the 1940s with orders for 50,000 pieces a year.

Samples of 160 different forms were displayed on shelves in the shop, each marked on the base with an order number. Although churns continued to be produced into the 1950s, numerous pieces were made for tourists. These novelty items included face jugs, wall pockets, ring jugs, vases, and nude-handled or horse's rear-end mugs. Cherokee shops ordered unglazed or unfired bowls and wedding jugs to be sold as authentic Indian crafts. Davis's and Javan's wives, Ella and Madeline, decorated ware with clay relief designs of dogwood, wild rose, wisteria, and grapes and leaves.

Charles Brown, Davis's grandson, continues to operate the pottery with his wife, Jeannette Bradley Brown. They continue to specialize in commercially-jiggered dinnerware and face jugs glazed with a traditional red-brown or vibrant blues, greens, raspberry or mauve. Brown's Pottery claims potting roots in England with eight generations of potters in America.

Evan's Pottery

Evan's Pottery, located on Clayton Road near Skyland, North Carolina, was opened in 1961 by Evan J. Brown. Evan had grown up in the pottery making business. His skilled father, E.J. (Javan) Brown, worked at many potteries in North and South Carolina, Georgia, Alabama, and Florida. As early as age seven, Evan was turning rabbit crocks and by age ten was making all forms except churns.

While in high school during the 1930s, he joined his father and Uncle Davis at the Brown shop in Arden, North Carolina. Here Evan made molds for the jiggered French-style cookware. Following service in the Air Force during WWII, Evan worked at his father's old shop at Forest Park, a suburb of Atlanta, Georgia. In 1955 the family moved from Atlanta to Skyland where they would be near Davis Brown's Arden Pottery.

In addition to working as a traffic controller at the Asheville Airport and helping at Brown's Pottery, Evan cleared the land in Skyland, built his home, shop buildings, and wood-burning kiln. Clay for the pottery was dug locally until the source ran out in 1981. Production at first consisted largely of churns. This changed gradually to the manufacture of kitchen and tableware, including pie plates, mugs, vases, urns, candleholders, umbrella stands, and water coolers. Folksy face jugs and large Rebecca pitchers were other specialties of the pottery.

Evan's basic glazes were two modifications of a Bristol stoneware glaze and Albany slip. Increasingly, coloring oxides and stains were added to create mottled green, brown, yellow, white, and sponged-on blue. Initially fired with wood, a shortage of fuel in 1971 caused Evan to switch to natural gas. First bisqued in a large gas kiln, the pots were then glazed and refired to cone 6 in small electric kilns.

Javan, his brother Otto, and Otto's son Jimmy occasionally turned ware at the pottery. Mercedes, Evan's wife, was a true partner, putting on handles, glazing, loading kilns, and selling. Ill health forced Evan's retirement in 1987, and he passed away in 1992. Following a decline in production, Evan's daughter, Cherry Corn, took over operation of the pottery. She continues making the traditional wares, specializing in face jugs, candle lanterns, and vases decorated with raised dogwood motifs.

Nonconnah Pottery

In May 1913, Walter Stephen settled in the Skyland community, a few miles south of Asheville. He had moved from Capleville near Memphis, Tennessee, where Stephen and his mother had established a pottery in 1904. The Tennessee pottery was named Nonconnah after a creek that flows around Memphis. Caught up in the Arts and Crafts movement, they had produced matte green or occasionally matte blue art pottery with multicolored raised slip designs of native flowers.

Following the death of both his parents in 1910, Stephen sought a new place to live and continue his pottery work. In western North Carolina he met a socially prominent couple, Mr. and Mrs. C.P. Ryman, who were influenced by examples they saw of the Tennessee pottery. With the Rymans' financing and Stephen's skills, a partnership was formed and a pottery established by late 1913 or early 1914.

The new pottery, also named Nonconnah, consisted of two buildings constructed of rough-sawn lumber, one with an inside kiln. Located on the east side of Highway 25, they hoped to attract summer tourists heading north to Asheville.

North Carolina Nonconnah produced mostly small souvenir items — vases, mugs, candlesticks, teapots, tobacco jars, pitchers, and match holders. Work was produced both in molds and on the potter's wheel. Their simple, well-designed shapes were glazed with matte or semi-matte glazes, usually with one exterior glaze and a contrasting interior glaze. Exterior colors frequently were chrome green, fawn brown, or charcoal gray while interior colors included gray-white, fawn, and blue-green.

Nonconnah art pottery shows a wide range of decoration. Stephen continued his mother's decorative technique of applying porcelain slip with a brush to create raised designs. Unlike his mother's Tennessee work with multicolored slip designs, Stephen appears to have only used white slip. The sharp contrast between the all-white patterns and their green or brown background created a classic look customers compared to the cameo decorations on English Wedgwood pottery.

The most commonly used white slip or cameo designs were of naturalistic ivy or grapevines and leaves. Less frequent patterns include arrowheads, butterflies, and geometric lines and shapes. While Stephen did some of the cameo designs, Mrs. Ryman is credited with the delicate vines and leaves. A local artistic high school student Artus Moser is also known to have decorated Nonconnah.

A line Stephen called "Terra Cotta" was also produced. These were created by spinning together contrasting colors of clay to create a marbleized or swirl effect. Glazed only on the interior, the exterior combinations of red-brown and cream or gray and orange were left unglazed. Niloak Pottery of Benton, Arkansas, manufactured similar swirled art pottery on a large scale which probably influenced the Nonconnah Pottery.

Other interesting decorated examples of Nonconnah include a five-inch molded vase with evenly spaced indented geometric panels, glazed with a satin matte blue-gray finish. This vase closely resembles the work of Marblehead Pottery in Massachusetts. Another flat-sided tapering vase with incised line decoration may have been influenced by Rookwood Pottery in Cincinnati.

Mrs. Jacques Busbee, who was to become famous for establishing the Jugtown Pottery in Moore County, North Carolina, visited Nonconnah Pottery in 1916. As chairperson of art for the North Carolina Federation of Women's Clubs, she wrote:

"The kiln of Skyland is very interesting. . . doing work that resembles Wedgewood (sic). He (Stephen) is experimenting with more intelligence than anyone in the state. He is studying and working constantly. His work is known as Nonconnah Pottery and will soon be in a class with the best work done in any of the states."

The pottery venture was not the financial success Stephen and Ryman had hoped. In 1916 Stephen left the partnership. Nonconnah Pottery continued another year under Ryman's direction, closing with the uncertainties and economic changes brought on by America's entry into World War I.

Pisgah Forest Pottery

Following his departure from the Nonconnah Pottery, Walter Stephen undertook a variety of masonry jobs. His love of pottery would not be denied however, and he read avidly and developed a new interest in Oriental forms and glazes. In 1920 Stephen worked part-time with Bachelder at his Omar Khayyam Pottery. He also constructed a small kiln at his home and experimented with local clays and formulated glazes. Little is known of what he made, but it is believed his experiments centered on recapturing the secrets of Chinese caledon and red glazes.

In 1925 Stephen began construction of a new home and pottery on property in Arden. Early in 1926

Stephen opened his new venture, Pisgah Forest Pottery, a name he had also apparently used on his previous experimental work. The pottery sold well, and in 1929 he expanded the shop building. A large round, up-draft wood-fired kiln was erected to accompany the coal kiln built in 1925.

More changes were made in the early 1930s. A filter press for clay preparation and carbide lighting were installed. Across the creek from the pottery Stephen constructed a small concrete library building. Nearer the highway a sales building of yellow-brown river rock was erected.

In 1927 Stephen had one assistant, Edgar Baker, who helped mix clay and fire the kiln. Early in 1929 Grady Ledbetter began working at Pisgah Forest. For several years Ledbetter prepared clay, cut wood, and assisted with glazing and firing. By 1934 he was turning pottery at the wheel.

Production reached a level where additional workers were needed. One of Stephen's stepsons, Herman Case, came to the pottery in 1931 and specialized in crystalline glazes. Three Rhodes brothers, James, Billy, and Woody, also assisted with the pottery duties. In 1936 Billy became a partner with Stephen and Ledbetter. Occasionally other potters, including Willy and Javan Brown, helped Stephen with special orders.

During World War II Stephen's coworkers left for other responsibilities. Stephen continued to run the pottery with the occasional help of Thomas Case, his step-grandson. After the war, Ledbetter returned, and in 1949 Case began full-time employment at the pottery.

Pottery production at Pisgah Forest shows a change from that at Nonconnah. Stephen continued some forms and decorative techniques but particularly explored his new interest in Oriental, especially Chinese pottery. Sung Dynasty and Ming Dynasty forms and glazes were produced. Other Oriental forms were adopted secondhand from the wares of Dedham, Rookwood, and other American potteries that were attracted to classic Chinese forms.

While the majority of Stephen's early production at Pisgah Forest consisted of vases, jars, and lamp bases in Chinese forms, non-Oriental forms were also made. Art novelties included molded rectangular match holders with relief images of a woman at a spinning wheel. Cast portrait busts of Robert E. Lee and Woodrow Wilson were produced as were bookends of sailing ships and of Chimney Rock, one of the area's

natural geological formations. Time consuming to produce, these novelty items were discontinued before 1930.

Vases and table wares, including plates, mugs, teapots, and pitchers were the predominant forms. Less frequently made items included lamp bases, lidded casseroles, cookie jars, candle lanterns, wall pockets, ashtrays, honeypots, flower frogs, fireplace tiles, and garlic jars. Unlike the molded Nonconnah wares, nearly all Pisgah Forest forms were hand turned at the potter's wheel.

Initially, Pisgah Forest produced semi-matte green or copper red versions of Chinese glazes. The gray to green caledon-like glazes resembled those developed over several Chinese dynasties. During the late 1920s Stephen added crackle glazes in blue and wine. Crackle glazes may be defined as glazes which have a tendency to craze or develop decorative patterns of cracks.

Aware of the growing popularity of brightly colored glazes during the 1930s, Stephen added white, light pink, rose, yellow, forest green, jade green, cobalt blue, and a variety of crystalline glazes to his palette. These new glossy formulas largely replaced Stephen's semi-matte caledon and copper red glazes. His brighter and glossier turquoise blue and wine glazes continued in use with his new colors and became trademark glazes of the pottery.

One of Stephen's special interests was in crystalline glazes. These glazes are characterized by crystal clusters of various sizes, shapes, and colors embedded in a more uniform and often opaque glaze. Herman Case helped Stephen, experimenting with various oxides of copper, cobalt, manganese, iron, and uranium to develop a wide variety of colors.

Methods other than colorful glazes were also used to decorate Pisgah Forest wares. While some were carved, painted, underglazed, or sculpted, it was the cameo work that brought Stephen the most recognition. Continuing his all-white cameo decorations, he selected new subject matter unlike that done at the Nonconnah Pottery.

Recalling his childhood experiences in the West, Stephen depicted covered wagons, cabins, buffalo hunts, Indian tepees, men with rifles or fiddles, square dancers, plowing with a steer, and the spinning wheel. Other scenes include sailing ships, deer chased by dogs, a Christmas dinner, the zodiac, and various Masonic designs.

Most cameo designs were free-hand, painted on in multiple layers to create relief. Stephen experimented with molded cameo decorations during the 1940s and 1950s. Clay reliefs were carefully removed from his original molds and sprigged-on to the pottery surface. Generally these designs were cruder than his handpainted reliefs. Some molded cameo designs are Masonic emblems, the spinning wheel, the Christmas dinner, a fiddler with a dog, Davey Crockett, Robert E. Lee, and religious themes such as the Good Samaritan, the Prodigal Son, and the Madonna with the Christ Child.

Two people other than Stephen created free-hand cameo designs at Pisgah Forest. In 1926 and 1927, Alton Case occasionally tried the cameo technique and is credited with doing a tile with an old bearded man pushing a loaded wheelbarrow. In 1951 and 1952, Sara Austin was taught the cameo technique by Stephen. Not wanting to copy his designs, she created her own. These include dogwood blossoms, a cobbler at his bench, a crowing rooster, three bears, Abraham Lincoln, an old church with cemetery, and the political elephant and donkey.

During the early 1950s, a set of square dancer and musician molds were made for Pisgah Forest by a Mr. Lawton. Lawton had moved to North Carolina from England where he had been employed as a mold maker by Wedgwood Pottery. Thomas Case assumed responsibility for the production of all cameo wares from Lawton's molds.

Some of the most unusual and attractive Pisgah Forest pottery was carved or painted with underglaze colors. In most cases these were not decorated at the pottery but by amateur artists in their homes or classes nearby. The person most responsible for these decorated wares was Nancy Jones, a local artist. Jones taught pottery carving classes from 1939 to 1941, and the names on many carved examples are attributed to her students.

Stephen started marking the bases of his wares with the figure of a potter at the wheel and words "Pisgah Forest Pottery" even before its official 1926 opening. In 1927 he began dating his production and continued to do so most years through 1954. Some potter figures were kneeling with others standing or seated. Different sized stamps were made for different sized ware. Over 60 variations of the Pisgah Forest mark are known.

In 1949, Stephen, now 73 years old, felt it was time to plan a semi-retirement that would allow him more time to concentrate on new cameo designs and crystalline glazes. He gave responsibility of the main pottery to his younger coworkers, Grady Ledbetter and Thomas Case. Near the sales building he built a small cinder block pottery shop equipped with an electric powered potter's wheel and an oil-fired, brick kiln. In 1953 he moved into his new shop that he called "Long Pine." Marking his creations "1953/Stephen/Cameo/ Long Pine," he worked here until his death in 1961.

Partners Ledbetter and Case continued to produce the forms and glazes made famous by Stephen. Tom Case's mother, Katherine Case, helped trim the freshly turned pottery and waited on customers in the sale shop. In 1956 when Case became employed at nearby Olin Corporation (later Ecusta), he worked part-time at Pisgah Forest Pottery. Ledbetter worked more regularly on his family's dairy farm and turned wares at the pottery only during warm weather. Production became limited, and the pottery was open only during the summer tourist season. Most of the pottery made by Ledbetter and Case was marked with an undated potter-at-the-wheel stamp. A few examples made during the 1980s and 1990s had added incised dates.

Between 1995 and 1998, local potter Rodney Leftwich assisted at Pisgah Forest Pottery. In addition to turning ware and assisting with glazing and firing, Leftwich made new dated stamps for the pottery. The first stamp created was the traditional potter-at-the-wheel with the added date 1995. The 1996 stamp commemorated 70 years of Pisgah Forest operation. It was dated 1926 – 1996 and depicted a vase form. The last stamp was dated but showed the upper half of a potter-at-the-wheel and not the full-bodied images on wares made earlier.

Ledbetter died in 1998, and Case still continues to make pottery on a limited basis. Visitors are welcome to drop by and walk around the pottery. It remains much the same as when Stephen worked there, a virtual museum to the early craft industry in western North Carolina.

Traditional Utilitarian Wares

During the past two decades there has been a resurgence of interest in the traditional folk wares of North Carolina. Utilitarian objects designed to fill the needs of a rural self-sufficient population have found their way to collectors' homes, galleries, and even art museums. Treated as aesthetic objects, these collected and displayed functional pots tell us more about our culture than the mountain people who made them.

Most mountain potters were skilled craftsmen concerned with form as well as function. What is it that makes these crocks, jugs, and jars of an earlier time appeal to collectors today? Their pottery forms were straightforward, usually unembellished, and had the formal simplicity of Shaker furniture. Glazes, such as the distinctive iron-infused, orange-brown-black mottled alkaline glazes of the Stones and Penlands, more often than not significantly enhanced the visual impact of the pottery. Although designed as practical utilitarian objects, they can now be seen, more or less, as art. Increasing numbers of sophisticated university educated Americans are collecting traditional folk pottery, displaying it in their homes rather than putting it to the uses for which it was intended.

Art Wares

The tourist industry in western North Carolina created a demand for souvenir items. Most mountain potteries, however, could not make the transition from functional to art pottery. Attempts to create art wares at the Penland and Donkel potteries were minimal at best. Bachelder successfully converted to art pottery at his Omar Khayyam Pottery, finding an eager market both locally and nationally.

Traditional utilitarian pottery was already on the decline by the time Brown Pottery arrived in 1925. By adopting modern production methods and catering to tourists, this pottery has survived until today. Commercially jiggered French-style cookware was produced in large quantities for a New York firm, and numerous vases and novelty items were created for the tourist trade. Collectible, tourist oriented items include horses' rear mugs, mini chamber pots with contents, multi-handled drunkard's jugs, and vases with applied clay leaves and flowers.

Popular with collectors are the whimsical (and occasionally frightening) folk art face jugs made by the Browns. Although the earliest North Carolina face jug was made in the mountains by Henry Stone during the 1890s, this was an isolated example. Brown Pottery has created face jugs on a regular basis since the 1920s. Recently one of Brown's large red-painted

devil jugs with advertising, made during the 1930s, sold for more than $40,000.

While face jugs have been produced near Asheville since the 1920s, other than rare examples they were not made elsewhere in the state until the 1970s. Burlon Craig of the Catawba Valley region was almost singularly responsible for a resurgence in their popularity, and now they are produced by numerous potters statewide.

Walter Stephen's Nonconnah and Pisgah Forest potteries near Asheville were art potteries from their inception. His Nonconnah Pottery was the first North Carolina art pottery and the only state pottery to manufacture slip decorated, matte green wares representative of the Arts and Crafts movement. At Pisgah Forest, exceptional Oriental forms were created glazed with celadon, copper red, crackle, and crystalline formulas. Stephen's crystalline glazes were the first in North Carolina and possibly the South.

Also notable are Pisgah Forest's cameo wares with hand-applied white porcelain scenes unique in American art pottery. These folk life scenes with covered wagons, native Americans, fiddlers, cabins, plowing oxen, and square dancers capture a lifestyle that is truly American. It has been predicted by several art pottery experts and auctioneers that Pisgah Forest pottery will become the next highly collected American art pottery.

Traditions Continue, Traditions Change

Groundhog kilns and mule-powered clay mills have disappeared from the western North Carolina mountains, but some potters continue historical traditions. Brown Pottery digs their clay locally and makes jiggered dinnerware and face jugs glazed with blue, raspberry, purple, green, mauve, or their traditional red-brown. Evan's Pottery creates dogwood decorated vases, face jugs, and spongeware similar to that of previous generations. Walter Stephen's step-grandson, Thomas Case, operates Pisgah Forest Pottery on a limited basis, producing mugs, bowls, and vases glazed with the blue, green, yellow, or brown formulas made famous at the pottery. Rodney and Kim Leftwich of Leftwich Folk and Art Pottery base their creations on the traditional forms, glazes, and scenery of the region. Their production includes vases and candle lanterns with incised and cut-out scenes of mountain life as well as face jugs and folk art figurals such as Noah's Arks and Pig riders. Locally available materials are mixed to create their traditional alkaline and slip glazes.

The mountain region has changed greatly during the last decade. Attracted by the beauty of the area, new inhabitants have brought a more diverse and cosmopolitan population. Organizations such as the Southern Highland Craft Guild and High Country Crafters, as well as folk schools such as J.C. Campbell and Penland, promote regional crafts. Numerous craft shops and fairs offer regionally made items and signs of potters are seen on every highway.

While a wide variety of quality pottery is available in the mountains, it is largely produced by college or technical school graduates who have moved to the region. Most are unfamiliar with the more than 150-year history of pottery making in the mountains. As is true, the one constant in life is change.

Buncombe County Area Marks

Potter	Mark	Method
Edward Stone	E. ƧTONE	stamp
John Henry Stone	J.H. STONE	stamp
Charles J. Penland	C.J. PENLAND	stamp
Joseph Sylvester Penland	J.S. PEN.	stamp
	J.S. PENLAND	stamp
William Marion Penland	W.M. PENLAND	stamp
	PENLAND POTTERY/ CANDLER, N.C.	stamp
Cash Penland	Cash Penland	incised
Benjamin Trull	B.R. Trull	incised
Jim O. Trull	J.O. Trull	incised
Oscar L. Bachelder	O.L. BACHELDER/ CANDLER, N.C.	stamp
	Omar Khayyam Studios/ Luther, N.C. also stamp that incorporated stylized initials "OLB"	incised
Mr. & Mrs. Thomas Throckmorton	Throckmorton of N.C. . . . of Candler, etc.	slip painted
S. Leverick Yoder	Y	incised
George & David Donkel	D. & D./THE BEST	stamp
George Donkel	key shape	stamp
Davis & Javan Brown	BROWN BROS.	stamp
Davis Brown and family descendants	BROWN POTTERY (variations)	stamp
Louis Brown	LB or Louis	incised
Robert Brown	RB or Robert	incised
Charles Brown	CB or Charles	incised
M. Shuford (?)	LEE SMITH/ HILLGIRT, NC	stamp
Evan J. Brown Jr.	Evans Pottery	stamp
E. Javan Brown	E.J. Brown	stamp
Walter B. Stephen and coworkers	NONCONNAH	incised or slip painted
Walter B. Stephen	PISGAH FOREST (over 60 variations)	stamps incised
Grady Ledbetter	Ledbetter	incised
Unidentified potter	☆	stamp

Suggested Reading on Mountain Pottery

Bridges, D. and K. Preyer (eds.), "The Pottery of Walter Stephen," Journal of Studies of the Ceramic Circle of Charlotte, North Carolina, 1978, Vo. 3, pp. 8-9.

Brunk, Robert S. editor, *May We All Remember Well*, Vol. II, published by Robert S. Brunk Auction Services, Inc., 2001.

Busbee, Mrs. Jacques "North Carolina Pottery and Pine Needle Baskets," *Every Woman's Magazine*, October 1916.

Carnes-McNaughton, Linda F. "The Mountain Potters of Buncombe County, North Carolina: An Archaeological and Historical Study," North Carolina Archaeological Council Publication, 1995, No. 26.

Dillingham, Deena "Reems Creek Pottery Works," unpublished manuscript on file at Mars Hill College, Mars Hill, North Carolina, 1981.

Eaton, Allen M. *Handicrafts of the Southern Highlands*, New York, Russel Sage Foundation, 1937.

Enka Voice, "Jugtown," *Enka Voice*, Vol. 9, No. 7, published by Employees of the American Enka Corporation, Enka, North Carolina, 1938.

"From Mountain Clay: The Folk Pottery Traditions of Buncombe County," N.C. Belk Art Gallery, Exhibition catalog, Western Carolina University, 1989.

Johnston, Pat H. editor, "Bachelder and Stephen," *The Antiques Journal*, September 1974.

Johnston, Pat H. editor, "Omar Khayyam Pottery," *The Antiques Journal*, September 1974.

Johnston, Pat H. & Daisy W. Bridges, "O.L. Bachelder and his Omar Khayyam Pottery," Vol. V, *Journal of Studies of the Ceramic Circle of Charlotte*, Mint Museum exhibition catalog, Charlotte, North Carolina, 1983.

Kovel, R. and T. Kovel, *Kovel's American Art Pottery: The Collector's Guide to Makers, Marks, and Factory Histories*, Crown Publishers, New York, 1993, pp. 2-274.

Purdy, Ross "The Craft Potters of North Carolina," *Bulletin of the American Ceramic Society*, Vol. 21, No. 6, June 15, 1942.

Ray, M. "Pisgah Forest Pottery," *The Spinning Wheel*, January/February 1971, p. 16.

Roberts, R. "Pisgah Forest Pottery: A Half Century of North Carolina Mountain Art," *Antique Week*, March 23, 1987, 19 (1).

Smith, Howard A. *Index of Southern Potters*, Old America Company, Mayodan, N.C., 1982 and 1986.

Sweezy, N. *Raised in Clay: The Southern Pottery Tradition*, Smithsonian Institution Press, Washington, D.C., 1984, pp. 234 – 238.

Zug III, Charles G. *Turners and Burners: The Folk Potters of North Carolina*, The University of North Carolina Press, Chapel Hill, North Carolina, 1986.

Uncommon shoulder decoration, 5-gallon molasses jug, Penland/Stone pottery, Buncombe County. Private collection.

5-gallon molasses jug, Penland/Stone Pottery, Buncombe County. Decorated shoulder, restored handles. $600.00 – 1,000.00. Private collection.

Right: Donkel monkey jug, Buncombe County. $600.00 – 800.00. Left: Monkey and ring jugs, Penland Pottery. $400.00 – 600.00. Private collection.

Decorated jar, George Donkel, Buncombe County, c. 1920s. Rare. Private collection.

Penland Pottery, Buncombe County, c. 1910 – 1935. Unsigned tourist wares. $85.00 – 400.00 each. Private collection.

Pitcher and wall pocket, George Donkel Pottery, transitional ware, unsigned, Buncombe County, c. 1920 – 1940. $100.00 – 200.00 each. Private collection.

Decorated vase, c. 1940s, Brown Pottery, Buncombe County. $100.00 – 200.00. Private collection.

Face jugs. Left: Robert Brown, 1970s. Right: Louis Brown, 1980s. Arden, Buncombe County. $300.00 – 500.00 each. Private collection.

Devil face jug, Brown Pottery, 1930s. Buncombe County. Albany slip. $1,500.00 – 2,500.00+. Private collection.

Rodney Leftwich face jug, 3-gallon. Iron clay slip glaze. $400.00 – 600.00. Private collection.

Pitcher and lidded jar, O.L. Bachelder, Omar Khayyam Pottery. Luther, Buncombe County, utilitarian ware. $500.00 – 1,000.00 each. Private collection.

Pitcher, c. 1895, signed Lee Smith, Hill-girt, Henderson County. Rare. Private collection.

Bachelder, Omar Khayyam Pottery, Buncombe County, c. 1920s. $300.00 – 1,500.00 each. Private collection.

Nonconnah Pottery, Tennessee, W.B. Stephen and Nellie Stephen, 1904 – 1910. 5" with lid. Rare. Private collection.

Nonconnah Pottery, slip and incised base markings, c. 1913 – 1916. Private collection.

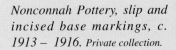

Pisgah Forest Pottery, Buncombe County. Workshop with kiln chimney extending through roof.

Pisgah Forest Pottery, shop interior, wedging table, potter's wheel.

Pisgah Forest Pottery, kiln, lower level, showing fire box.

Pisgah Forest Pottery, kiln interior, showing handmade shelves for stacking wares.

Pisgah Forest Pottery, saggars in which pottery pieces are fired.

Photos on this page by Rodney Leftwich.

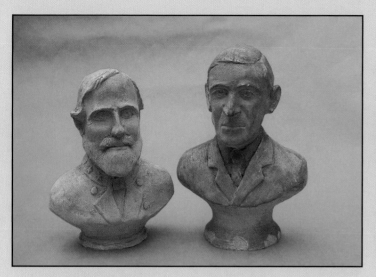

Pisgah Forest Pottery busts, c. 1926. Left: Robert E. Lee, 8½";
Woodrow Wilson, 9⅛". Unsigned, rare.

Pisgah Forest Pottery, cameo plate with crystalline,
1930, d. 6⅞". $800.00 – 1,000.00. Private collection.

Pisgah Forest Pottery, 1934 jug at left, incised base marks.

Pisgah Forest Pottery, crystalline, 1934, 17⅜".
$3,000.00 – 5,000.00. Private collection.

Pisgah Forest Pottery, drip
glaze which was caused by
crystalline glaze that flowed
rather than crystallized dur-
ing firing, 1938, 7". $600.00 –
1,000.00. Private collection.

Pisgah Forest Pottery, decorated by Nancy Jones, 1934 – 1935 teapot h. 5¼", part of 23-piece set. Private collection.

Pisgah Forest Pottery, pitcher with tumblers. Pitcher, 6¼", tumblers 4⅛". 1938. Part of set decorated by Nancy Jones. Rare. Private collection.

Pisgah Forest Pottery, cameo by Sara Austin. Left, 1951, h. 6⅛". Right, 1952, h. 3½". Pitcher, $600.00 – 800.00; mug, $500.00 – 700.00. Private collection.

Pisgah Forest Pottery, crystalline, 1941, 8", exceptional. $1,800.00 – 2,200.00. Private collection.

Pisgah Forest Pottery, cameo with crystalline, 1936, 7½". $800.00 – 1,200.00. Private collection.

Pisgah Forest Pottery, cameo lamp base, glaze behind cameo matches 1948 pieces H. 13⅛". $2,500.00 – 3,000.00. Private collection.

Pisgah Forest Pottery, crystalline glaze, by Rodney Leftwich. Photo by Tim Barnwell. $300.00 – 500.00.

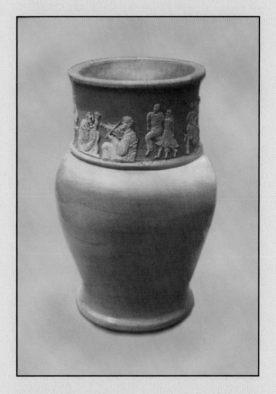

Pisgah Forest Pottery, crystalline glaze by Rodney Leftwich. Photo by Tim Barnwell. $200.00 – 300.00.

Pisgah Forest Pottery, sprigged cameo, by Thomas Case, 1952, h. 11½". $1,000.00 – 2,000.00. Private collection.

Pisgah Forest Pottery, crackle glazes. Left: 1941, 6¾", right: 1938, 5½" . $100.00 – 200.00 each. Private collection.

Pisgah Forest Pottery, base marking on carved vase, 1941, potter kneeling facing left. Private collection.

Pisgah Forest Pottery, carved by Nancy Jones, made by W.B. Stephen, turquoise crackle glaze. 1936, 10¼". Rare. Private collection.

Cameo decorated vase with pedestal, by Rodney Leftwich. Pisgah Forest Pottery technique, 16", 1990s. Photo by Tim Barnwell.

Double bodied vase with small handles, 6¾", crystalline glaze, Pisgah Forest. The form of this example is unusual. George Viall collection.

Vase, 6¼", decorated with applied face reliefs; boy and girl application to Bachelder piece by Ann S. Gaudens, signed "Ann St. Gaudens, Charlotte, NC 1923." George Viall collection.

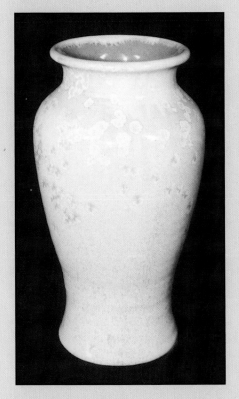

Vase, 8¾", crystalline glaze, Pisgah Forest. George Viall collection.

Lidded jar, 8¾", faintly signed O.L.B. Attributed to Oscar Louis Bachelder (1852 – 1925) at Omar Khayyam Pottery. Albany slip glaze at high temperature. St. James Place Museum.

Pisgah Forest pottery. George Viall collection.

Wares, O.L. Bachelder (1862 – 1935), Candler, North Carolina. Bachelder, an itinerant turner, has become a potter of mythic proportions because of his simple elegant forms and the glazes he developed. St. James Place Museum.

Pisgah Forest vase, circa 1930, note small kiln crack on rim at right. This represents a defect from the natural formation process of the object. Its implications for value are less than defects caused by in-use trauma.

Vase, 13", crystalline glaze, by Pisgah Forest Pottery. George Viall collection.

Pisgah Forest, small 4½" vase, stamped.

Pisgah Forest stamp, 1936.

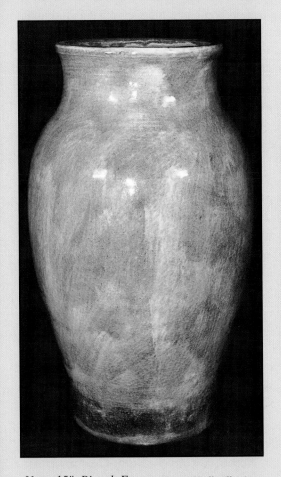

Vase, 15", Pisgah Forest. George Viall collection.

Pisgah Forest (except three-handled pot in right foreground), W.B. Stephen (1876 – 1961). St. James Place Museum.

Cole Pottery: A Tradition

The present-day Cole potters can trace their family legacy over seven generations to their ancestors in Staffordshire, England. This pottery dynasty has been making wares in North Carolina for over two centuries, and the contributions of this family to the American pottery tradition are truly monumental if one considers the variety and numbers of wares they produced, the potteries they founded, and the wide geographic distribution of their productivity. However, there are significant contributions by the Coles in technical and aesthetic areas as well.

William Cole, according to folklorist Charles Zug, settled in the south central Piedmont of North Carolina in the seventeenth century. Most scholars believe that he and his sons were potters. The oldest known wares of a Cole, however, were turned by Raphael "Rafe" Cole (1799 – 1862) who built the first "groundhog" kiln in the Seagrove area. Rafe had three sons who were all potters, and the best known was Evan Cole (1834 – 1895) who with his seven sons became the owners of the largest pottery firm in the area. Their wares were stamped "Cole & Co." if they were signed at all.

While Cole and Co. was an important operation, it was the future activities of several of the brothers and their progeny that have been of ever greater significance. "Ruff" Cole's son, Charlie, "C.C.," was the founder of C.C. Cole and Co. This shop was famous for their multiglazed pottery. Their smaller wares were shipped by the thousands to resorts and sold to tourists. C.C. Cole's daughter, Dorothy Cole, married Walter Auman, and they founded Seagrove Pottery. Dorothy Auman was not only an outstanding potter, but she and her husband Walter were the archivists/historians who preserved many of the records of the Seagrove area pottery tradition and started the first Potters' Museum there. Their collection of over 2,000 pieces is now in the permanent collection of the Mint Museum in Charlotte.

Another of Ruffin's sons, Arthur Ray "A.R." Cole, started Rainbow Pottery around 1926 and in 1941 renamed his operation, A.R. Cole Pottery. His daughters Celia (1924 –) and Neolia (1927 –) continue to operate this business as Cole Pottery where grandson Kevin George is the principal turner. A.R. Cole's legacy in the forms he turned and the glazes he used is very important.

The pure colors in the glazes of his Rainbow facility duplicated the hues and colors of the rainbow and created a distinct and highly collectible line of pottery. For the collector, most of the pieces from this Rainbow establishment will be unsigned as Cole used an ink stamp which often proved not to be permanent. However, certain shapes and glazes from this pottery are unmistakable to permit identification as we have discussed elsewhere in this text.

Cole was a very disciplined potter, exercising rigid quality control. His handles were often potting triumphs and certain of his glaze combinations striking. Almost all of his large and unusual forms are very desirable. Many of A.R. Cole's pieces were sent to eastern cities and sold by florists, and some have even appeared in museums. His large porch vases (22"+) often had intricately curved handles which identify his work by form alone.

There were several stamps used at various times at A.R. Cole Pottery, and some pieces were hand signed. His daughters now not only stamp their wares but write short messages on them as well. A son of A.R., General Foister Cole (1919 – 1991), after working for his father, started C.F. Cole Pottery, Cox Mill Road, Sanford, and employed his brother, Truman Cole (1922 – 1989), who had also worked for A.R. Truman Cole's daughter, Sandy Cole, who now operates North Cole Pottery.

Another son of Evan Cole, Lorenzo or "Wren," operated Carolina Pottery in Candor, North Carolina (circa 1920 – 1930s). After he bought the pottery from Joe Steed, Wren employed several other potters. Later he turned wares for C.C. Cole (Smith). The wares from Candor Pottery are often distinctive in their blue color, handles, and shouldered ridges, and most are not signed. Some may be identified by the thick lustrous glazes or suggest the hired potter in Wren's employ by its form.

Jacon B. (J.B.) Cole, who was the brother of Ruffin and Wren, founded the large operation of J.B. Cole Pottery in 1922. His children included Herman Cole (1895 – 1982) who operated Smithfield Pottery (1926 – 1932) and Nell Cole who married Philmore Graves, a fellow potter. Nell Cole Graves, North Carolina's first woman potter, continued to make pottery for the J.B. Cole Company until several years ago but did so at

Holly Hill Pottery. She was known for the delicate, thin edges of the curves and lips of her work. There was recently an exhibition of her work at the Chapel Hill Museum in Chapel Hill, and a collection of her small wares was given to the Seagrove Museum. With the closure of the J.B. Cole Pottery and her death, Nell's small delicate wares have increased in value. She along with the oldest living male potter, M.L. Owens at Seagrove, are subjects of vignettes in this text.

Nell Cole Graves, according to local lore, is said to have had the first electric wheel in Seagrove. This was made for her by her brother-in-law, Harwood Graves, in the 1940s. A.R. Cole had one in Sanford almost a decade earlier which not only reflects the leadership of the Coles in technical innovation but the opportunities available in the town of Sanford located along U.S. Highway 1 and the relative isolation of the rural community of Seagrove.

J.B. Cole Pottery had the first belt sander in the Seagrove area. This was an expensive item and could only be justified if one had a large volume of production. The sanding marks along with the telltale stilt remains assist in identifying the works of the J.B. Cole Company from the 1950s until they began signing pieces in the 1980s. This is useful in differentiating wares from A.R.'s, C.C.'s, or Dorothy Cole Auman's facilities because many glazes and forms were shared in the Cole family, although each had their "signature" pieces. The signature alone of a J.B. Cole piece greatly enhances its value, or the label of some resort like Sunset Mountain or Mrs. Smith's will be present.

The reach of the Cole influence in pottery through marriage is illustrated not only in the union of Dorothy Cole and Walter Auman but also in the marriage of J.B.'s daughter Vellie to potter, Bascomb King. Their daughter, Doris King, operates King Road Pottery and son, Evan J. King, owns E.J. King Pottery. Another daughter, Virginia Shelton (1923 – 1991), potted at J.B. Cole Pottery for almost 30 years until her death. Virginia's wares rival Nell's in delicacy and are often signed VS. Her son, Mitchell Shelton, owns Shelton's Pottery and daughter, Linda Shelton Potts, operates Potts Town Pottery. Thus, the legacy of the Coles will extend well into the twenty-first century and predictably for several more generations.

While at present all appears alive and well among the potters in south central North Carolina, this has not always been the circumstance. In the most challenging of times the Coles showed an attentiveness to changing markets, the ingenuity to adapt, and perseverance when the rewards were not immediately apparent or forthcoming. A.R., J.B., and C.C. Cole managed to survive by creating new, sometimes elaborately formed, decorative pieces.

Charlie Cole in 1939 purchased the Teague Shop when James "Jim" Teague joined the Fulper Pottery Company in New Jersey as a demonstration potter. This site operated until 1971. From the grays and greens of their utilitarian ware they later developed vibrant, aesthetically appealing glazes. Son Thurston was responsible for much of the large output as he was a prodigious worker. In addition to the changes in molding the clay and use of modern chemicals in their glazes, the Coles embraced technological innovations such as the electric kiln, motorized wheels, and the belt sander.

Probably as important regarding the impact of this work was the adoption of "state of the art" distribution methods. Certainly, it was no accident that A.R. Cole located his shop on U.S. 1, and Herman Cole's Smithfield Pottery was positioned along U.S. 301. For well into the twentieth century these were the major North-South arteries in North Carolina. But this was only the beginning of mass distribution as shipments of thousands of pieces were later made by rail and truck to distant parts of America.

C.C. and his brother Everette (1890 – 1974) had a shop in New Hill, Wake County (1927 – 1933) before Charlie began the large operation of C.C. Cole. C.C. Cole had contracts with the Shenandoah Candy Company and Great Smoky Mountain Industries for thousands of wares per shipment. These mass-produced examples in general are not of great importance to the collector, but some of the smaller contracts allowed the production of larger and more important wares. For example, the arrangement between J.B. Cole and Sunset Mountain is well documented by very collectible examples of interesting forms and glazes.

J.B. Cole's catalog allows us to appreciate the variety and forms they offered beginning in the 1930s. It unfortunately does not allow us to appreciate the glazes they advertised such as periwinkle blue, brown on white, crystal blue, and crystal green and brown sugar (Gilson).

At J.B. Cole there were four principal potters, and others came in for short periods of time when they had a large order to fill. The 1932 catalog (order information for copies is on page 25) will help you determine whether a particular vase was done by Nell Cole

Graves, her husband Philmore, Bascomb King or Waymon Cole. The larger pieces were usually turned by Waymon, and these are usually the most expensive of the unsigned Cole examples.

The Aladdin lamps fashioned by Waymon are rare and valuable. This particular form was difficult to turn, and only a few potters in the Seagrove area were able to keep the angular walls from collapsing (Teague). The very best wares of the J.B. Cole Pottery are desirable, and one should look past the volume of undistinguished wares made in this intensely active operation. Their best examples are equal to other potteries with less volume and more time for creativity.

There are certain legendary families of the pottery tradition which must include Craven, Auman, Owen (Owens), Teague, Hilton, Brown, and others; but in sheer numbers and in management of potteries, the Cole family is among the first rank in their importance to this method of creative expression.

References: Kenneth George, Richard Gilson, Nell Cole Graves, Howard Smith, Archie Teague, Neolia Cole Womack

Vase, 12½" h, with split handles, Rainbow Pottery (stamped) by A.R. Cole. Cole developed the muted, pastel colors in the 1930s. $225.00 – 250.00

Rainbow pottery glazes by A.R. Cole. This pottery (1926 – 1941) produced some of the most beautiful and simple glazes with mellow, warm tonalities for a decade and a half, taking advantage of the Mitchfield clay. Vase on left with ruffled top, $175.00 – 200.00; two-handled vase on right, $200.00 – 250.00.

A.R. Cole, Rainbow Pottery, circa 1930. These solid color bowls are very decorative. $150.00 – 175.00.

Cole Family 1830 – 1960 and Cole Pottery

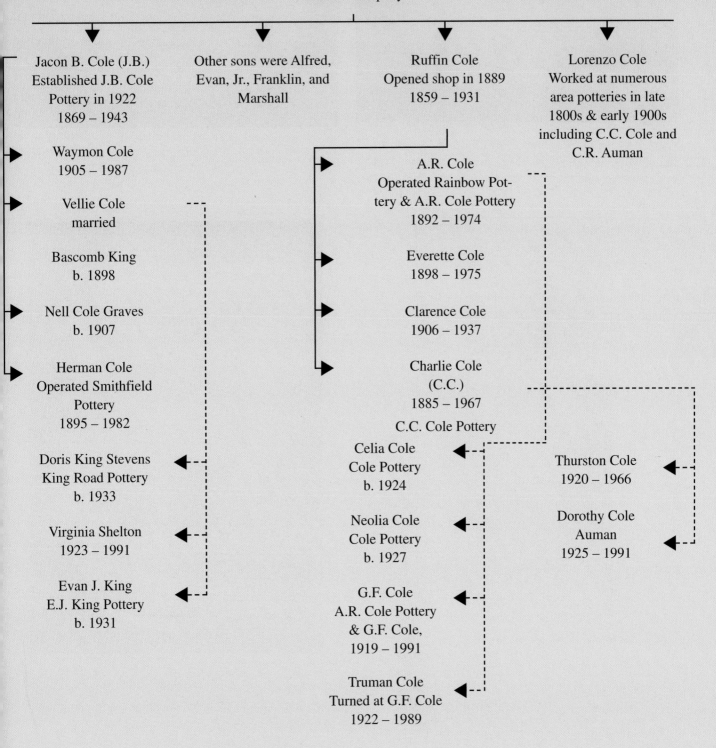

Evan Cole
Son of Raphael Cole
1834 – 1895
Cole & Company

Jacon B. Cole (J.B.)
Established J.B. Cole
Pottery in 1922
1869 – 1943

Other sons were Alfred,
Evan, Jr., Franklin, and
Marshall

Ruffin Cole
Opened shop in 1889
1859 – 1931

Lorenzo Cole
Worked at numerous
area potteries in late
1800s & early 1900s
including C.C. Cole and
C.R. Auman

Waymon Cole
1905 – 1987

Vellie Cole
married

Bascomb King
b. 1898

Nell Cole Graves
b. 1907

Herman Cole
Operated Smithfield
Pottery
1895 – 1982

Doris King Stevens
King Road Pottery
b. 1933

Virginia Shelton
1923 – 1991

Evan J. King
E.J. King Pottery
b. 1931

A.R. Cole
Operated Rainbow Pottery & A.R. Cole Pottery
1892 – 1974

Everette Cole
1898 – 1975

Clarence Cole
1906 – 1937

Charlie Cole
(C.C.)
1885 – 1967
C.C. Cole Pottery

Celia Cole
Cole Pottery
b. 1924

Neolia Cole
Cole Pottery
b. 1927

G.F. Cole
A.R. Cole Pottery
& G.F. Cole,
1919 – 1991

Truman Cole
Turned at G.F. Cole
1922 – 1989

Thurston Cole
1920 – 1966

Dorothy Cole
Auman
1925 – 1991

Apothecary jar, 6¼", for Arthur Ray Cole, operating as Rainbow Pottery (1926 – 1941). The position of the arms in relation to the rim and the upper arms insertion is characteristic of A.R. Cole. $225.00 – 275.00.

View from above A.R. Cole apothecary jar. Note insertion of the handles. The external grooves are prominent as well.

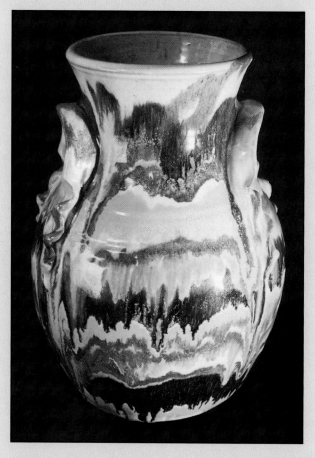

Grecian/Roman pitcher, fritted glaze, 19¾", made in 1950s by General Foister Cole working at A.R. Cole. The example demonstrates an elegant thumb groove handle with inside finger grip. G.F. Cole (1919 – 1991) was brother of Neolia, Celia, and Winfred Cole. Operated his own shop after 1960. $250.00 – 325.00. St. James Place Museum.

Reverse side of unusual A.R. Cole vase shown on page 31. Note shape of lug handles as an adaptation of historical shapes in North Carolina employed by the Moravian potters.

Three-handled vase, 8¼", by A.R. Cole. Rainbow Pottery, aqua glaze, circa late 1930s. $225.00 – 275.00.

Grecian, sometimes described as Roman, pitcher, 16" by General Foister Cole at A.R. Cole, circa 1940s – 1950s. This was the form for which he was known. $175.00 – 250.00.

Large porch vase, 21". A.R. Cole, Rainbow Pottery (1926 – 1941), stamped. $600.00 – 900.00.

Aqua two-handled bulbous jar or lidded vessel. Stamp has been washed away. Attributed to Royal Crown Pottery or A.R. Cole. Note similar glaze and form to yellow jar below left. $250.00 – 275.00.

Multiglazed, two-handled porch vase, 12½", circa 1930s, A.R. Cole. $325.00 – 450.00. Farmer/James collection.

Lidded jar with lug handles, 10¾", soft yellow, Rainbow Pottery, circa 1930, stamped. Turned and glazed by A.R. Cole. $225.00 – 275.00. Chapel Hill Museum collection.

Two-handled vase, yellow glaze, very unusual handles, 10½", attributed to A.R. Cole, circa 1930s. This was probably an experimental form.

Oblong low bowl with unusual handles, mirror black glaze, by Arthur Ray Cole, circa 1940. $135.00 – 170.00.

Underside of above bowl, showing A.R. Cole stamp.

Low bowl with handles, 14", A.R. Cole, stamped Rainbow Pottery. $145.00 – 200.00. Farmer/James collection.

Two-handled vase with scalloped rim, 10¼", stamped Rainbow Pottery. Turned by A.R. Cole. Some of the more subtly compelling glazes were applied to the wares of this pottery from 1927 to 1941. $145.00 – 175.00. St. James Place Museum.

Candle plate, 9½", gunmetal glaze, attributed to A.R. Cole. Candle plates this size are rare. $65.00 – 85.00. Ray Wilkinson collection.

Teapot by Arthur Ray "A.R." Cole, 8", with "mistake crystal blue" glaze. Some glazes were fortuitously successful. A.R. thought this would be blue so he named it "mistake." $135.00 – 185.00. Ray Wilkinson collection.

Tall vase, 15½", large arms and narrow neck, by A.R. Cole. This striking glaze was used mainly by A.R. and C.C. Cole potteries. $225.00 – 275.00. Ray Wilkinson collection.

Bowl with handle and spout, 8", decorative "striped" glaze, most closely associated with A.R. Cole. $110.00 – 130.00. Ray Wilkinson collection.

Large 12¾" folded low bowl, by A.R. Cole (stamped, circa 1940s). The brown edges and runs are caused by rutile in glaze. Some fritted glazes also have a similar appearance. $150.00 – 200.00. Ray Wilkinson collection.

A.R. Cole bud vases, 6½", probably commercial glaze with rutile providing darker contrasts.

A.R. Cole "signatures" (stamps) on bud vase indicating they were made at different times.

157

Typical wares of A.R. Cole pottery, split-handled pitcher turned by Foister Cole. Courtesy of Mick Bailey.

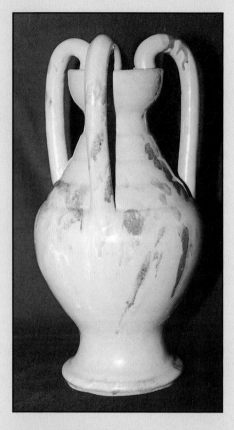

Vase with three handles, yellow glaze with green decoration applied digitally. A.R. Cole, unusual glaze color. North Carolina State University Gallery of Art and Design collection.

Birdhouse, 8", A.R. Cole. In general, these whimsical items are interesting but not very collectible.

Rainbow Pottery stamp, 1926 – 1941. Arthur Ray (A.R.) Cole.

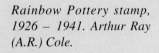

Rebecca pitcher, 21", multiglazed, unsigned but glaze and form make the piece attributable to A.R. Cole, circa 1940s. Courtesy of Mick Bailey.

Apothecary jar, 14½", with multiglazing (Mason stain) by A.R. Cole, Rainbow stamp. David Blackburn collection.

Rebecca pitcher, 21", stamped A.R. Cole. Note reaction of glaze to firing. David Blackburn collection.

Apothecary jar, 11¼", decoration over mirror black glaze. A.R. Cole Pottery as Rainbow, circa 1930s. David Blackburn collection.

Low, three-handled bowl, 6¼", with decorative band, incised stamp J.B. Cole. Ink stamp A.R. Cole Pottery rare, origin uncertain. David Blackburn collection.

Tiered cylinder, 9¾", A.R. Cole as Rainbow Pottery.

Vase, 14", attributed to J.B. Cole. Note the patina of the base from Mitchfield clay (Auman clay pit). The linear decoration is probably caused by use of manganese. Wilkinson collection (1994). Farmer/James collection.

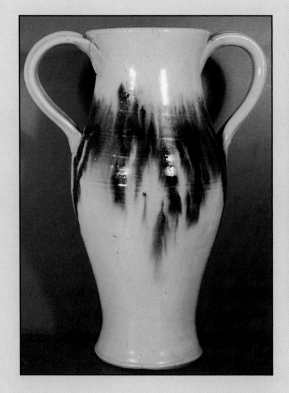

Two-handled vase, unsigned. 16½" chrome red. Handle and lip probably 1920s. Attributed to Jacon B. Cole, see Robert C. Lock, The Traditional Potters of Seagrove.

Two-handled vase, 14", clear lead glaze, ink stamp. Black and green runs on tan surface. Attributed to J.B. Cole, 1920s – early 1930s. $275.00 – 350.00.

"Handmade pottery J Palmer" stamp on two-handled vase at left. Palmer was a business man who contracted with J.B. Cole Pottery.

Two-handled vase, 11", unusual form, chrome red glaze, J.B. Cole Pottery (attributed), late 1920s or early 1930s. $175.00 – 225.00. Bailey collection.

Vase with exotic, elongated lug handles, circa 1920s – 1930s. Chrome red, 17¼", attributed to J.B. Cole. Bailey collection.

Pitcher, 14¼", chrome red reduction glaze with variations due to reaction of temperature in kiln, early J.B. Cole. $250.00 – 400.00. Bailey collection.

Vase, two handles, raised line at center of body, 8¾", chrome red glaze, J.B. Cole Pottery (early example 1920s). David Blackburn collection.

Series of plates made for stand. Attributed to J.B. Cole Pottery, rare. Bailey collection.

Set of graduated bowls, chrome red glaze, unsigned, attributed to J.B. Cole, rare. Very successful glaze to clay match and excellent reduction changes. Bailey collection.

Vase, 4¾", chrome red, J.B. Cole Pottery, attributed to Nell Cole Graves. Stamped Goose Creek. Goose Creek was a resort in South Carolina.

Long neck, two-handled vase, chrome red, 19". Attributed to J.B. Cole, circa 1930s. Very rare. Edwards collection.

Large, long neck vase, 16", by J.B. Cole Pottery. Unusual shape and large size. $350.00 – 400.00.

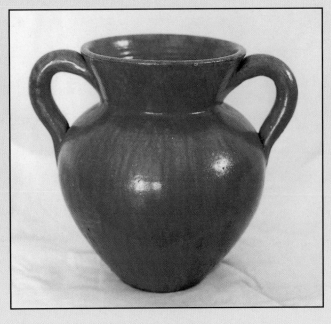

Two-handled low vase, 6¾", salt glazed, cobalt secondary, unsigned, attributed to J.B. Cole.

Vase, two-handled, 11¼", J.B. Cole, chrome red glaze, stamped "Sunset Mountain." Courtesy of Mick Bailey.

Pitcher, chrome red, 9½", stamped "Shenandoah Valley", attributed to J.B. Cole. David Blackburn collection.

Vase, 9¾", unusual ovoid form with lug handles, chrome red, attributed to J.B. Cole Pottery, signed "Unaka," significance unknown. Bailey collection.

Rare J.B. Cole stamp, from wares at left.

Signed J.B. Cole wares, both chrome red, rare stamp, three-handled (strap handles) vase, 13", and two-handled vase, 7¾", by J.B. Cole.
David Blackburn collection.

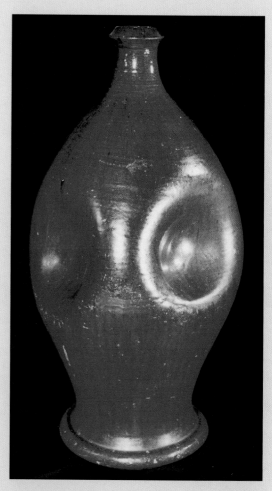

Pinch bottle, 13½", chrome red, attributed to J.B. Cole, very large size for this form. Edwards collection.

Large porch vase, 24", by Waymon Cole, circa 1930s. Made in small numbers initially and because of damage from use, vases of this size are rare. Waymon's signature pieces were these heroic-sized examples, and chrome red was a desirable glaze. When available, these are worth several thousand dollars. $1,600.00 – 2,200.00.

Compote with folded edges, 8¼", J.B. Cole Pottery, circa 1950s – 1960s. $100.00 – 120.00.

Vase, 9", by Philmore Graves. Unusual double handle. *Farmer/James collection.*

Swirl handle vase, 11¾", J.B. Cole Pottery. $250.00 – 350.00.

Double ring handle vase by Waymon Cole, green glaze with contrasting tonalities. $275.00 – 350.00.

Vase, 10½", unsigned blue commercial glaze. Attributed to J.B. Cole Pottery, circa 1940s. No evidence of stilt marks and belt sander. J.B. Cole in the 1932 catalog had 524 items. $70.00 – 90.00. *Chapel Hill Museum collection.*

"Buzzard vase", 16¾", mid green glaze, by Waymon Cole. Rare form. $450.00 – 600.00.

Two-handled vase, attributed to J.B. Cole, late 1930s. Large vases (often designed as porch vases) are rare. $525.00 – 750.00.

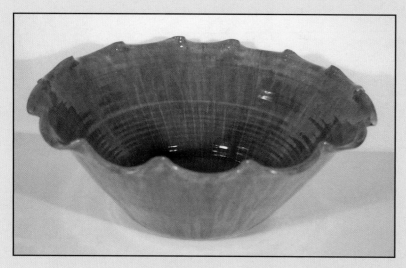

Large bowl, 16¼" x 6", fluted edges, green glaze with rutile. Attributed to J.B. Cole. Large bowls with thin walls and without edge chips are rare. $175.00 – 225.00. Farmer/James collection.

Wide low bowl, 12", brilliant yellow, lead glaze, attributed to J.B. Cole. $110.00 – 125.00.

J.B. Cole stamp, "J.B. Cole Pottery Steeds, NC." The most prolific of all North Carolina pottery establishments stamped less than 1% of their production. They would stamp orders, Sunset Mountain, Goose Creek, Marion, Virginia, Williamsburg, and others. *Arthur Baer.*

Multistepped or "accordion" vase, 5¾", J.B. Cole Pottery. $225.00 – 350.00. *Farmer/James collection.*

Large bowl with handle, 12½", aqua glaze, circa 1930, small glaze loss to rim. These handles, because of weight of bowl, are particularly susceptible to breaks in use. Intact, this form is valuable. Attributed to J.B. Cole Pottery.

"Accordion" or multistepped vase with fluted rim, attributed to J.B. Cole. This form appears to be specific for J.B. Cole Pottery. *Edwards collection.*

Footed bowl, J.B. Cole, 4½" h, 11" across, with lovely green/blue rutile glaze. The form makes this a collectible item. Circa 1950. $125.00 – 150.00.

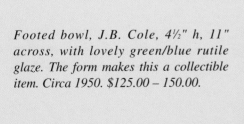

Ice pitcher, Nell Cole Graves (1908 – 1998), J.B. Cole Pottery, circa 1940 – 1950. $145.00 – 175.00.

Large earthenware pitcher, 19", Waymon Cole, J.B. Cole Pottery. Matte glaze with variation of glossy glaze (described by Robert Lock as containing rutile). $175.00 – 225.00.

Porch vase, 19¾", with double rope or cord handles, gunmetal glaze (note double thickness on upper part of the body of vessel). Graceful taper to well-turned pedestal. $375.00 – 500.00. Farmer/James collection.

Small pitcher, J.B. Cole Pottery. Nell Cole Graves was able to achieve the most delicate handles and thinnest edges on small wares. Fritted glaze with rutile, creating the dark streaks over the body. $95.00 – 115.00.

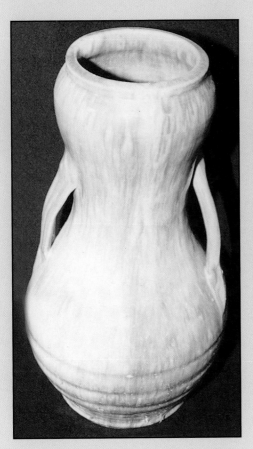

Vase, 8½", intricate handle formation, multiple glaze with rutile, J.B. Cole Pottery, Sunset Mountain stamp. George Viall collection.

Vase with small slightly swirled handles, 12½", stilt marks, and evidence of belt sander. J.B. Cole Pottery. Subtle (fritted) glaze. $95.00 – 125.00.

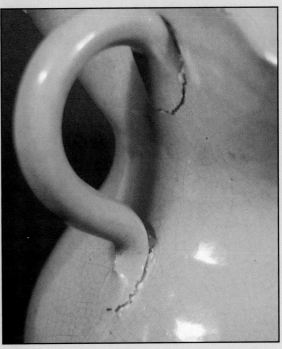

Vase with square, fluted top, 7½", by Philmore Graves at J.B. Cole (see p. 32 of catalog). Graves (1904 – 1969) was brother of Harwood and husband of Nell Cole Graves. $145.00 – 165.00.

Detail of handle on Philmore Graves vase at left. Working at J.B. Cole, he was overshadowed by Way-mon Cole but was an outstanding potter in his own right.

Vase, with split handles, green glaze, note thinness at the under-rim attachment. Two circular incised lines at the handle base. Unsigned, attributed to J.B. Cole Pottery. Collection of North Carolina State University Gallery of Art and Design.

Pitcher, 13¾", copper green glaze, J.B. Cole by Waymon Cole. This glaze was also used at Log Cabin (circa 1930s). Bailey collection.

Stamp on bowl at left, Carolina Craft Hand Made.

Dark green oblong two-handled bowl. Unusual handles, probably A.R. Cole for "Carolina Craft," also form seen in J.B. Cole 1932 catalog for ware of Bascomb King but without Roman-styled handles. $125.00 – 175.00.

Porch vase, 19", unsigned, attributed to Joe Owen. However, the J.B. Cole 1930s catalog pictures similar ware produced by Waymon Cole. Both potters' work is very collectible. $325.00 – 450.00. Farmer/James collection.

Vase, 11", early form, incised lines, attributed to J.B. Cole. Bailey collection.

Large strap handle bowl, 16", note glaze thinning and small glaze chips randomly about the rim edge. No clay loss of significance. Attributed to Cole Pottery. These chips will probably devalue this rare example only 10 – 15%. $175.00 – 225.00. Farmer/James collection.

Elephant trunk pitcher, 11¾". Chrome red, J.B. Cole. David Blackburn collection.

Undersurface of the apothecary jar below, more vividly display-ing the chrome red glaze. The glazing on these makes each unique. Attributed to J.B. Cole, 13¾".

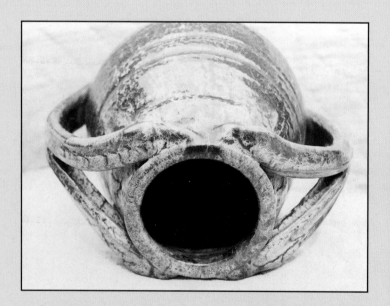

Two-handled vase, 16", probably chrome red glaze that matured to a creamy white. Unknown maker, attributed to J.B. Cole. Note handles. David Blackburn collection.

View of the arms and orifice of an apothecary jar. This very thick glaze gives a three-dimensional effect as one often sees in double glazed wares. The overglaze may dominate but chrome red may be the single glaze employed here.

Two-handled vase, 8¾", J.B. Cole Pottery, turned by J.B. Cole, unusual handles, rare. David Blackburn collection.

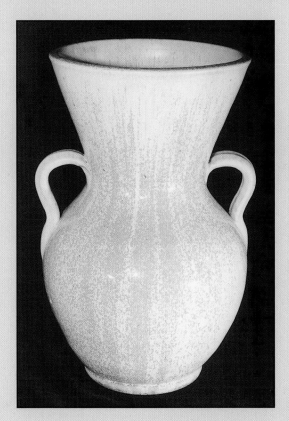

Candlesticks, 14¾", gunmetal glaze, attributed to J.B. Cole. Edwards collection.

Vase, two handles, 13½", turned by Bascomb King at J.B. Cole Pottery. David Blackburn collection.

Candlesticks, 14½", thick Oriental white glaze, attributed to J.B. Cole. Edwards collection.

Rebecca pitcher, 16¾", stamped Williamsburg Pottery, attributed to J.B. Cole. Most wares turned on contract were not so elegant as this example. David Blackburn collection.

173

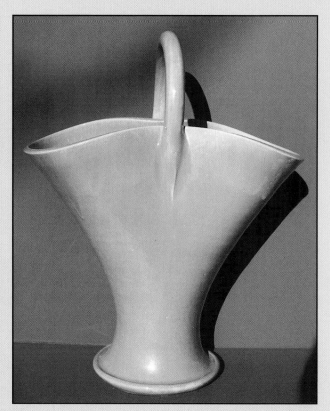

Basket, green glaze with rutile providing the darker linear contrast areas. J.B. Cole Pottery. Collection of North Carolina State University Gallery of Art and Design.

Basket, 18¾". Earthenware, light aqua glaze with thinning at rims. Unsigned, attributed to Philmore Graves at J. B. Cole Pottery, 1930s. By the appearance of glaze, one might consider Royal Crown Pottery and Porcelain Company. Very collectible example. $145.00 – 195.00.

Basket, 11" with "flambe" green glaze, unsigned, attributed to J.B. Cole Pottery. Note the small rim chip which will devalue this large format example of a desirable form. $125.00 – 145.00.

Undersurface of basket by J.B. Cole, at left. Note light clay and several small base chips.

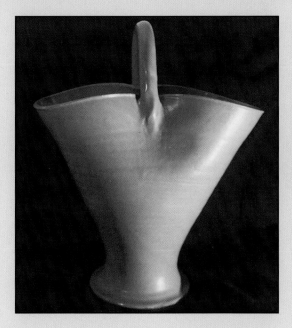

Basket, 14", pink/cranberry glaze, J.B. Cole Pottery, attributed to Philmore Graves. $125.00 – 175.00. Chapel Hill Museum collection.

Fluted vase, 8¾", stamped Sunset Mountain Pottery, J.B. Cole Pottery, attributed to Bascomb King or Philmore Graves. The Sunset Mountain label has become quite popular with collectors, especially on wares glazed with chrome red. $95.00 – 115.00.

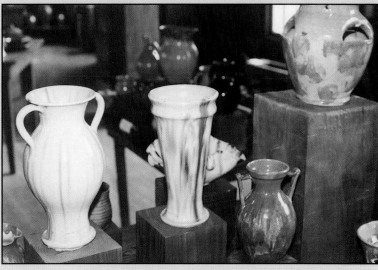

Multiglazed fan, 6", probably C.C. Cole, circa 1930.

C.C. Cole Pottery pieces (1887 – 1967), multiglazed. St. James Place Museum.

Detail of two-handled vase by C.C. Cole. Charlie Cole bought Teague Pottery shop in 1939 which remained in operation until 1971. The larger wares such as this vase from C.C. Cole are highly desired as are the rare signed pieces.

C.C. Cole Pottery. The "C.C. Cole" is clearly seen but "Pottery" found on other stamps is not seen. Vase appears to be circa 1930s – 1940s.

Multiple glazing, C.C. Cole Pottery. Cole was a high volume pottery, shipping thousands of wares to resort areas. Sometimes the vessels were filled with a liquid and corked.

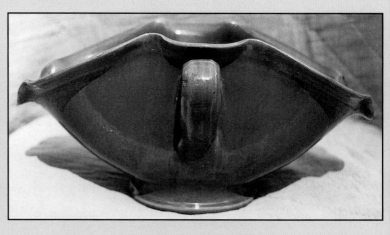

Two vases by C.C. Cole Pottery, each over 8". This was a high production pottery making small wares for the tourist trade. Larger pieces are very collectible. Note the excellent glaze work that is well exhibited across the large surfaces. Left vase: $125.00 – 175.00; right vase: $115.00 – 145.00.

Bowl, 5" x 11" oblong, unsigned, shape attributed to Thurston Cole (1920 – 1966). Thurston turned for his father C.C. Cole (1885 – 1967) and could throw hundreds of wares in a day. He also rode a horse through the local schoolhouse for which he expressed no remorse. $110.00 – 135.00

Strawberry planters, pair, 21¼", multiglazed, unsigned. Attributed to C.C. Cole. Large planters are rare, and pairs even rarer. $175.00 – 225.00. Farmer/James collection.

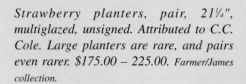

A pottery that made significant contributions during the transitional period of the Seagrove movement from 1917 – 1935 was the one operated by Charlie R. Auman. Auman began making utilitarian stoneware with Paschal Marable, Wendell Richardson, and Lorenzo "Wren" (Wrenn) Cole as potters. Wren Cole is believed to have influenced C.R. Auman to make earthenware art pottery. Cole also taught Charlie Auman's brothers, Ray and James Auman, to turn art pottery.

In the late 1920s Floyd Hilton, from the Catawba Valley Hiltons, joined C.R. Auman and replaced Wren Cole as the principal turner. Charles Masten, who is abundantly represented in this text, arrived from Indiana and began to fashion salt-glazed stoneware with colored oxides applied in a very creative and unique manner. Masten is thought to be a graduate of the well-known ceramics program at Alfred University in New York.

From approximately 1929 to 1935, this pottery may have produced the only salt glaze wares decorated in this very abstract style in America. These examples have become quite valuable.

Some of the works from the 1920s are also particularly desirable as they feature the warm buff tones of Mitchfield clay covered by a clear lead glaze. They are usually decorated with cobalt and occasionally manganese. These pieces were most often turned by Wren Cole and advertised in the "Clay Crafters" advertising flyers. Certain of the glaze combinations are similar to those of D.Z. Craven Pottery and forms not unlike many of Jacon B. (J.B.) Cole's wares. Jacon and Wren both turned at the Baxter Welch Shop in Chatham County in the early 1900s. Some early Auman examples by Wren Cole may have been fired in a low-temperature kiln at the Cole homeplace where Wren lived at the time.

The low, wide angular vases with blue and yellow glaze from the Auman pottery are signature pieces and were most often turned by Wren Cole. Ray Auman made some of the vases in trophy form in the 1926 – 1928 period at Auman Pottery. Certain pitchers, if decorated in a cobalt wash, bespeak the work of Floyd Hilton. The spouts in these examples will be well defined (Hussey). In the period 1931 – 1932, Floyd Hilton was the major potter at C.R.

Auman Pottery. C.B. Masten would dominate the production later in the 1930s.

C.B. Masten (1872 – 1938) grew up in Hendricks County, Indiana. His half-sister, Mrs. Simon E. Allen, lived in Randolph County, North Carolina, and Masten visited her in 1894 and met his future wife, Ida Ingold. They were married at the Ingold residence in 1895. Living in Bloomington, Masten studied ceramics at Indiana University and for 10 years visited Asheboro and Seagrove in Randolph County during the summers.

In 1928 Masten may have studied at the well-known program at Alfred University (Hussey). After the summer course by Charles F. Bennis, Masten came directly to Seagrove and remained there until November, working at the C.R. Auman Pottery. Masten's pieces are rarely stamped with an oval impression stating "handmade." Most wares by this potter will be attributed, but his glazing style is very distinct and can be identified using these criteria.

The Auman Pottery remained in the family until 1936. Their shop was located approximately four miles north of Seagrove. After the Depression, Ray left the pottery to work in the furniture industry. Masten died in 1938 of leukemia, and Floyd Hilton returned to the Catawba Valley area.

The legacy of the C.R. Auman Pottery is a very significant one. In the late teens and early 1920s, they, along with the Cravens and J.H. Owen, were the leaders in the art pottery movement, and examples are very reflective of their progress.

Walter Auman was the son of George Hadley Auman and grandson of Fletcher Auman at whose pottery J.B. Cole turned. His uncle was Herman Cole who operated Smithfield Pottery where Walter worked as a youth. Walter married Dot Cole, daughter of C.C. Cole. She was an accomplished potter and the historian of the Seagrove pottery tradition. In 1953, they opened Seagrove Pottery.

While still working at C.C. Cole Pottery, Dot turned and Walter glazed their wares at Seagrove. In the 1960s with a decline in interest in Seagrove area pottery, Walter and Dot, along with public figure and philanthropist Hargrove "Skipper" Bowles, began active promotion of the south-central Piedmont-based industry. They had the first pottery museum and were major forces in organizing the Seagrove Pottery Festival, a very popular annual event. In 1969 they opened the Seagrove Pottery Museum (Ivey.) In the 1990s the Aumans were tragically killed in a vehicular accident. Their collection was purchased by the Mint Museum in Charlotte, and Quincy Scarborough has written a text about their contributions.

References: Billy Ray Hussey, Bill Ivey

Lidded jar, 10", salt glaze, stamped Auman Pottery. Note the decorative frogskin appearance on this signed utilitarian example of Auman Pottery. Bill Ivey collection.

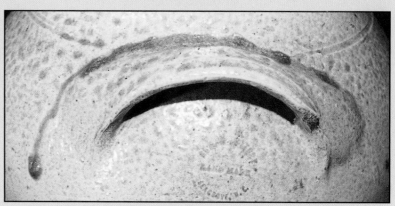

Auman stamp on jar at left, Auman Pottery, Hand Made, Seagrove, North Carolina. Bill Ivey collection.

Pitcher, 11½", Auman Pottery, excellent decoration of simple, clear lead glaze, circa 1920 – 1925. David Blackburn collection.

Vase, 10½", with flat fluted rim, thumbprint design around middle of body. Rare Auman piece which is early, circa 1920, and may be one-of-a-kind. David Blackburn collection.

C.B. Masten pieces. North Carolina State University *Gallery of Art and Design.*

Medicine jar, unusual form, 7", Auman, glazed by C.B. Masten.

Vase, 8¼", glazed by C.B. Masten at Auman Pottery, cobalt over salt glaze, circa 1930s.

Low vase with fluted rim, 5", attributed to C.R. Auman, c. 1919.

Vase, 11½", 1929, Auman, glazed by C.B. Masten, salt glaze, cobalt.

Vase, 13¼", cobalt and chrome drips, C.R. Auman Pottery, attributed to Ray Auman, circa 1920s.

Vase with flat, thin lip, 7", salt glaze with cobalt. Form attributed to Wren Cole. Bailey collection.

Rectangular bowl, 6" x 12¼", ribbon handles, clear lead glaze with decorations. Unusual form. Auman Pottery, 1920s or early 1930s. David Blackburn collection.

Vase, 12¾", unusual ribbon handles. Early Auman Pottery example. Clear lead glaze with cobalt wash. David Blackburn collection.

One of the most successful forms from the Charlie R. Auman Pottery's (1922 – 1937) offering. At first they made utilitarian wares but in the early 1920s changed to lead glazed earthenware art pottery. Wren Cole taught Ray and James to turn, and Floyd Hilton came from the Catawba Valley. C.B. Masten arrived in 1929. This low, wide angular two-handled vase is very collectible. $250.00 – 400.00. Farmer/James collection.

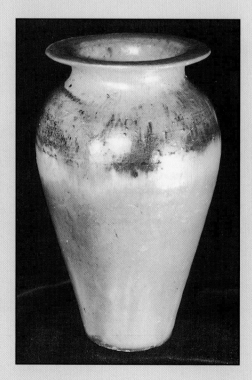

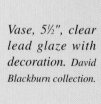

Vase, 5½", clear lead glaze with decoration. David Blackburn collection.

Vase with wide, flat rim, 9", clear lead glaze decorated. David Blackburn collection.

Three-handled hanging vase, 12", and two-handled shoulder vase, both have clear lead glaze with cobalt decoration. Auman Pottery, circa early 1920s. David Blackburn collection.

Vase with wide flat rim, 6¾", by Auman Pottery, 1920s. The buff color is achieved by the clear lead glaze over Mitchfield clay, and this background makes the cobalt decoration dramatic. $275.00 – 325.00. Chapel Hill Museum collection.

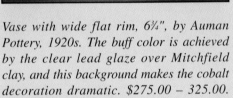

Undersurface of vase above. The clear lead glaze over the white/yellow Mitchfield clay has undergone some cracking or spidering as one might see in an oil painting 80 – 100 years old. Such crazing has little effect upon value.

Candlesticks, 8", Auman Pottery, clear lead glaze with cobalt decoration. Edwards collection.

Vase, 7", with bulbous lower body and stepped pyramidal form. Several incised border lines. Rare and important example of early North Carolina art pottery, c. early 1920s. Bill Ivey collection.

Wide low bowl, 6¾" w x 3¼" h, circa 1925. C.R. Auman Pottery. Clear lead glaze, Mitchfield clay. $125.00 – 175.00. Farmer/James collection.

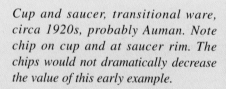

Cup and saucer, transitional ware, circa 1920s, probably Auman. Note chip on cup and at saucer rim. The chips would not dramatically decrease the value of this early example.

Ovoid low vase, 5½", circa 1920 – 1925, probably by C.R. Auman Pottery. The sophistication of this vase is remarkable for a transition piece. $200.00 – 250.00.

Appearance of clay from Auman clay pit on bottom of low vase at left.

182

Vase, 9", cobalt over salt glaze, definition due to incised edges. Auman Pottery, glazed by C.B. Masten. $3,000.00 – 3,500.00. *Bailey collection.*

Vase, 6½" by C.B. Masten at C.R. Auman Pottery. Salt glaze with blue glaze decoration. *George Viall collection.*

Long necked bud vase, 11", Auman Pottery, circa early 1920s, with Mitchfield clay and transparent lead glaze. $125.00 – 175.00. *Farmer/James collection.*

Low wide vase, 6" and pitcher 11". Auman Pottery, glazed by C.B. Masten. Masten examples sell for well into the thousands of dollars. *David Blackburn collection.*

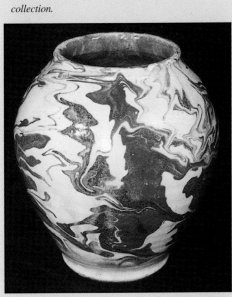

Ovoid vase, 7", C.R. Auman Pottery by C.B. Masten. Masten came from Indiana to turn and glaze for C.R. Auman Pottery. Examples like these are now valued in the several thousand dollar range. *George Viall collection.*

Bottom of Auman bud vase at top left. Mitchfield clay was used and lead glaze covers the bottom of the ware.

183

Vase, decoration over salt glaze, produced at Auman Pottery by C.B. Masten. Masten experimented with unique combinations of salt glaze with decoration. His results were unique and only recently have been appreciated. Collection of the North Carolina State University Gallery of Art and Design.

Vase, two handles, decoration over salt glaze provides a textured surface with unique visual imagery, almost as far as from traditional decoration as is seen in North Carolina pottery. Recent exhibitions have emphasized the contribution of this creative potter. Collection of the North Carolina State University Gallery of Art and Design.

Pitcher, 10¾", by C.R. Auman Pottery. Probably turned by Floyd Hilton. Glazed by C.B. Masten. Chocolate from thinner chrome green oxide mix (Hussey). Bailey collection.

Pitcher, stoneware, salt glaze, 12½", decorated in manner of C.B. Masten at Auman Pottery (1919 – 1936). Same piece is shown on page 22. $350.00 – 450.00 (rim chip). Wilkinson collection.

Small vase, blue salt glaze by C.B. Masten. Masten wares are rare, and the work of this Indiana transplant is becoming increasingly recognized. Farmer/James on loan to North Carolina State University.

C.B. Masten, 7¼" vase, blue over salt glaze. $400.00 – 600.00. Farmer/James collection.

C.B. Masten, left, signed bowl, pure salt glaze; the vase at right is more typically decorated. David Blackburn collection.

St. James Place Museum, Martin County, North Carolina. Pattie Royster James, at age 95, to whom the museum is dedicated. Porch vase which she painted in the 1920s, also pictured on the cover with a detail photo on page 43, is from Auman Pottery.

Seagrove Pottery represented a marriage of two of the most revered pottery families in North Carolina. The Aumans and the Coles had been influential in the traditional/utilitarian era and leaders in the transition to art pottery.

Walter Auman was the son of Hadley Auman. He learned many of his pottery skills with Herman Cole at Smithfield Pottery. His wife Dorothy Cole Auman was an eighth generation potter, the daughter of Charles C Cole. Charlie Cole was the owner of C.C. Cole Pottery, a volume operation serving the tourist trade largely with multiglazed small jugs and Rebecca pitchers. Dot was ten years old when her father gave her a small treadle wheel. At the Westmoore shop she also turned beside her uncle, Everette Cole, and her brother Thurston.

In 1953 Walter and Dot bought a building on Highway 220 just north of Seagrove, opened a pottery, and called their establishment Seagrove Pottery. However, they both also worked at C.C. Cole as Dot's father's health restricted his participation in the turning and burning processes. Brother Thurston died in 1966 and father C.C. in 1967. C.C. Cole Pottery closed in 1971.

Walter and Dot now devoted their efforts to establish a line of pottery that would reflect their interpretation of this genre. From their interest in Seagrove lore, knowledge of the existent pottery families, and their collection of rare and historical wares, they founded the original Potters Museum. They were, along with Greensboro businessman and civic leader Hargrove "Skipper" Bowles, the major forces in re-creating interest in and further knowledge of North Carolina pottery.

Walter glazed the wares, fired the kiln, and sold from their shop. Dot turned the pieces, apparently with great speed. Their forms were traditional and many matte glazes were used. "Seagrove" was signed in script.

In 1991 the Aumans were tragically killed when a truckload of timber fell on their van.

Seagrove Pottery, Dorothy Cole Auman and Walter Auman. Dorothy was the daughter of C.C. Cole and Walter was the son of Hadley Auman. She learned the trade at C.C. Cole and Walter worked with his uncle Herman Cole at Smithfield Pottery. In the 1960s they engaged in public relations for the Seagrove area potteries.

Seagrove candlesticks. Various potteries.

Matte green glaze compote, 11¾", by Dot Auman at Seagrove Pottery. Dot and Walter often used matte glazes. $125.00 – 150.00.

Various wares from Seagrove Pottery (Walter and Dot Auman). Note the matte glazes. Dot and Walter Auman were the historians and chroniclers of Seagrove lore. They were tragically killed in an automobile accident in the 1990s, and their collection of several thousand examples was sold to the Mint Museum in Charlotte.

Bowl, two rings, orange/red glaze, 7¼", by Dot Auman at Seagrove Pottery. Glazed by husband Walter. Note the thickness of the rings. $125.00 – 175.00.

Vase with rings at left. Note rings' thickness.

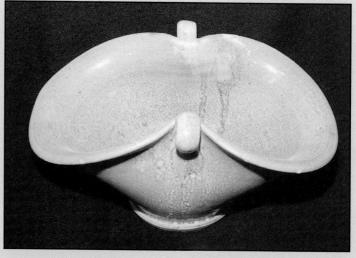

Low bowl, folded sides, rudimentary handles, 4½" x 7¼", matte brown finish. Seagrove Pottery used more matte glazes than any other pottery in the area. $115.00 – 125.00.

Rebecca pitcher, 7¼", matte brown glaze attributed to Seagrove Pottery, unsigned. The matte finished glazes are relatively opaque but at high firing temperature may become translucent. $45.00 – 65.00.

Coffeepot, brown glaze with varied reaction to kiln temperature. Turned by Dot Auman. Glazed by husband Walter. Note elongated handle. North Carolina State University Gallery of Art and Design.

Rebecca pitcher, 6½", multiglaze. Attributed to Seagrove Pottery.

Seagrove signature, Walter Auman signature, probably on ware made by Charlie Owens. Signatures from Seagrove were scribed by Dot Cole Auman, Walter, or Bob Armfield.

Vase, ring-handled, incised rings at mid-body of vase. Fired at matte glaze temperature. Outstanding brown/green variation. North Carolina State University Gallery of Art and Design.

Chicken pot, articulated, Seagrove Pottery, Dot Auman, circa 1960. Ray Wilkinson collection (1994). David Blackburn collection.

189

The turning and glazing of pots for utilitarian purposes in America has been predominantly a male profession. This was indeed the circumstance in the south-central Piedmont of North Carolina in the first several decades of the twentieth century —— they thought it was too difficult for women. Certainly digging one's clay, drying, separating the debris from usable clay, running it through the pug mill or whatever processor available, preparing the glaze, and then turning the piece that could take up to 25 to 40 pounds of clay for the large storage vessels was followed by the firing of the wares. Just this final process was physically taxing and dangerous. The "burning" began with stacking a kiln with several hundred pieces carefully arranged in a space that did not conform to the human anatomy. Remember they were called "groundhog" kilns.

The tour de force of firing the wares was part witchcraft, some dead reckoning through uncharted skies, and a great deal of reaction based upon the potter's unstructured experience. The firing process lasted 10 to 12 hours. At "blastoff," the temperature in the kiln could reach more than 1500 degrees F. making it dangerous to be in the area. Consider the added risk of opening a "peek" hole to observe the process. Kilns have been known to fall in; others have exploded and potters have been burned in the course of their observations. This was, indeed, dangerous, hard labor that was aesthetically unappealing.

Conventional wisdom reasoned that this combination of disincentives excluded women, but yet another factor may have been as important. The end result of this arduous task was a utilitarian object that had little aesthetic merit, the value of which was based upon its volume rather than its intrinsic beauty. One might logically question why any woman would wish to have more than a supporting role in such an endeavor.

Nell Cole was born in 1908, the daughter of Jacon B. Cole, the patriarch of a family of potters and at that time the owner of the largest operation in the Tarheel State. J.B. Cole's pottery employed a number of men, some were accomplished, and the personnel changed over the years from 1922 until the present. The constants in this mix of talent were Nell, her brother Waymon, her husband Philmore, and Bascomb King. Her older brother, Herman, operated Smithfield Pottery.

One might imagine that Nell was accepted in this male-dominated activity for a multitude of reasons. Certainly the Cole legacy in pottery was a factor as was the encouragement of her influential father. Another overlooked but very important factor was the conversion from utilitarian objects to decorative fancy ware. Art pottery may have provided the entree for a skilled woman who was facile in the demands of fashioning the often small and delicate forms. Nell was particularly adept at this specialized activity. She had learned to turn alongside her brother Waymon since they were children, and it was soon recognized that she had a facility for fashioning the small decorative wares that many of the men were having difficulty with. Nell was particularly adept with the thin edges that the public found so appealing. The established potters who were all male were far down on the learning curve; some either could not or would not make these smaller wares with their curved surfaces and delicate edges.

In times of change, new opportunities present themselves. One might well imagine that with the innovations being introduced by Jugtown (1922 –), Auman Pottery (1919 – 1936), North State (1924 – 1959), and J.B. Cole, gender became less important than the skill with which one could address the challenge — and Nell could produce wares with the very best.

Nell married fellow potter Philmore Graves, and her sister Vellie married Bascomb King. Vellie was 10 years older than Nell. She could turn ware and later helped her husband when he started his own pottery in 1939. She was not a full-time potter and was not listed in the 1932 Cole catalog. In contrast, the acceptance of Nell is evidenced by the numerous illustrations of her work in that seminal publication. Her specific wares were easily distinguished from the three male potters also illustrated.

The J.B. Cole Pottery became a volume operation of almost unprecedented magnitude for North Carolina, making thousands of pieces and shipping them all over America. There were contracts with resorts for large numbers of the smaller examples which Nell was particularly adept at making. The small delicate trays, baskets, cups, and bowls were the bulk of these orders. Over the years, many potters passed through the J.B. Cole operation, including Jack Kiser, Virginia Shelton, Harwood Graves, and Margaret Shelton Mabe, some for only a short period of time.

At the death of Jacon Cole in 1943, Nell and her brother Waymon took the helm of a company in great need of renovation and modernizing. This was to require a capital expenditure that was unprecedented and at a relatively uncertain time because of the war. Many of the younger potters were gone and when they would return, if they ever did, was problematic. Materials for the glazes were difficult to obtain and the post-war market unknown. Gas rationing had markedly decreased the tourist trade and made what shipments there were unpredictable.

While there had been some modernization in the 1930s such as the electric wheel Harwood Graves had fashioned for Nell, much more substantive measures were needed. For volume production a belt sander was felt to be essential. This and the renovations required a loan rumored to be in the high five figures, a debt greater than other potteries in the area had. Waymon was reported to have remarked, "I hope we live long enough to pay this off." Presumably this happened long before his death in the mid-1980s. From what is known, Nell was an equal partner in this family indebtedness.

Over the course of the next three decades J.B. Cole Pottery produced wares in great, almost unprecedented volume and sent these all over the country. Glazes came and went as did potters. Experiments with shapes and forms were a constant exercise for Nell and the other potters. It had been related that she became the champion of quality control, insisting upon the adherence to the images and descriptions in their catalog. At the same time Cole wares represented their personal response to changes in public tastes. Many of the wares, even the decorative ones, had a functional purpose. Those having a traditional Cole brown border were among the more identifiable glazes whether the base was cream or light turquoise. Younger members of the Cole family came to turn at Cole Pottery following the death of Philmore Graves and the departure of Bascomb King to start his own business.

Nell assisted her brother with a number of the administrative tasks and nominal oversight of quality control. There are several accounts related to her exercise of quality control by literally destroying wares in a dramatic fashion if they did not measure up to her personal standards. One of the younger generation of potters told of her clearing an entire table with a sweep of her arm, cleaning away the offending substandard wares. One might imagine the reaction of a young and fragile apprentice.

She wanted to continue as a full-time potter but recognized that her efforts at that time might be more appropriately directed in the business operation of J.B. Cole and as a glazer. Nell Graves in her later years made wares at Holly Hill and graciously received visitors, potting into her late 80s. She died in 1998.

Nell Cole Graves at Seagrove Festival in the mid-1990s. Note the osteoarthritic changes in her hands and fingers. She remained amazingly facile in her later years.

The Potting Legacy of the Cravens

Potting traditions in North Carolina often involve families that have engaged in this occupation for a number of generations. They have also married into other families of potters, creating what could be accurately characterized as dynasties. Such is true of the Craven family.

The Cravens arrived in the south-central Piedmont of North Carolina in the mid-1700s. Peter Craven appears on the tax roles about 1760, residing in the northern part of present Moore County. There exists a deed in 1764, and a land grant from Lord Granville indicating that Peter purchased almost 200 acres on the Deep River.

Whether Peter Craven was a potter is subject to considerable speculation, but there is documentation that his grandson John was. At his death in 1832, an inventory of John's property listed "one potter's wheel and crank." By the time one traces this Craven line to the fourth generation, potters abound, working in several states. However, a full contingent of Cravens were plying their trade in North Carolina and were among the leaders in the production of utilitarian ware. Enoch Craven (1810 – 1893) produced a substantial body of work. Much was signed "E.S. Craven" and decorated with Masonic emblems and cobalt bands. His stamp was of two types, one with large block letters and the other printed in smaller type. He also decorated with a toothed cogglewheel. Enoch married into the Hayes family in 1883 and probably trained James (J.M.) Hayes who produced jugs and jars very similar in form and configuration to Enoch's wares.

Anderson Craven (1801 – 1872), brother of E.S. Craven, was a minister and a potter. His wife Elizabeth was a member of the renowned Fox family of potters including Nicholas and his son Himer who were very well-respected practitioners of the art. All four of Anderson Craven's sons were potters. They appear to have used cobalt decoration on their stoneware, a rarity in the South. By 1860, of the four brothers only Dorris remained in North Carolina, but he was clearly the driving force in fostering the craft in Moore County, having moved from Randolph County around mid-century. Initially he made wares stamped "J.D. and T.W. Craven." The pottery was located several miles west of Jugtown along the plank road connecting Salem and Fayetteville.

By 1870 J.D. Craven had four employees and was producing annually 6,000 gallons of pottery. Among his turners were William Henry Luck and William Henry Hancock. W. H. Chrisco lived with the Cravens and potted there in his late teenage years. Ben Owen's family were neighbors of the Cravens, and J.D. may well have taught the aspiring young Ben the foundations of technique. Owen was later to become the master potter for Jacques and Juliana Busbee at Jugtown. Most of the wares were stamped "J.D. Craven," but it said that he impressed the tip of a reed at the base of the handles on wares he personally turned.

Daniel and Isaac were sons of J.D. Craven and both established potteries near their father's business. While both Isaac Franklin (1863 – 1946) and Daniel Z. (1873 – 1949) initially made utilitarian ware, the Daniel Craven Pottery participated in the transition to art pottery in the second and third decades of the twentieth century. Examples of Daniel Craven's art pottery are somewhat rare, and many are unsigned. The forms appear to reflect the early attempts at change from somewhat crude shapes and features of utilitarian ware to graceful turning with fairly sophisticated refinements and elegant glazes. The most characteristic glaze pattern appears to be clear glaze over the native clay, decorated with copper, manganese or cobalt drips. Both the Cravens and the Aumans made wares with many similarities in both glaze and form, but the Auman pieces are lighter in base color with tans and buff hues, whereas the wares of Craven Pottery were more orange or yellow brown. A few of the early North State wares bearing the first stamp (circa 1924) or very early stamped pieces also featured the glaze combinations like the Daniel Z. Craven pieces.

There is no real documentation that Isaac Craven made decorative wares, although he continued to produce pottery until sometime after World War II, long after there was a practical need for utilitarian pieces.

The sons of Daniel Craven were potters who made significant contributions in a number of sites and had careers with great variety. Both Farrell and Charles (C.B.) worked first at Teague Pottery in Robbins. Farrell later worked at Smithfield Art Pottery with Herman Cole, Glenn Art Pottery with Joe Owen, at Royal

Crown Pottery, and with Ben Owen at Old Plank Road Pottery. In the early 1960s some of the pottery stamped "Ben Owen Master Potter" was turned by Farrell Craven. There were a number of pieces signed "F. Craven Teague's," but those wares produced at Royal Crown, Smithfield Art Pottery, Glenn Art, or with Ben Owen can only be identified by the distinctive style of this accomplished journeyman potter.

Grady Craven (1917 –) and Braxton Craven (1901 – 1984) were two lesser-known brothers who were also potters. Grady spent his career working for his father. Braxton was a journeyman potter whose work is difficult to identify as he neither signed his pieces nor had a known mark. For a time he worked with his brother Charlie Craven at North State for Henry and Rebecca Cooper. His duties were glazing and various activities related to the kiln but not turning. According to Zug in *Turners and Burners*, Braxton opined that he "didn't learn much except how to work hard" and left North State's employ after only a few months. In the late 1930s and 1940s, Braxton turned for his father.

Charles Boyd (C.B.) Craven, also addressed as "Charlie," had a long and varied career as a potter, chronicled recently by Steve Compton. His earliest experiences were at his dad's shop, Craven Pottery. He also worked at North State in the early years after the pottery was founded (circa 1924 – 1925). When Herman Cole started Smithfield Art Pottery, Charlie went with him and remained for a dozen years until it closed in 1940. Since Smithfield did not stamp their wares and the individual potters are not identified, it is difficult to evaluate the work of these men or what singular contributions they made to North Carolina art pottery. Certainly some of the pieces show remarkable turning skills, but one cannot always attribute these accomplishments to an individual potter.

After Smithfield Pottery closed, Charles Craven went to work at Royal Crown Pottery, an operation financed by Victor Obler, a New Yorker who had made his mark in the silver business. The administration of Royal Crown was under the direction of Jack Kiser, an accomplished potter. When Royal Crown closed in 1942, allegedly due to the fact that chemicals for glazes were not available (others believe it was an economic decision), both Jack Kiser and Charlie Craven retired as potters. Charles Craven moved to Raleigh and went into the wholesale grocery supply business. For several decades Charlie did not make pottery but later began turning wood-fired pieces for Jugtown as well as for the Teagues. He also made traditional forms such as two-handled jugs that resembled the work of his forebears which he displayed and sold locally.

Several admirers of Craven's work formed an interesting business, Tobacco Road Pottery, and he began turning and burning at the same location in Raleigh. Another facet of this arrangement was the turning of the works in Raleigh and transporting them to the Catawba Valley where Ernestine Hilton Sigmon (of the renowned Hilton family) painted scenes on the green ware that would later be fired at Jugtown. This complex arrangement lasted well into the 1980s. Charlie Craven died in 1990 at the age of 81.

In sheer numbers the Cravens do not rival the Owens or the Coles in the dominance of potters in their family lineage. However, their contributions were substantial, especially those of J.D. (Dorris) Craven, in shaping the style of North Carolina utilitarian pottery in the latter quarter of the nineteenth century. This is expressed in the descriptions of unsigned pieces as "Craven like", "Craven school" or even "Cravenesque." The shape of the opening at the top of the vessels and the application of the strap handle are indeed distinctive. In art pottery, their skills in turning and their glazes set apart the rare examples from the Daniel Craven Pottery as unique and desirable for the collector, and the variety of wares from Tobacco Road Pottery shows great originality.

Thus, the Craven family can rightly take their place among the leaders in the development of North Carolina pottery from Peter Craven's advent to the end of Tobacco Road.

Group of early Daniel Z. Craven wares, early 1920s, very rare. David Blackburn collection.

Candlesticks, 14¼", Daniel Z. Craven, circa 1920, rare form. David Blackburn collection.

Two-handled, bulbous vase, 14¾", cogglewheel decoration, clear lead glaze with cobalt or manganese decoration. Attributed to Daniel Z. Craven. Edwards collection.

Royal Crown Pottery, 1939 – 1942

Royal Crown was established by Victor Obler, a Russian immigrant, in the Merry Oaks area of Chatham County in 1939. Obler already owned a silversmith company in New York City with his brother, Henry. He had shown a fascination with the production of art wares and had purchased North Carolina pottery for resale. He expressed a desire to have his own shop and purchased land adjacent to old US Highway 1.

Obler hired Jack Kiser, an accomplished potter, to run the North Carolina shop for him. Kiser was designated as the chief potter but also handled the daily operations related to production and quality control. In 1940 Charlie Craven joined them and later Everette and Thurston Cole as well as Lesley Stanley (Hussey). They used Kentucky and Tennessee clay and mixed it with other clays from Sanford and Smithfield, pits that were nearby. Oil-fired kilns were employed at Royal Crown as were both kick wheels and the newer electric-powered designs for turning wares.

Although most of their early output was shipped north (according to Hussey, as much as 75%, most to supply the New York Florists Association), examples from the remaining limited production can be found in other states, especially North Carolina. Most often these examples are identified by one of three versions of ink stamps.

The shop closed in 1942 when Obler declined to produce chemical stoneware for the war effort and found obtaining raw materials to make decorative wares too difficult (Smith). Several years later Obler and his wife Maxie Smith converted the building to a restaurant and dance hall.

Victor Obler hired seasoned and accomplished potters, and Royal Crown wares reflect their skills. Many of these are very collectible and bear witness to the quality control exercised during the short life of this pottery operation.

References: Billy Ray Hussey, Howard Smith

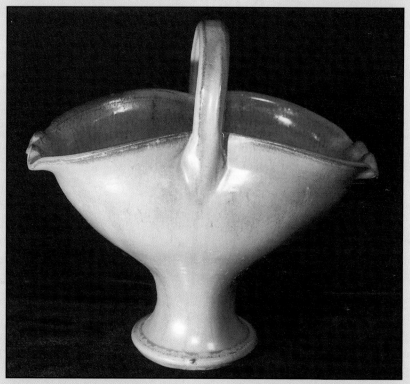

Basket, 9¾", with mirrorlike brown sugar glaze, Royal Crown Pottery (1939 – 1942). Royal Crown wares are rare since much of their early production went to florists in New York and thus had short duration of existence. Victor Obler hired very good potters, and the quality of the pieces reflects his choices. $175.00 – 225.00. Farmer/James collection.

Vase, two handles, 12¼", Royal Crown Pottery (stamped). David Blackburn collection.

Low vase (6") with wide mouth, aqua glaze by Royal Crown Pottery (1939 – 1942). Victor Obler established this pottery at this site near the north/south railroad line. $125.00 – 175.00.

Three-handled vase (handles sometimes described as Roman style). Note the almost porcelain-like appearance. Made at Royal Crown Pottery, Merry Oaks, in Chatham County, (circa 1930s). Probably turned by Jack Kiser. Leslie Stanley may have glazed this elegant 6" vase. $225.00 – 275.00. Farmer/James collection.

Royal Crown Pottery (1939 – 1942). Two-handled vase, 12", chrome red. Each pottery had their own version of this popular glaze. Royal Crown Clay from Kentucky and Tennessee was mixed with North Carolina clay from Sanford and Smithfield. Royal Crown's electric-powered wheels allowed easier production of large wares. $275.00 – 325.00.

Wide cylinder vase (11"), Royal Crown Pottery and Porcelain Co., Merry Oaks. Owned by Victor Obler, a New York silver merchant. First potter was Jack Kiser. Royal Crown employed ink stamp, and their wares appear highly vitrified. $135.00 – 165.00.

Two-handled urn, wonderful light blue glaze, thinly applied, circa 1930s. The ware is unsigned, but clay is white. Considerations are A.R. Cole as Rainbow or Royal Crown Pottery; clay favors Rainbow Pottery.

Three-handled shouldered angle vase, circa 1930. Attributed to Charles Craven (1909 – 1991) while at Smithfield Pottery or Royal Crown Pottery. Clear glaze with cobalt decoration, 8¾". Cinnamon interior, exteri- of buff colored glaze, three cord-style handles. $325.00 – 400.00. Chapel Hill Museum collection.

Oversized 19½" apothecary jar, turned by Jack Kiser, probably at Royal Crown Pottery but possibly while he was in the employ of A.R. Cole, circa 1930s. George Viall collection.

Vase, two handles ("rat tail" handle). 19½". Royal Crown Pottery, 1939 – 1942. Attributed to Jack Kiser. Edwards collection.

Bowl with six fluted areas, 14¼", aqua/turquoise glaze. Royal Crown Pottery. Some of the most elegant bowls from the Seagrove area were made at this Merry Oaks pottery. $225.00 – 325.00. Farmer/James collection.

Fluted vase, 5½". Royal Crown Pottery (1939 – 1942), attributed to Everette Cole. Thin coating of glaze over ruffled edges is common with Royal Crown wares. Possibly glazed by Lesley Stanley, supplied to New York Florists Association.

Undersurface of large fluted bowl from Royal Crown Pottery, circa 1940. $200.00 – 300.00. Farmer/James collection.

Royal Crown stamp (1939 – 1942).

Bowl, 6" x 12¾", matte brown finish by Royal Crown Pottery (1939 – 1942). Advertised in catalog as "matte cream." David Blackburn collection.

Pitcher, 17¾", chrome red glaze, Royal Crown, attributed to Jack Kiser. Edwards collection.

Bowl, two handles, 14", matte green glaze, advertised as moss green.

In the transition period from 1915 to the late 1920s, certain potteries in the Seagrove area took advantage of the local clay which burned to produce a tan to almost white color. Pieces were decorated with clear lead glazes and with cobalt and manganese to produce some of the more collectible examples of North Carolina art pottery. Principally, these were from the Aumans, the Cravens, and the Teagues.

John Wesley Teague (1867 – 1916) was the patriarch of the family. After turning for J.D. Craven and William Criscoe, he opened a pottery on N.C. Route 705 and stamped his ware "J.W. Teague, Longleaf, N.C." Teague hired Frank Moody and Rufus Owen to turn for him and sold his wares from a wagon. He might venture as far east as the port town of Wilmington. There is the apocryphal story that once when rain flooded the roads he was gone almost a month with no communication with his anxious family.

John Wesley's brother Alex was a potter, but it was a member of the next generation, Bryan "Duck" Teague (1898 – 1983), who was to carry the Teague name forward in the North Carolina art pottery movement. He opened a shop on Highway 27 south of the railroad shipping area of Robbins (Hemp). Teague was an accomplished potter and hired his brother-in-law, Farrell Craven, a journeyman with talent and experience. Daughter Zedith worked there and later ran the pottery after her father's death.

Early Teague pieces are rare as evidenced by the fact that most of the Teague examples in Lock's text on Seagrove pottery have pieces fashioned after 1980 as illustrations. If unstamped, they are sometimes difficult to distinguish from Auman and D.Z. Craven, but all are very desirable, so this differentiation may be unimportant. The stamp is rare, but interestingly, when seen is often multiple. The alternating linear drips of black (cobalt) and green (manganese) over a tan body are supposedly a distinguishing characteristic (Bailey).

Charlie Teague (1901 – 1938) was the first potter for the Busbees at Jugtown. He and others made wares for Jacques Busbee before Jugtown was a true entity. The early wares were, very rarely, signed in script "Charlie Teague." After seven years at Jugtown, Charlie joined the large operation at Smithfield Pottery operated by Herman Cole. There production was not signed, and four or five turners were in the employ.

The individual example can only be attributed by stylistic evaluation of the form.

James G. Teague (1906 – 1988) opened his own shop in the 1930s which he then sold to C. C. Cole when he went to work for Fulper Pottery Company. Fulper, located in northern New Jersey, was a factory type operation. The owner came to Seagrove and induced James to become a demonstration potter for visitors to the factory. They fashioned a log cabin near the entrance, and visitors passed through the building to see Teague at work before taking the factory tour.

In 1941 James Teague returned to North Carolina and reopened a shop, making large pieces mainly for other local potteries such as Joe Owen at Glenn Art, Duck Teague, and M.L. Owens Pottery. He continued to do this through the 1950s. Archie Teague (1935 – 1999) opened Hand T Pottery in the 1960s with his wife Yvonne's father, Homer Hancock. Archie has previously turned for a year at C.C. Cole and for five or six years at J.B. Cole in the 1950s.

When Hand T Pottery closed, Archie went to work for the Asheboro Fire Department. In 1986 he reopened a pottery and worked with his wife Yvonne Hancock Teague until his death. Yvonne died the following year.

Archie was known for his ability to turn difficult forms, including the elusive Aladdin lamp, which would become his signature piece. If there are examples of this form by other potters from the 1950s when Waymon Cole was making them, they have not been uncovered.

Teague examples are rare, especially those of the 1920s and 1930s. In the 1930s and early 1940s they were a volume operation, offering 200 shapes in 11 different colors. They would ship pottery in eight-bushel plywood boxes acquired from a local textile mill. Tourist items were sold to residents and guests of Pinehurst, and they adopted several elegant styles such as the Greek amphora and the Portland vase which are rare. Some of the pieces from the 1970s reflect the artistry of Farrell Craven who turned at Teagues with Zedith after he left Ben Owen's shop.

The legacy of the Teagues is an important one and continues today through descendants and relatives still working in Seagrove.

Reference: Mick Bailey

Teague Family of Potters

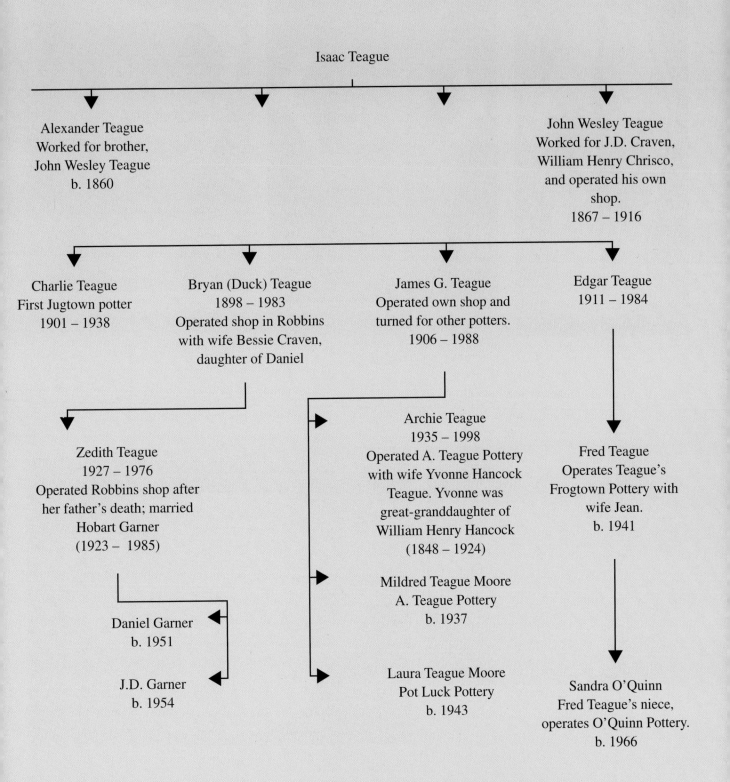

Isaac Teague

Alexander Teague
Worked for brother,
John Wesley Teague
b. 1860

John Wesley Teague
Worked for J.D. Craven,
William Henry Chrisco,
and operated his own
shop.
1867 – 1916

Charlie Teague
First Jugtown potter
1901 – 1938

Bryan (Duck) Teague
1898 – 1983
Operated shop in Robbins
with wife Bessie Craven,
daughter of Daniel

James G. Teague
Operated own shop and
turned for other potters.
1906 – 1988

Edgar Teague
1911 – 1984

Zedith Teague
1927 – 1976
Operated Robbins shop after
her father's death; married
Hobart Garner
(1923 – 1985)

Archie Teague
1935 – 1998
Operated A. Teague Pottery
with wife Yvonne Hancock
Teague. Yvonne was
great-granddaughter of
William Henry Hancock
(1848 – 1924)

Fred Teague
Operates Teague's
Frogtown Pottery with
wife Jean.
b. 1941

Daniel Garner
b. 1951

Mildred Teague Moore
A. Teague Pottery
b. 1937

J.D. Garner
b. 1954

Laura Teague Moore
Pot Luck Pottery
b. 1943

Sandra O'Quinn
Fred Teague's niece,
operates O'Quinn Pottery.
b. 1966

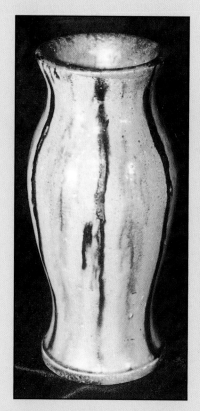

Vase, 9", Teague Pottery, Hemp, NC stamped, Hemp was former name of Robbins. Bill Ivey collection.

Two-handled vase, 8¾", chrome red, stamped several times, Teague Pottery. Rare and valuable. Bill Ivey collection.

Two-handled vase, 12¼", clear glaze with decoration. Attributed to Teague Pottery, circa 1920s. David Blackburn collection.

Teague Pottery, Hemp, NC stamp. Bill Ivey collection.

Three-handled (Grecian), low wide bowl with shoulder, 8" x 11½" by Teague. Popular form among Aumans, Cravens, and Teagues in early 1920s. David Blackburn collection.

Undersurface of early Teague example showing white/tan Mitchfield clay with clear lead glaze.

Unusual pitcher 12¾" attributed to Teague Pottery. Clear lead glaze, manganese decoration. View of handle on page 94. Later Farrell and Charlie Craven worked at Teague Pottery. George Viall collection.

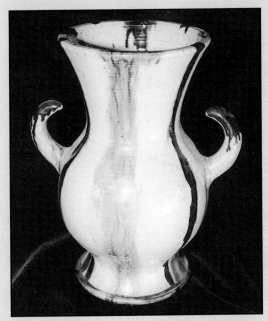

Vase, 11¼", with unusual handles, circa 1920s, clear glaze, manganese decoration with alternating green (thin) and black (thick) runs. Attributed to Teague Pottery. Bailey collection.

Three-handled vase with three rows of concentric rings, 14". Thin blue/aqua glaze by Teague Pottery (1928 near Robbins), Turners were B.D. "Duck" Teague, Farrell Craven, Zedith Teague, and Hobart Garner. Examples are relatively rare. $225.00 – 325.00. St. James Place Museum.

Two-handled vase, 12", attributed to Teague Pottery, Hemp, circa 1920s. Probably made by B.D. Teague or Farrell Craven. Bryan P. (Duck) Teague moved the pottery west of Robbins in the 1920s. $175.00 – 250.00.

Small 5½" "decorative" vase/pencil holder/vessel, Teague Pottery. John Wesley Teague (1867 – 1916) was the first potter learning the trade from J.D. Craven. He and neighbor David Z. Craven used the same clay and recipes. At John Wesley's death, Charlie, James, and Bryan (Duck) ran the shop. After WWII, B.D. operated a shop in Robbins, closing in 1984. $95.00 – 115.00.

Stamp, Teague Pottery, Hemp, NC.

Lug handles, maker unknown. Attributed to Teague Pottery (Charlie Teague) or early J.B. Cole. George Viall collection.

Two-handled vase, 13¾", stamped Teague Pottery, rare form. David Blackburn collection.

Note turning of large wide, sometimes called "Moravian", handles on vase, circa 1920s.

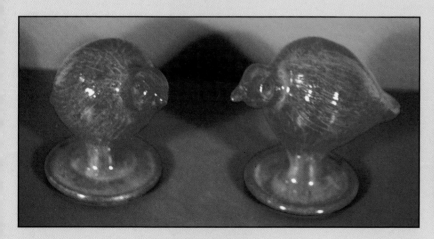

Pair of partridges, also known as "turtle doves". Figures are considered by most collectors and scholars as a different but related genre of art pottery. Farmer/James collection. Gift of Archie and Yvonne Teague.

Piece with multiple Teague stamps. Bill Ivey collection.

Carolina Pottery

Carolina Pottery was located in the small town of Candor along Highway 220, which was originally described as a clay road. The pottery was first known as Steed's Pottery as it was started in 1925 by C. L. Steed. He employed Emerson "Bud" Luck to make utilitarian wares with the traditional salt glaze.

Over the next several years C. L.'s son, Joseph D. Steed (1901 – 1978), began attempts at the production of decorative ware using lead glazes. In 1929 Lorenzo "Wren" Cole leased the pottery from Joe Steed. Wren Cole turned and glazed wares with his sons Lacy and Woodrow, and also attended to the other duties necessary to produce the art pottery. For short intervals, other potters were hired.

Two identifying marks were used by Carolina Pottery, "Carolina Pottery, Candor" and an earlier one with "Steeds NC, Handmade". Wren Cole closed the shop in 1932 (*NCFPS Newsletter* #19).

Vase, 6½", Carolina Pottery, stamped, very unusual glaze. Bill Ivey collection.

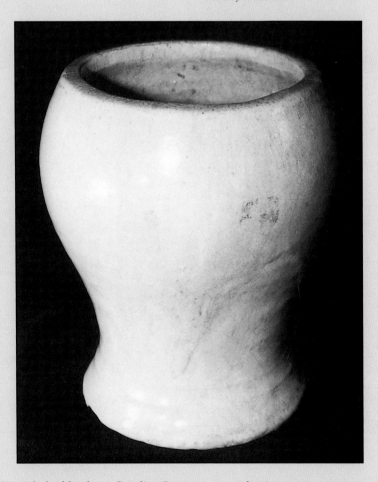

Vase, 8½", with double glaze, Carolina Pottery, stamped twice. David Blackburn collection.

Carolina Pottery stamp on basket at left.

Basket with unusual, striking glaze, 9", attributed to Wren Cole, stamped. Bill Ivey collection.

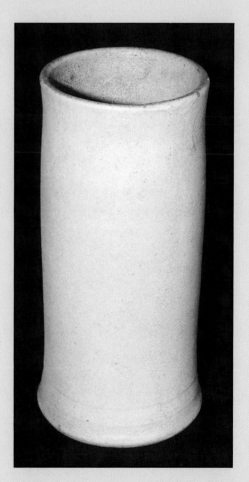

Cylinder vase, 12¾", stamped Carolina Pottery. Turned by Lorenzo (Wren) Cole (1871 – 1931).

Two-handled vase, 12" with "finger" handles, decorative glaze. Attributed to Carolina Pottery, Candor, Wren Cole. Bailey collection.

207

Low bowl with shoulder, 5¼", stamped "Carolina Pottery, Steeds," (other stamp, Candor, NC). Carolina Pottery was begun in 1925 by C.L. Steed who employed Bud Luck; later operated by Joe Steed and sold in 1929 to Wren Cole who operated it until 1932. $75.00 – 100.00 (glaze loss).

Low bowl, 6", Carolina Pottery, Candor. Unusual variegated glaze. The glazes in North Carolina express such variety that they represent a very wide spectrum. There were several potters at this location who may have experimented with this glaze.

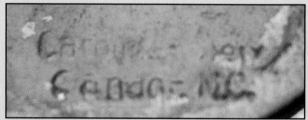

Bottom of vase at left. "White" clay, 1920 – early 1930.

Carolina Pottery, Candor. Two-handled vase, multiple glazes. Form and glaze are typical of this pottery. $175.00 – 200.00.

The color of the glaze along with the prominent form/clay combination identifies this piece with the Highway 220 pottery. Attributed to Lorenzo Cole (1871 – 1931). $145.00 – 175.00.

Tall vase, 13¼", with striking mottling due to glaze with copper base, referred by some as "flame" or even "flambe". Attributed to Carolina Pottery.

M.L. Owens is the undisputed dean of the Seagrove Potters. However, when you visit him, you will not find a doting old man or someone who has even heard of the slow lane. Instead you will encounter a blur of activity at the wheel and a flood of observations, past and present, very definite opinions, and multiple truths. As you talk, or rather listen, handles and teapots will appear before your eyes. Observing M.L. moving about the shop you can hardly believe that he was born in 1917, but you can certainly document the fact that this operation began in 1910 with his father. J.H. Owen was a pioneer in fashioning traditional ware and the early attempts in the late teens to make the transition to art pottery. He made some of the very earliest wares that were sold by Jacques Busbee when Jugtown was in its most formative stages. The Owens legacy remains intact some 80 years later.

With little provocation, M.L. will talk to you about the past and offer comments about the activities of the potters in the Seagrove area, especially his own kin. "Cousin Joe (Owen) liked to throw big stuff. He did a lot of Rebecca jugs but couldn't make them with the narrow base like me and old man Cole," he said. M.L. related to us that on one of his Rebecca pitchers he inserted the handle origin inside the rim. The other potters had "stand off" handles, and you could not see the back portion of the rim in its entirety.

Among the more interesting aspects of a visit with M.L. is the opportunity to receive firsthand, purely unabridged lore about his family, the Owens. However, when you consider how many families were linked by marriage, commerce, common interests or even mutual distrust, you realize that these are more than just the revelations of Melvin's dynasty. During some of M.L.'s observations, you feel the need of a scorecard or program to help keep the players straight.

M.L. has a very negative opinion about the wanderlust evidenced by certain Seagrove potters past and present. He believes turning is a serious business, and you only can remain competent if you do it daily, not "running off somewhere." He takes great pride in having worked in the same place and "stuck with the same things" most of his life. He admitted, however, that some of the glazing innovations brought from elsewhere represented significant aesthetic advances

and also agreed that some of the journeyman potters brought new ideas with them. He told us about his common practice of turning or burning wares upon request for other potteries, especially Log Cabin which was a rather complex operation run principally from Guilford, North Carolina. He believes you will always have difficulty with quality control if you turn a piece at one site and transport it to be glazed and fired at another location.

In any description of North Carolina art pottery there is invariably the statement that a significant advantage that potters from the Seagrove area had was the presence of light-colored, almost white clay. The virtue many believe is that this clay does not alter significantly the color of the glaze. Therefore, the color would be "true." This allowed use of translucent glazes and a wider choice of colors and shades than with the red or orange clay from other areas. While there was white clay available from the Candor area where Carolina Pottery was located, the principal source is Mitchfield clay from the Auman clay pit. The other common source is near Smithfield on Highway 301. M.L. must be a true believer as he stated matter-of-factly, "I leased the pit and when it got hard to get, I got this fellow with a bulldozer to make me a bank so I can get down to it." The discussion was closed.

When asked what his signature piece was, M.L. didn't immediately respond, so we reminded him of Joe Owen's Rebecca pitchers or Waymon's porch vases as a comparison. "I guess my teapots are what everybody talks about," which we took to be his pronouncement on that. We asked M.L. how we could differentiate the teapots from the 1930s to 1950s from the more contemporary ones, and he stated "the handles, they're different." The shape of the handles for his vintage teapots are squarer in shape than the new ones. We had several pieces as well as photographs and slides of others for him to identify which he did while working away at his passion. He also admitted his early pitchers were a source of pride.

M.L. never stopped turning during our talk and offered his diagnosis in short, unequivocal utterances. "Walter made that. That's mine. Never saw that glaze before." One piece, a refrigerator jar with a so-called elephant trunk spout we feel certain that M.L. made, as do other collectors and two potters familiar with his work, evoked "not mine, must be a Cole." So much for science, but later we recognized that M.L. was becoming bored with this "authentication" process and had something else on his agenda.

M.L. Owens was born in 1917, the son of J.H. Owen and brother of potters Jonah (Jonie), Elvin, and Walter (W.N.). His potter children are Boyd, Vernon, Nancy Owens Brewer, Bobby, and Lula Bell Owens Bolick. His older brother Walter (1904 – 1981) was the potter for the Coopers at North State and later inherited the business in 1960 and operated it as Pine State until the late 1970s. About Walter, M.L. opined, "Walter was a good potter, but he never looked under a single piece. You gotta bend over and look at the bottom. That's important." M.L. said that he believed that some of the North State glazes were unique and that the double and triple glazes made very identifiable pieces. Some that we brought he "authenticated" as to the origin. We asked why his brother Elvin's work was relatively scarce. M.L. said he "didn't pot much after he went away." We found out that Elvin again turned wares with his son in Winston-Salem in a pottery/concrete operation for several years before his death in 1994.

Jonah was the first potter at North State (1924 – 1926) and was the principal potter at Log Cabin for Bessie Myrtle Hunter (1926 – 1933). He then opened his own shop with his wife Myrtice. Jonah (1895 – 1966) was the second oldest of James H.'s sons after Harrison (1892 – 1972). M.L. said Jonah was a very creative turner but made no further comment about any of Jonah's life or work. He then moved the conversation to his children.

Although you get the idea Melvin is very proud of his children, every pronouncement has a disclaimer attached. Bobby and Vernon along with Vernon's wife Pam are the driving forces in Jugtown Pottery which has been making wares since the 1920s. Jugtown is usually thought of as the best known pottery in the Seagrove area. The traditions of Jacques and Juliana Busbee and M.L.'s relative, master potter Ben Owen, have been well maintained.

Vernon recently won the North Carolina Folklore Award, awarded in the past to Burlon Craig and Ben Owen. M.L. subsequently received the honor. Son Boyd acquired M.L. Owens' (we asked about the inspiration for the added 's' but obtained only this definitive answer from Melvin, "looked better") pottery in 1975. M.L. exclaimed, "potting and playing baseball don't go, so we had to get that straight. I kept on potting cause that's what I can do best."

M.L. related a story about the collaboration process in the early days of art pottery in North Carolina. "Jacques (Busbee) came over and said he needed 95 pieces for a contract he had and they had to be ready in a couple of days. Ben (Owen) couldn't get it all done for at least two weeks. I turned them that night and put the handles on the next morning — made 100 pieces so we would be sure we had enough and only lost one when we fired them."

Nancy Owens Brewer works in the shop with M.L. "Nancy can turn work, any kind of thing," he said. Son Boyd glazes, fires the kiln, and fills the various volume contracts with large companies such as Eveready Battery. Lula Bell Bolick who lives near Blowing Rock in the area north of Hickory also turns wares for her family business.

M.L. also wanted to share his future plans. He and a photographer friend plan to open their own shop on the property. Melvin will turn the wares, and she "will be out front. We aren't going to make any of the pieces that will compete with Boyd and them but may glaze some in the old style," he said. The results of this arrangement will be interesting.

Epilogue

In February 2002 while we were photographing the M.L. Owens collection housed in the gallery above the salesroom, M.L. drove over from his house in the golf cart he now uses. From upstairs I was able to observe the interchange between M.L. and the staff; he was still in charge.

After a few minutes I came down and greeted him and reminded him of our 1994 visit. He recalled it well, asking about the other interviewer who had been with me.

He then told me a story about his brother Elvin who decided he had a full life and was ready for the hereafter, so he refused to eat. M.L. went to see him in Winston-Salem, believing his culinary skills would snap Elvin out of this nonsense. Despite his best efforts, M.L. found Elvin resolute, so "I came on home and he was dead in three days."

I told M.L. we hoped he had no such plans. His reply was "Doc, I gotta stay around 'cause of all the women that want to marry me." At 84, M.L. was still thinking creatively.

The Dean of North Carolina Pottery, M.L. Owens, age 84, in M.L. Owens Pottery. Photo taken February 13, 2002.

Lidded jar with two lug handles (swirl pattern). M.L. Owens Pottery, attributed M.L. Owens. M.L. Owens Museum.

Pitcher, 12½", multiglazed, M.L. Owens. Unusual form and glazing pattern. M.L. Owens Museum.

Teapot, 11", by M.L. Owens, stamped Steeds NC. Present location of M.L. Owens Pottery and M.L. Owens Museum is on Busbee Road near site of J.H. Owen's shop. M.L. Owens Museum.

Two hanging bowls by M.L. Owens. Melvin Owens (b. 1917 –) is a traditional potter whose production over his long career has been phenomenal. The forms are traditional and the pattern of green glaze in vertical runs over a yellow base typical of his work. Left bowl: $65.00 – 95.00; right bowl: $60.00 – 75.00.

Pitcher, M.L. Owens (1917 –) M.L. took over his father's shop in the 1930s. Father of Boyd b. 1948, Nancy b. 1953, Lula Bell b. 1943, Bobby b. 1939, Vernon b. 1941.

M.L. Owens Pottery, Steeds, NC. Oldest continuously working pottery in Seagrove.

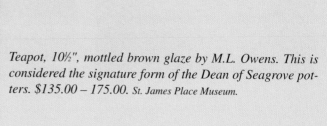

Teapot, 9¼" x 10¾", by M.L. Owens. The rings at the base of handle and spout are characteristic as is the bottom curve of the spout, circa 1950s. $175.00 – 250.00. Farmer/James collection.

Teapot, 10½", mottled brown glaze by M.L. Owens. This is considered the signature form of the Dean of Seagrove potters. $135.00 – 175.00. St. James Place Museum.

Teapot, M.L. Owens (1917 –). When asked what was his signature piece, M.L. replied, "folks like my teapots." The bands from base of handle to base of spout are characteristic. 8½" x 9", circa 1940 – 1950s.

Teapot, 16¾", by M.L. Owens. This is the second largest example of the M.L. Owens signature piece. M.L. Owens Museum.

(Right) Wild Turkey jug, made in the style of R.E. (Emmitt) Albright, 12" x 5½". Made by his son using the same clay and salt glaze. Emmitt turned at North State, with Everette Cole and M.L. Owen. $90.00 – 125.00. St. James Place Museum collection.

(Far right) Wild Turkey jug with stopper. Salt glaze stoneware. Made by R. Emmitt Albright (1910 – 1996). After turning for a number of potters, he developed the "turkey jug" at M.L. Owens Pottery which became his trademark. His son continues to make this signature piece. $250.00 – 500.00. Made at M.L. Owens Pottery.

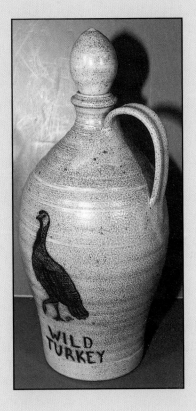

The Owens family is another that can trace its lineage to many of the important developments in the North Carolina art pottery movement. They also play very significant roles today in the artistry of Seagrove pottery.

Joseph Owen (1823 – 1905) and his brother James J. Owen (1830 – 1905) were the first recognized potters in the Owen family. Manley Owen was a potter for the well-known shop of Edgar Allan (E.A.) Poe.

Benjamin Franklin Owen had two sons whose lineage began the very distinguished and distinctive branches of the Owen family tree of potters. Rufus Owen (1872 – 1948) was primarily a utilitarian potter but according to family lore (M.L. Owens) made the dirt dish that was seen by Juliana Royster Busbee at the North Carolina State Fair and attracted her to the Seagrove area to later found Jugtown.

Rufus's brother, James H. Owen (1866 – 1923) was a very important figure in the North Carolina art pottery movement. He worked for utilitarian potter Pascal Marable and then opened a shop with his brother Rufus and his father, Benjamin Franklin Owen. Rufus's three sons, Joe, Charlie, and Ben (Ben Sr. or Ben Wade) are also part of Seagrove art pottery history.

Charlie worked for his father Rufus and then for his brother Joe at Glenn Art Pottery (1948 – 1968) and at Joe Owen Pottery (1968). In the 1930s he went to Williamsburg, Virginia, to turn wares for the tourist trade there. He also worked with the Aumans at Seagrove and retired in 1988.

Joe Owen operated Glenn Art Pottery mainly as a wholesale operation (1948 – 1968) and later operated Joe Owen Pottery. Joe Owen is best known for his large pieces such as porch vases and Rebecca pitchers. He often used cogglewheel decoration around the body of his wares. His glazes at times would be so varied in color and so abstract in technique or placement of the decoration that they resembled a modern-day abstract painting. As noted elsewhere in the text, the Glenn Art foil label was pasted on and usually removed or became detached with use.

Ben Wade Owen in 1923 at age 18 went to work for Jacques and Juliana Busbee at Jugtown. This was a fledgling operation but laden with creativity. The Busbees wished not only to revive the North Carolina pottery traditions but also to take it in new directions, seeking national and international recognition. While Juliana tested some of their new forms and glazes in her Greenwich Village tea room on the denizens of New York, Jacques was receiving wares from some of the older potters and traditional operations in the Seagrove to sell.

From 1918 to 1923 Jim (J.H.) Owen worked for Jacques Busbee. Jim would turn the ware, and Jacques would glaze it (Sweezy). Busbee would often design his own shapes, and Owen would turn them and fire the bisque in the two kilns on the Jugtown property.

Ben Owen (Sr.) was a young man when he came to work at Jugtown. Some feel this helped him embrace the "new" ideas of the trained painter, Busbee. Owen was adept at translating the Oriental and sometimes European imagery to the realities of the technology and clay available in North Carolina's south-central Piedmont. This became the best known pottery in the Seagrove Area.

Ben Owen (1904 – 1983) remained at Jugtown for 36 years. Jugtown closed for a year (1959 – 1960) and was reopened by John Mare with Vernon Owens, son of M.L. Owens and grandson of J.H. Owen, as the chief potter. Ben opened Plank Road Pottery and at first signed wares, "Pottery by Ben Owen" and later, "Ben Owen, Master Potter." He continued many of the forms and glazes that had been successful at Jugtown.

At that time Jugtown was going through a series of ownership changes, and in some ways the Busbee tradition was being carried on by Ben Owen. Ben, troubled by arthritis in his later years, hired a very talented potter to assist him in turning wares, Farrell Craven (B. Owen). Gradually his son Wade assumed operation of the pottery assisted by his son, Ben Owen III. In 1983 Ben Owen died, but his widow Lucille lived into the late 1990s.

Ben Owen III has become one of Seagrove's more celebrated contemporary potters. He has had one-person exhibitions at the Chrysler Museum in Norfolk and the Mint Museum in Charlotte. Ben uses his academic training to embellish traditional forms and glazes, creating noteworthy examples of both the new expressions while preserving a number of his grandfather's forms and glazes.

It is ironic that the grandson of the first potter of Jugtown would today be its owner and master potter. When J.H. Owen opened his pottery in 1910, one might opine that he was evaluating the market and assessing whether or not there would be a future demand for utilitarian wares. We can find rare and important examples of the transitional forms produced from 1915 to the early 1920s where J.H. Owen, the D.Z. Craven Pottery, and the Aumans were exploring the avenues of adaptation. This was an evolutionary process with a number of obstacles and a very unclear mandate. The Owen(s) were at the forefront of this change.

Among the seven J.H. Owen progeny there were some very talented potters. Jonah (1895 – 1966) was one of the most creative potters to ever work in the Seagrove area. His forms and glazes show great imagination, and most of his work is very collectible. Jonah worked with the Coopers at North State Pottery from 1924 through 1926 before his brother joined them. He turned at Log Cabin (1927 – 1932) for Bessie Hunter and then opened Steeds Pottery at Steeds (1932). The pottery was operated for 10 years by Jonah and his wife Myrtis (1908 – 1993). They stamped their wares "hand made." These were primarily for the tourist trade in Luray, Virginia, and this stamp was probably to assure the purchasers that they were getting "the real thing." (M.L. Owens) Jonah's early pieces at his father's pottery, North State, and Log Cabin are very desirable.

Walter (W.N.) worked with Henry and Rebecca Cooper at North State from 1925 – 1977. He was the principal potter, but others working there included Thurston Cole, Charlie Craven, and Jack Kiser. At the Coopers' deaths, W.N. Owens inherited the pottery and changed the name to Pine State. In the 1970s the output of Pine State was sporadic and the quality irregular; later pieces were signed "W.N. Owen."

Elvin Owen also worked at North State (1935 – 1936) but principally with brother M.L. at M.L. Owens after 1942. Elvin left the pottery in 1948 and ran a carpet wholesale business in Florida and later in Winston-Salem. "Elvin liked a steady job where he knew the money was gonna come in," M.L. said. Elvin made some pottery after 1960 but principally made concrete garden ware with his son in the Winston-Salem area.

M.L. Owens, the family patriarch, took over Owens Pottery (J.H. Owen's 1910 operation) at his father's sudden death. Having worked there in the interim, he was 22 when he assumed the leadership. This was then reformatted and designated as "M.L. Owens, Steeds, NC." in 1942. M.L., a tireless worker and taskmaster, made his own wares and contracted with other potteries in the Seagrove area. Many of the larger Log Cabin pieces were fired there (M.L. Owens).

Two of his larger contracts were Goosecreek Pottery, a wholesaler in South Carolina (in the 1950s and 1960s) and the Carolina Soap and Candle Company in Pinehurst. These pieces were often labeled. M.L.'s signature pieces are considered to be his teapots. His legacy, however, includes the number of young potters he has encouraged and assisted and the kilns he has built for others. At 84, he is still promoting the value of this art form.

Currently, M.L. Owens Pottery is operated by son Boyd (since 1975) and Nancy Owens Brewer. Billy Ray Hussey, Melvin's grandnephew, directs the Southern Folk Pottery Collector's Society. Their auctions are an excellent source for rare examples of North Carolina art pottery, and the catalogs are quite informative.

Vernon Owens is the master potter at Jugtown. His wife Pam is a potter there and is primarily responsible for the glazes. Brother Bobby is in charge of the operations of the kilns and the deployment of the clay, woods, and other elements essential to the process. This is a formidable team, reflected by the quality of their wares which is reflected by the numerous illustrations in their text.

When Vernon came to Jugtown, he was hired by John Mare in 1960. Mare also hired Bobby Owens and Charles Moore to prepare clay, glaze, and fire the kilns. Mare was a business man who owned radio stations and a friend of Juliana Busbee. He loved Jugtown and the simple yet beautiful pots that had been made there. He offered the job to Ben Owen, who declined to carry on with his own shop. Vernon began to learn the Jugtown shapes and the old glazes, with the exception of Chinese blue, were continued. Mare Blue was the beginning of new glazes being developed at Jugtown. Unfortunately Mare never had a chance to prove his love of Jugtown since he was taken ill and died suddenly from liver cancer in 1962. This was the same year that Juliana Busbee died.

The pottery was run under the Mare estate until 1964. Vernon leased the pottery from 1964 – 1968, when a suitable buyer was found. Jugtown could not be sold until a buyer was found who would carry on the pottery in the same way that the Busbees and then Mare had run it. This stipulation was part of John Mare's last will and testament.

Country Roads, a nonprofit operation directed by Nancy Sweezy, bought Jugtown in 1968. Their mission was the preservation of hand crafts, and along with Nancy, on the board were weaver and folk singer Norman Kennedy, and founder of the Smithsonian folk life program Ralph Rinzler.

Somewhat symbolic of the changing circumstances was the confusing saga of the stamps. The "original" stamp had been used since it was designed in the 1920s. It featured a central jug and was almost the same size as a U.S. quarter. These were "lost".

When John Mare came to work in 1960, the stamps were not to be found. One was thought to have been taken by Ben Owen, the other was found in 1962, but they had to make new stamps in the meantime. A new stamp was made from a piece of fired ware, smaller by approximately 20% due to the burning. The two new stamps featured either a central jug (as in the original) or a pitcher and could both be covered by a quarter.

After 1962 the one original stamp that was found was put back into use, confusing the dating of the ware. When Vernon was made aware of this quandry, he started dating the salt glaze examples, and after 1977, all of the pieces. The Mare stamps were used again in 1968 – 1969 while imprints made from an original stamped pot were used to make the new stamps. This was done because the old stamp was becoming worn and with several apprentices working, they needed more than one available stamp. The new stamps are similar but slightly smaller than the originals (P. Owens).

Both M.L. Owens and Jugtown potteries are in operation today, producing wares that demonstrate their legacy. Jugtown has a fine museum as does Ben Owen Pottery. M.L. Owens has a small historical collection of Owens pottery.

Throughout this text you will encounter testaments of the Owens' contributions to the North Carolina art pottery movement. At present Vernon and Pam and Ben III stand at the forefront of present-day Seagrove potters. They link the present with the traditions of the 1920s and 1930s.

References: Ben Owen III, M.L. Owens, Pam and Vernon Owens, Nancy Sweezy

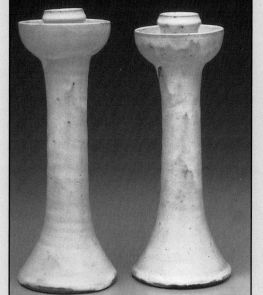

Chinese white candlesticks, wood-fired stoneware, Ben Owen, Jugtown period (1923 – 1959), 14" h. Courtesy Ben Owen III.

Tobacco spit tea set with charger, wood-fired earthenware, Ben Owen, master potter (1959 – 1972). Courtesy Ben Owen III.

Owen (s) Family 1880 – 1960

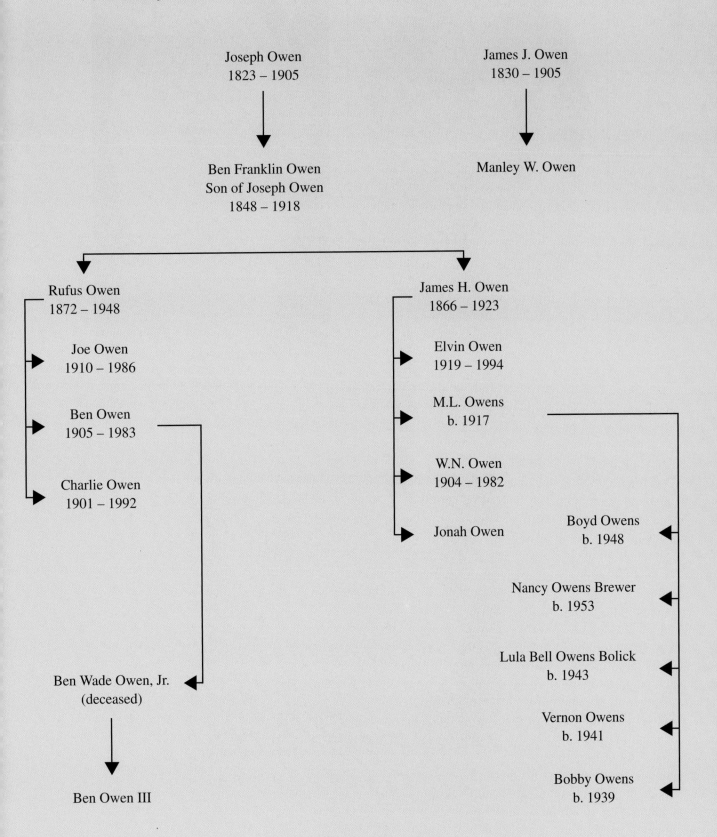

Joseph Owen
1823 – 1905

James J. Owen
1830 – 1905

Ben Franklin Owen
Son of Joseph Owen
1848 – 1918

Manley W. Owen

Rufus Owen
1872 – 1948

James H. Owen
1866 – 1923

Joe Owen
1910 – 1986

Elvin Owen
1919 – 1994

Ben Owen
1905 – 1983

M.L. Owens
b. 1917

Charlie Owen
1901 – 1992

W.N. Owen
1904 – 1982

Jonah Owen

Boyd Owens
b. 1948

Nancy Owens Brewer
b. 1953

Lula Bell Owens Bolick
b. 1943

Ben Wade Owen, Jr.
(deceased)

Vernon Owens
b. 1941

Bobby Owens
b. 1939

Ben Owen III

Vase, 11", cobalt decoration over clear glaze. Note the sine wave at shoulder and mid-section of body. Attributed to J.H. Owen. Very rare. Edwards collection.

Vase, 21", three-handled, clear lead glaze, cobalt decoration. Note sine wave pattern. Attributed to J.H. Owen. Rare.

Two-handled vase, 11", stamped J.H. Owen. Attributed to J.H. Owen, could have been turned by Jonah Owen. Characteristic handles of J.H. Owen Pottery of that era (circa 1920s). David Blackburn collection.

J.H. Owen bowl salt glazed, since wave incising, raised and cobalt decorations, 9¾".

J.H. Owen (1919 – 1925), Persian vase, 18½". One of the most desirable forms in all Seagrove wares.

Persian vase, 21¾", Chinese blue, Ben Owen, Jugtown, 1927 – 1933. This is an important, sophisticated form with a most desirable glaze, a very valuable piece. Detail of the rope decoration is on page 53.

Vase, two lug handles, 10½", North State Pottery, Jonah Owen, circa 1924 – 1925, rare pre-mark.

Orange teapot, wood-fired earthenware, Ben Owen, Jugtown period, 6" h.

Buff and orange Grueby jar, wood-fired earthenware, Ben Owen, Jugtown period, 11" h. Courtesy Ben Owen III.

Orange oil bottle, wood-fired earthenware, Ben Owen, master potter, 14" h. Courtesy Ben Owen III.

Chinese blue Tang vase, wood-fired earthenware, Ben Owen, Jugtown period, 11" h. Courtesy Ben Owen III.

Chinese blue Tang Vase, wood-fired earthenware, Ben Owen, Jugtown period, 8" h. Courtesy Ben Owen III.

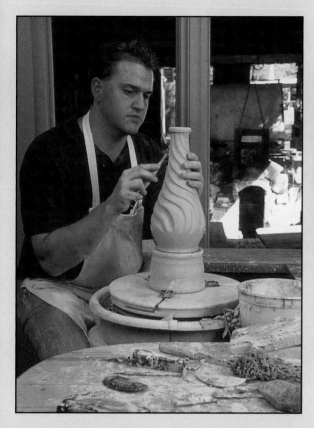

Ben Owen III at work in his studio.

Ash glazed tea set, wood-fired stoneware, Ben Owen III, 2001.

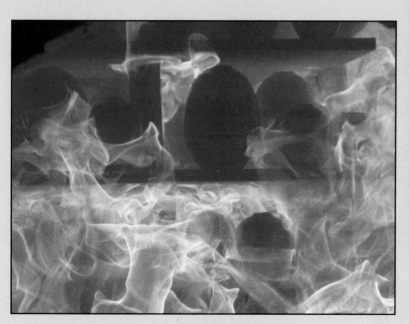

Wood-fired groundhog kiln during firing.

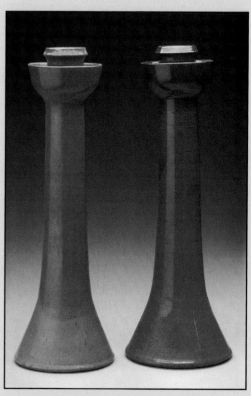

Burnt orange candlesticks, wood-fired earthenware, Ben Owen, master potter (1959 – 1972), 18" h. Courtesy Ben Owen III.

Although the attraction of North Carolina pottery is part of the phenomenon of heightened awareness of the virtues of American art pottery, specific reasons can be cited for this growth in interest, especially in those collectible wares previously made in North Carolina's south-central Piedmont region. These stimuli include several informative texts such as Terry Zug's *Turners and Burners*, Nancy Sweezy's *Raised in Clay*, and Robert Lock's *The Traditional Potters of Seagrove, North Carolina*; numerous museum exhibitions with catalogs; auctions featuring North Carolina art pottery, as well as the activities of the Southern Folk Pottery Collectors Society, the North Carolina Folk Art Society, and the North Carolina Pottery Guild; and the North Carolina Pottery Museum at Seagrove.

With the growing interest of the collecting public and the increasing scholarship has come recognition that various potters, families of potters, and pottery shops had individual forms and glazes that might separate their wares and be specifically analyzed and acquired. One such pottery that has now come into its own in this regard is North State Pottery.

North State Pottery has a very interesting origin as it did not evolve as a family tradition as Owens Pottery or Owen Pottery and J.B. Cole did or from the skills and organization of a dominant potter such as at A.R. Cole Pottery.

Rebecca Palmer Cooper first because interested in pottery as a hobby. She lived in Winston-Salem near the Randolph/Moore county border. Her husband, Henry, was employed by the R.J. Reynolds Tobacco Company as a salesman. In 1924 Mrs. Cooper employed Jonah (Jonie) Owen, a member of the Owen potting dynasty, to turn wares for her, and this small operation became a thriving enterprise.

Apparently realizing his wife's commitment and having an interest in the glazes from a technical and decorative bias, Mr. Cooper joined the endeavor after leaving his position with Reynolds. In 1925 the Coopers hired another potter, Walter N. Owen, Jonie's brother, who was to remain associated with North State for his entire career. At Henry Cooper's death in 1960, W.N. Owen inherited the business.

One of the events that must have given the Coopers confidence in their new venture was the success they enjoyed with the exhibition of their wares at the 1925 North Carolina State Fair. According to the late pottery historian Howard Smith, North State sold almost all of the 5,000 pieces they displayed; however, W.D. Morton, North State Pottery scholar, relates that some archives indicate it may have been only 1,000.

Henry Cooper became very interested in the chemistry of glazes and studied the process as well as collaborated with members at nearby North Carolina State College (University) in Raleigh. Also, students from the college interned at North State. The Coopers were truly a team effort as wife Rebecca directed the turning and the handling of the greenware prior to glazing which was the province of her husband. She was responsible for a number of innovations in shapes and forms, adding to the desirability of their wares.

In 1926 the company was incorporated, and although Jonie Owen left to open his own business in Seagrove, they hired Charlie Craven who represented another of the important families of potters. Certainly any member of the Owen, Craven, Cole, Teague, or Auman families brought not only tradition but also skills and knowledge to any pottery. While Walter was the principal turner, Rebecca probably was the innovator regarding new shapes and forms, and Henry developed the original glazes and their unique combinations for which North State is known. Jonah was also a very creative potter, and his contributions to the desirability of North State wares may have been significant early (1924 – 1926) in the life of the operation.

By 1927 the Coopers were widely advertising the availability of their wares in periodicals and magazines, and several newspaper accounts had illustrated their work. They donated 35 pieces of their pottery to the North Carolina State Museum of Natural History in Raleigh. National exposure resulted from their garnering a silver medal at the 1926 Sesqui-Centennial Exposition in Philadelphia. Henry Cooper and Jonie Owen built a log cabin on-site there to display and sell their wares. They remained in Philadelphia from May 1 to December 1.

Braxton Craven, Charlie's brother, began working at North State assisting with the glazing and the burning process. Garland Williams was also employed to assist in the kiln preparation and burning process. Both advertising and sales by that time had transcended regional boundaries. North State wares in cartons and barrels were shipped all over the United States. Dorothy Cooper Foster, a daughter, had a pottery sales room 12 miles north of Washington, D.C. (Morton). Many tourist shops in North Carolina carried North State wares, and Rebecca Cooper had a shop near the pottery in addition to the on-site sales room. They printed catalogs in the 1930s and 1940s.

One of the great virtues of North State wares for the collector is the variety and strength of the glazes, a testament to the interest and creativity of Henry Cooper. Robert Lock notes that North State was the most successful pottery in the glazing process of double and sometimes triple "dipping". Some of these combinations rival the glazing of any American pottery on a purely visual basis.

The swirl ware by North State is distinctive in that it was made using different clays, creating a somewhat indistinct pattern, and embellishing a piece with a glaze chosen to enhance the appearance. By experimenting with the firing process, North State could offer a line of "aged" ware that came with crackle (crackleur or crazing), a term often used to describe the appearance of oil pigment in paintings with minute lines across the glaze in a spider web pattern. North State, like the neighboring pottery operation of Jugtown in the 1920s and 1930s, was attempting to use forms and glazes reminiscent of the Chinese works displayed in museums, and they were the favorites of important and sophisticated collectors of other American pottery genre.

In the 1930s the Depression affected the economy broadly, and even the most successful potteries in Seagrove area had a very difficult time surviving. Due to financial needs, the land on which North State was located was sold, and the facility was relocated a short distance away in a low-lying area. This proved to be a poor choice of venue because in the mid-1940s this area flooded, making it necessary to relocate the pottery again.

They settled west of Sanford on Highway 42 in the Pocket Creek area. In 1954 Rebecca Cooper died. Henry and Walter Owen continued to run the pottery until Henry's death in 1959. The pottery was given to Walter Owen who, according to the Coopers' wishes, changed the name to Pine State. After that time output was sporadic, and the examples not as collectible except as documentary pieces.

Dating signed pieces of North State is a relatively simple procedure — if the piece is stamped. Some are not, which are the earlier and quite interesting pieces, especially those probably made by Jonie Owen. The first stamp (1924 – 1926) which is rare and thus inherently valuable, has North State encircling the words "hand made." The letters in "hand made" are all written in capitals or are of the same height with the words slanted, passing upward from left to right. Both stamps #2 and #3 are more common, embracing longer time periods (1926 – 1938, 1939 – 1959) and, on a relative basis, are less valuable. With the second stamp, the words "hand made" are enclosed by North State, but only the first letter of each word is capitalized. The third stamp "hand made" encompasses the description "North State."

Since Walter Owen was the primary turner for the duration of the pottery, "Pine State" might well be considered the fourth stamp (1960 – 1965). At the end of the life of the pottery, Walter signed his wares "W.N. Owen." The output was sporadic and varied greatly in quality. According to brother Melvin (M.L Owens), Walter "just got tired and his health wasn't that good." While almost all North State ware is collectible, the earlier examples, especially the rare salt glaze and those with hues from reduction firing in the wood kiln as well as the multiglaze or dipped pieces with striking color contrast, are the most valuable. Low, wide-style bowls were a trademark of Walter Owen and North State. Large ovoid vases with a footed base are also characteristic and highly desirable as are a number of their unique and unusual forms.

Although Jacques Busbee took the formula to produce Chinese blue with him to his grave, every pottery seems to have attempted to produce this same glaze appearance, and North State was probably the most successful with their version. Their "flambe" or reds and blues from the smoking (reduction firing) process most closely resemble the effects achieved by Busbee. In the combinations of glazing colors and textures, the decorative pieces from North State equal any from a contemporary North Carolina pottery. The variety of their wares is incredible. Certain very knowledgeable collectors specialize in North State wares.

Any discussion of North Carolina pottery should include the legacy of the families of potters, and that is certainly appropriate as some have been making wares for seven or eight generations, almost two centuries. However, "outsiders" and non-potters made significant contributions as well; certainly Jacques and Juliana Busbee at Jugtown and to a lesser extent Victor Obler at Royal Crown did. Some like Jude Palmer, Rebecca Cooper's brother, and Obler were entrepreneurs but were not A.R., C.C., and J.B. Cole astute businessmen as well? In fact, many artistic and cultural innovations and advances have occurred under the stimulation of free enterprise.

North State Pottery was indeed a business, but one that had to appeal to the tastes and aesthetic values of the public. For a period of time they did this, and now their wares are very collectible.

I am indebted to the scholarship of W.D. Morton on North State Pottery. He was gracious in reviewing personal research with me and evaluating the examples chosen for this text. We look forward to the publication of his text on the Cooper family and North State Pottery.

Reference: W.D. Morton

North State first stamp, "hand made" is slightly slanted to the right and all letters are capitalized.

Vase, well turned and double or possibly triple glazed, very rare example. $525.00 – 750.00. Farmer/James collection.

Vase, 8½". Intricate and sophisticated turning with stepped rings on shoulder and raised ring at mid-body. Clear glaze with manganese decoration. North State Pottery (first stamp). Danielson collection.

North State pitcher, 10¼", second stamp. The rich brown double dipped glaze and the excellent form of this early (circa 1926 – 28) North State piece are very desirable. $125.00 – 170.00. Ray Wilkinson collection.

North State first stamp.

Shouldered vase, 6½", note gradations of color from golden to brown due to temperature variations in the kiln. North State Pottery, rare first stamp. George Viall collection.

Ring jug or "water holder," 7½", first stamp, North State, early salt glaze ware for this pottery. Courtesy Phillip Fulton.

Wide, ovoid vase with shoulder at mid-body. Glossy multicolor lead glaze. North State. This glaze pattern has been seen with J.B. Cole wares in the 1920s and 1930s. *Bailey collection.*

Swirl arms with exotic multiglazing. Attributed to Hilton Pottery, but demonstrating the influence if not the hand of Jonah Owen.

Two-handled vases, Jonah Owen. Hired by Rebecca Palmer at North State Pottery in 1924. Brother Walter Owen joined in 1925. *Bailey collection.*

Three examples of North State Pottery, circa 1930s. Chinese blue type glaze. *David Blackburn collection.*

Two vases with Chinese blue glaze, North State Pottery (third stamp). Turned by W.N. Owen. David Blackburn collection.

Elixir pitcher, 14", with double glaze or single attempt at North State version of Chinese blue (second stamp). David Blackburn collection.

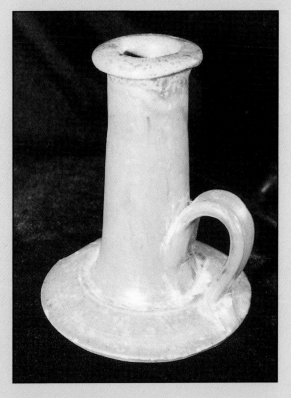

Vase, three-handled, Chinese blue, unusual shape and successful reduction firing. North State (second stamp). $800.00 – 1,100.00. Bailey collection.

Candlestick, 6½", with double glaze, early North State (first stamp). Edwards collection.

Salt glazed vase at left, undersurface, showing North State pottery (second stamp). The early salt glazed wares from North State are very collectible. Farmer/James collection.

Vase, salt glazed, with fluted edge, 8¾", cobalt decoration. North State (second stamp). Salt glazed examples by this pottery are very desirable. $350.00 – 400.00. Farmer/James collection.

Teapot, 8¾", salt glaze with cobalt decoration. North State (second stamp). David Blackburn collection.

Pitcher, 7⅔", Chinese blue glaze by North State (second stamp). David Blackburn collection.

Elixir pitcher, 13½", Chinese blue glaze with almost total reduction to oxblood red color. North State. David Blackburn collection.

Vase, two-handled, 12½", triple glaze or double glaze with different reactions to kiln temperature. Second stamp. David Blackburn collection.

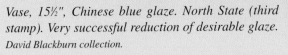

North State Pottery, rare first stamp. David Blackburn collection

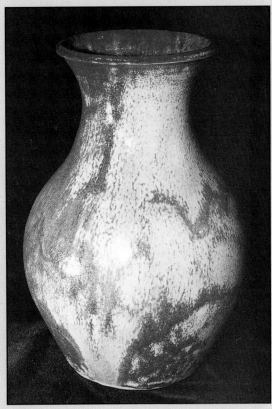

Vase, 15½", Chinese blue glaze. North State (third stamp). Very successful reduction of desirable glaze. David Blackburn collection.

229

Two-handled vase, 8½", swirl, North State (second stamp). David Blackburn collection.

Ovoid vase, 4¾", and large (beer) mug, double glaze with Chinese blue overglaze, second stamp, North State. W.D. Morton collection.

Vase with unusual low set handles, green double glaze, 10¾". North State Pottery (third stamp). W.D. Morton collection.

Apothecary (medicine) jar, 4⅝", split handles, uranium yellow. North State (second stamp). W.D. Morton collection.

Two one-handled small jugs, 4¾", left, cobalt blue. Right, Chinese blue over clear glaze. North State (second stamp). W.D. Morton collection.

Low wide bowl, 6½". Double glazed with runs, reduction glaze above with large oxblood coloration, North State Pottery.

Bulbous vase, 7¾", stoneware, white glaze drips over gunmetal glaze. Second stamp, (stamped twice). Important example. W.D. Morton collection.

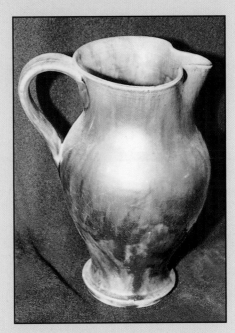

Two-handled shouldered vase, 10½", mottled yellow/red glaze, North State Pottery (second stamp). Note the excellent turning with the handles conforming to the slope of the shoulder. Bailey collection.

Pitcher, 8", double glazed, attributed to Jonie Owen at North State. May represent combination of green and turquoise blue.

First stamp, North State, 1924 – 1925. The first stamp is rare especially when applied to aesthetically collectible wares.

Double glazed, two-handled vase, 8¾". The glaze allows moderately certain attribution to North State Pottery. $225.00 – 350.00. *Farmer/James gift to Chapel Hill Museum.*

Bowl, three handles, 5¾", elegant double glaze. Unmarked, attributed to North State, probably by one of the early potters before W.N. Owen became the master potter there. $125.00 – 145.00. *Ray Wilkinson collection.*

Fan, 8½", Chinese blue glaze, North State Pottery (third stamp). Edwards collection.

Vase, three Grecian handles, 7", cobalt decoration, North State Pottery (third stamp). Edwards collection.

Vase, 9", with double glaze, North State Pottery, second stamp. George Viall collection.

Large, 13", stoneware pitcher with salt glaze and second decoration of North State version of Chinese blue, second stamp. George Viall collection.

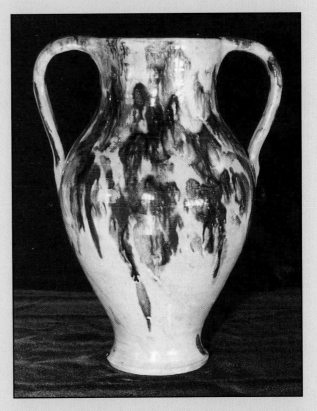

Cylindrical tall jug, 11½", North State Pottery (second stamp). Small base chip. $250.00 – 450.00. St. James Place Museum.

Vase, 10¾", earthenware, variegated glaze. North State second stamp. Attributed to Jonah Owen. Bailey collection.

Basket, 7⅝", multiglazed, unusual form. Attributed to Jonah ("Jonie") Owen (1896 – 1966). Started at his father's shop in 1921. When father died in 1923, he went with Clarence Cole at Log Cabin, then North State (1924), and later had his own pottery at Sodom. Bailey collection.

Swirlware vase, 13¼", unsigned. Note vertical brown run downward, suggesting that much of the color differential might be due to the glaze. Attributed to North State Pottery. Three and possibly four contrasting colors due to clay and glaze mixture. $275.00 – 325.00. Farmer/James collection.

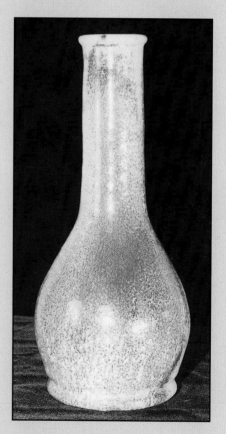

Candle lamp, 7¾", double glazed, North State (second stamp). Henry Cooper developed glazes with scientists at NCSU. Many potters turned at North State, including Jonah Owen, Thurston Cole, Charles Craven, and Jack Kiser. $145.00 – 175.00. Farmer/James collection.

Long neck (bottle) vase, 12¼", reduction glaze. North State (second stamp). Bailey collection.

Rebecca pitcher, 10", with variegated glaze, attributed to Walter Owen. Fine example of North State's glazing abilities. Chapel Hill Museum collection.

Rebecca pitcher, 6¾", double glazed, upper glaze much thicker than underglaze. Unsigned, attributed to North State Pottery (circa 1930s – 1940s). Provenance Baynes collection. $95.00 – 125.00. St. James Place Museum collection.

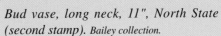

Low vase with shoulder rim, 6½", glaze with decorative overlay, less definite glaze placement than C.B. Masten. North State, second stamp, attributed to Jonah Owen. Bailey collection.

Bud vase, long neck, 11", North State (second stamp). Bailey collection.

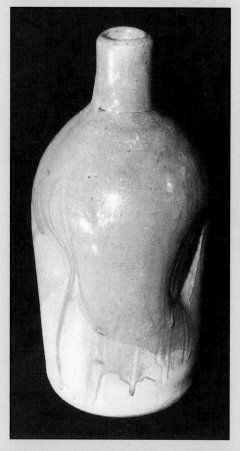

Wide vase with slip decoration, W.N. Owen signature. Many of the examples were dull and uninteresting, but this represents an outstanding ware of this era. Collection of the North Carolina State University Gallery of Art and Design.

Pinch bottle, 7¾", by Walter Owen operating as Pine State (stamped). David Blackburn collection.

North State Pottery (1924 – 1959). Double dipped wares.

"Jugtown" to some is a pottery state of mind and not a location, while for others it is a generic art form and the characterization of an entire industry. When most refer to Jugtown, they mean the decorative pottery that comes from the central Piedmont in the land of the long-leaf pine. Nestled between many natural attractions for the collector and lover of folklore is one of America's great concentrations of traditional and folk potters who today make fancy ware.

In the south-central North Carolina Piedmont is the Seagrove area where most of the potteries are found. Families like the Owen(s), Cravens, Teagues, and Lucks (they also market beans) have been producing utilitarian objects and art forms from clay for over 200 years. The Coles can trace their pottery lineage back to Staffordshire, England, and the matriarch Nell Cole Graves who until a few years ago made pots but "only" six days a week. There are over 100 recognized potteries in the counties of Randolph, Chatham, Moore, and Lee in south-central North Carolina. The little villages have quaint names like Whynot, Hemp (ne: Robbins), Seagrove, Merry Hill, and as expected, Jugtown.

The Moravians from Pennsylvania in the eighteenth century established the settlement of Bethabara near present-day Winston-Salem and brought with them centuries of the master/apprentice pottery tradition. They initially made earthenware fired at 1200 – 1800°F which was subsequently replaced by stoneware (fired at 1900 – 2400°F). They glazed their products with either traditional salt or sometimes alkaline glaze. Although some decorative ware was made around the turn of the century, the utilitarian ware was the largest type of production in the nineteenth and the first decades of the twentieth century. Thus, examples of this period would most appropriately be crocks, cream risers, churns, plates, jugs, and storage vessels. After the turn of the century due to the introduction of refrigeration, improvement in transportation of perishable goods, the temperance movement, and later Prohibition and the Great Depression, the demand for utilitarian wares declined and many potteries failed.

Certain resourceful inhabitants in this area changed their product to open up another market — decorative pottery, referred to first as transitional pottery, art pottery, or simply fancy ware. Besides the fortunate location of the clay nearby, the facts that the technology has many common elements and potting skills often translate, the folks in the Jugtown/Seagrove area enjoyed other significant advantages. Among these were the presence of their affluent neighbors in Pinehurst and Southern Pines, the heavily traveled north-south artery, U.S. Highway 1, that ran "right through the middle," and the railroad at Hemp (now Robbins) to ship "what they couldn't cart back up North were all factors."

Certain of the new participants in this art pottery industry realized that the clientele wanted things that, were different, reflecting art forms with which they had little experience. They began to experiment with shapes and forms not unlike those of classic decorative objects of Europe and the Orient. Jacques Busbee, founder of Jugtown (circa 1917 – 1921) even had his future master potter Ben Owen, Sr. (of the famous Owen family that had been making traditional forms for seven generations) travel with him to museums in the U.S. Northeast to see these objects, and they fashioned wares that reflected this exposure. This observing and reproduction continue today with grandson Ben Owen III.

Glazes became as much of a passion as did the forms and shapes. Colors were bold, varied, and suitable to decorate a room or even an entire home. These glazes were given such names at Jugtown as frogskin, tobacco spit, and Chinese blue.

Potteries in the Seagrove area became large cottage businesses with some division of labor and employed several turners and often a separate burner responsible for the kiln. Many of these businesses were composed of merchants and investors hiring these potters. Sometimes a potter would learn the trade from a neighbor, become a journeyman, and then establish his own business.

Jacon B. Cole was an itinerant potter for 25 years until he started a business so large that it was affectionately known as "the warehouse." North State Pottery (1924 – 1960) was begun by Rebecca Palmer Cooper as an extension of her hobby when she hired Jonah Owen and later Walter Owen to turn the goods. Two years later they incorporated when she was joined by her husband Henry, an R.J. Reynolds employee. North State, as did Royal Crown, A.R. Cole, and others, packed their goods in barrels and shipped them all over the U.S.

Today collectors are avidly seeking examples of this transitional pottery of the 1920 – 1930 era while others wish to acquire those shapes, forms, and glazes that are being produced in this area today. Some of the potteries such as Jugtown, Owens Pottery, A.R. Cole, and others are a continuation of family businesses and some who went out of business, where others represent new potters with innovative techniques that have been applied in the last decade. All of these efforts have their own intrinsic beauty and merit. Additionally, both the uninitiated and the aficionado can observe the people and the process of tradition.

The art pottery movement in North Carolina was often a marriage of the traditional pottery dynasties and the new ideas and energy brought to the area by outsiders. Jugtown, which was to become Seagrove's best known pottery, was initially a result of the former but its continued prominence has been the presence of one of the most renowned pottery families, the Owens.

Jacques and Juliana Busbee must have represented a truly different culture with an unusual agenda for most of the natives of the Seagrove area in the early 1920s. Jacques had trained at the Art Students League in New York where William Merritt Chase and Robert Henri taught. He had witnessed the wane of Impressionism and the ascendancy of Realism as well as the celebration of the Arts and Crafts movement.

Busbee was convinced by his wife Juliana that the fledgling art pottery movement in the south-central Piedmont area of their native North Carolina had sufficient promise and attraction to warrant their moving there and become active participants.

Jacques Busbee's interests were in the traditional Chinese and Korean forms and in new glazes that reflected the ancient Oriental cultures. In the early years of Jugtown (1917 – 1926), Juliana lived principally in New York and operated a "tea room" there. Jacques enlisted several well-known

Seagrove potters to make wares for him. Ben Owen, son of Rufus Owen, in 1923 at age 18 came to work at Jugtown. Owen became the master potter of Jugtown and remained there until 1959.

A new pottery shop was built in 1921, and Juliana moved to the Westmoore community in 1926. In the ensuing decades, Jugtown forms and glazes came to be nationally and internationally known.

After Jacques' death in 1946, Juliana operated the pottery until 1959. That year Ben Owen left to open his own shop, Plank Road Pottery. In 1960 John Mare, owner and local businessman, hired Vernon and Bobby Owens (sons of M.L.) at Jugtown. Mare died in 1962, and in 1968 Jugtown was acquired and managed by Country Roads, a nonprofit organization. Jugtown was administered by Nancy Sweezy, a potter who has written a well-known text on Southern pottery.

Vernon Owens acquired ownership in 1983. He, wife Pamela, Charlie Moore, and Boyce Yow continue to be responsible stewards of the Jugtown legacy of the Busbees and Ben Owen.

We are indebted to Steve Compton, collector and founder of the North Carolina Pottery Guild, for his assistance with this chapter.

References: Billy Ray Hussey, Vernon and Pam Owens

Teapot, 6½", Jugtown, circa 1920s. Note mottled appearance of clay seen through translucent glaze. Bill Ivey collection.

Jugtown, typical forms glazed in white, turned by Vernon Owens. Courtesy of Mick Bailey.

Lily vase, 13¾", thick white glaze with unusual decoration at four equal intervals around the body. According to Vernon and Pam Owens, possibly unique. Collection of North Carolina State University Gallery of Art and Design.

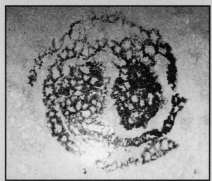

Detail of applied decoration on lily vase, referred to by Busbee as tenth century Chinese translation. Highly fired earthenware, circa 1930, attributed to Ben Owen. Curved, flat handles resemble petal of lily flower.

Bowl with ruffled rim. Oriental white glaze, four brushed decorations on rim, evenly spaced. Note gradation of glaze thickness on lower part of body. Slight color change is due to glaze thinning and clay becoming visible. Collection of North Carolina State University Gallery of Art and Design.

Interior of the museum at Jugtown Pottery, a private museum open to the public. Funded by gifts and the Owens family. Some examples are on loan. Houses an excellent Busbee memorabilia collection.

Vase, 10⅞", black ankle glaze, Jug, 11". One of glazes developed at Jugtown during the John Mare era, uses Albany slip with white slip glaze layered (Hussey). Difficult to control. David Blackburn collection.

Two-handled vase, 13¼", double glaze, incised line decoration. Attributed to Charles Teague at Jugtown. Very rare. Edwards collection.

Large, low angular bowl, exterior glaze, mirror black. This is an unusual glaze combination. Collection of North Carolina State University Gallery of Art and Design.

Early (1925 – 1926) Jugtown wares. Bill Ivey collection.

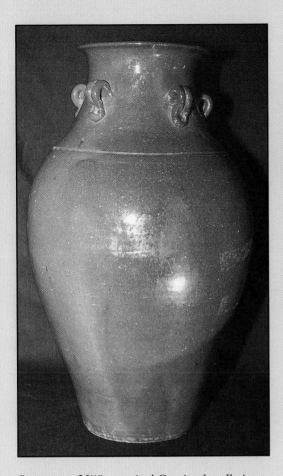

Sung vase, 23½", a typical Grecian handle interpretation in rich brown glaze. The size and form of the Jugtown vase are unusual if not unique. Collection of North Carolina State University Gallery of Art and Design.

Jugtown, 1930s – 1940s. White glazed earthenware. Bowl has four edges of Chinese blue applied to flat rim. Bailey collection.

Salt glazed Jugtown wares.

Shouldered bowl, 8", with Oriental white glaze by Jugtown. George Viall collection.

Pedestal angular bowl, frogskin glaze, Jugtown (original stamp). Collection of North Carolina State University Gallery of Art and Design.

Ovoid vase, frogskin glaze, Jugtown (original stamp). Frogskin glaze provided basically an olive drab appearance but browns and yellows may be interspersed. Collection of North Carolina State University Gallery of Art and Design.

Three-handled vase, 11½", Oriental hanging form. Tobacco spit glaze. $225.00 – 325.00. Farmer/James collection.

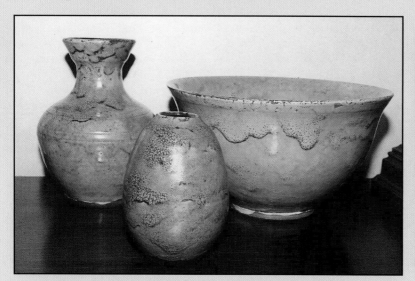

Jugtown, three examples of Chinese blue. George Viall collection.

Han Dynasty vase, 14¼", Chinese blue. Although it is believed Jacques Busbee favored only slight delineation of aqua with the reduction oxblood color, the collecting public prefers this appearance. One sold in 2001 at auction for $8,500.00.

Two Han Dynasty vases from Jugtown Pottery. Note the difference in reduction of the Chinese blue glaze. It is said Jacques Busbee favored only a small linear oxblood pattern to delineate the aqua color.

Vase, 9¼", Chinese blue over salt glaze application. Note white areas in this unusual Jugtown piece. Mick Bailey collection.

Bowl, 7" x 11¼", Chinese blue glaze, Jugtown, 1930s. David Blackburn collection.

Ovoid vase, wide mouth, Jugtown Pottery, circa 1920s. Chinese blue glaze. This very desirable glaze was developed by Jacques Busbee and has not been successfully reproduced since his death in 1946.

Note the large area of reduction phenomenon. This "blood red" color is very desirable as it contrasts well with the aqua in the non-reduction part of the glaze. Jacques Busbee wanted the glaze to extend to the base but wife Juliana did not. $425.00 – 650.00. Farmer/James collection.

Persian vase, four handles, Chinese blue glaze, large areas of reduction. Outstanding example of desirable glaze and form. Present attempts to reproduce the Busbee appearance are hampered by the absence of lead and occasional use of wood-fired kilns. Collection of the North Carolina State University Gallery of Art and Design.

Bowl with lid, Jugtown Pottery (1922 –), typical Jugtown orange, circa 1920s. $125.00 – 145.00.

Bowl, 14" x 4¾", Chinese blue glaze, note interior with excellent reduction. Jugtown, circa 1930s. Edwards collection.

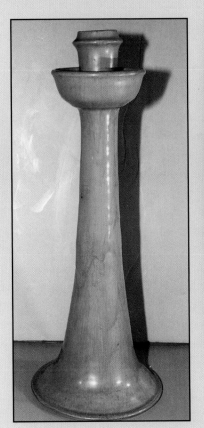

Jugtown jar, stoneware with Chinese blue glaze; 12" h, 10" d. North Carolina State University Gallery of Art and Design.

Measuring container, 12¼", salt glaze, Jugtown, circa 1950. This is a rare if not unique example.

Candlestick, 18", Jugtown (stamped), unusual glaze for Jugtown, rare. Edwards collection.

Jugtown stamp.

Catfish, 11", by Boyce Yow at Jugtown Pottery. Many figures, whimsies, and other collectibles have been made by North Carolina potters. Most are interesting to the general public but less so to the serious collector.

Jugtown; Korean bowl, stoneware with Chinese blue glaze; 3½" h. North Carolina State University Gallery of Art and Design.

Jugtown; egg vase, stoneware with Chinese blue glaze; 7¾" h, 5" d. North Carolina State University Gallery of Art and Design.

245

~ Smithfield Pottery ~

Smithfield Pottery, located in Johnston County, was in existence from 1927 – 1940. Herman Cole operated the pottery and employed a number of well-known potters, including Charlie Craven, Charles G. Teague, Guy Daugherty, and Jack Kiser.

One of their kilns was a very large bottle-shaped facility. This kiln was designed to achieve a more uniform heat distribution over the interior. Herman Cole was never satisfied with the performance of this unusual configuration and believed it to be a grave financial mistake.

This pottery was built adjacent to Highway 301 because "there are a lot of travelers north and south," Cole said. Also, there was a plentiful supply of clay in the vicinity. For a time, business was good, and there were reports that Mrs. Cole experienced days with $100 in sales despite the Great Depression.

There is no recorded stamp, logo, or label for Smithfield Pottery. No wares were signed in script, and there were many accomplished potters who worked there. Thus, shape, form, and glaze must be assessed to even reach a reasonable attribution. Certain Smithfield wares have a light gray to charcoal discoloration of the undersurface. This has been thought by some to be compelling evidence of the origin. Provenance, if available, provides the best documentation of a Smithfield made piece. Those that have been identified are usually quite collectible.

Vase, 12¼", with swirl handles, flambé, copper glaze over mirror black, Smithfield Pottery. $145.00 – 175.00. St. James Place Museum.

Vase with rudimentary rope handles, 18¾", thick white glaze over mirror black. Smithfield Pottery, attributed to Farrell Craven. $350.00 – 475.00. Farmer/James collection.

Two vases turned by Farrell Craven. The dark vase with the variegated glaze over mirror black was turned at Smithfield. The larger with ringed handles and sine wave decoration may have been turned there as well, but Craven worked at many different locations.

Large 13" low serving bowl with slightly folded edges. Mottled interior, thick edges, attributed to Wren Cole. The dark gray dusky bottom is thought to be due to the coal-fired kiln used by Smithfield Pottery. $225.00 – 235.00. Farmer/James collection.

Bottom of serving bowl above with typical appearance from Smithfield Pottery. Not all wares will have this appearance of the bottom since Smithfield had more than one kiln for this large operation on U.S. 301 Highway.

Pitcher, Smithfield Pottery, 10½", mirror black, undersurface gray to black. The potters were Herman Cole, Charles Craven, Jack Kiser, and Farrell Craven. Even with small chips, this is a collectible piece. $145.00 – 175.00. Farmer/James gift, Chapel Hill Museum.

Two-handled vase, 11½", with glaze variation of spatter-ware, circa 1940 – 1950, Seagrove area, attributed to Smithfield.

Blue flambé basket, 9¼", attributed to Herman Cole, Smithfield Pottery (1927 – 1942). Wilkinson collection.

Vase, 7¾", double glazed with striking combination of pink (flesh colored) glaze over somewhat translucent black, undersurface is dark gray. Maker unknown. Attributed to Smithfield Pottery or possibly North State. Unusual example. Leland Little Auction.

Buzzard vase, 16¼" with flambé glaze by Lester Farrell Craven at Smithfield Pottery. Farrell was an excellent potter and worked as a journeyman for B.D. Teague, Royal Crown, Smithfield, and Ben Owen. $900.00 – 1,100.00. Bailey collection.

Double ring handled vase. Subtle glaze of buff and light green. Sine wave decoration framed by two horizontal lines. Turned by Farrell Craven but a similar form was produced by others.

Basket, 8½" (handle), chrome red, unusual shape, attributed to Smithfield Pottery. Danielson collection.

Porch vase, 23", chrome red glaze, Smithfield Pottery.
George Viall collection.

⤬ Log Cabin Pottery ⤬

Log Cabin Pottery was a short lived (sources disagree; 1927 – 1932 or 1924 – 1927) small tourist pottery located in the Guilford College area along Market Street in what was then Greensboro, North Carolina This business was owned by Mrs. G. N. Hunter and her husband known as "Tweet."

In about 1923, Clarence Cole asked Jonah "Jonie" Owen to work with Cecil Auman for the Hunters. This shop was to make decorative wares and would be called Log Cabin Pottery. The distinctive logo was drawn by hand by Myrtice Owen, a cabin sketched onto the greenware and covered with the glaze.

The arrangement for production was that the pottery was turned and often glazed on the Hunter site but was fired in several Seagrove potteries. Because of this complex pattern for producing the art pottery, quality control was understandably difficult. This is reflected in a somewhat limited number of available collectible examples of Log Cabin pottery. However, Jonah Owen was one of North Carolina's most creative potters, and truly outstanding examples of his work can be found from this underappreciated pottery.

There is no consensus as to why Log Cabin closed after only a few years of operation. Complexity of their operation and the economic effect of the Great Depression must have been factors. Great examples from Log Cabin Pottery are quite valuable.

Two-handled vase, 8¼", glazed with wash and overall vertical runs applied. Turned by Jonah Owen at Log Cabin Pottery (1926 – 1933). Incised cabin mark. George Viall collection.

Vase, 11", gray-blue glaze with applied vertical decoration, signed Log Cabin Pottery, attributed to Jonah Owen. George Viall collection.

Vase, three handles (Grecian), 6¾", Log Cabin Pottery. Bailey collection.

Vase, 12¾", Log Cabin Pottery, attributed to Jonah Owen. This was an operation with several locations and major wares are somewhat rare. Outstanding examples are very collectible and valuable. $425.00 – 650.00. Farmer/James collection.

Vase, 8¼", dull gray/green glaze, possibly underfired at matte temperature. Log Cabin Pottery, probably turned at Market Street location, Greensboro, and fired elsewhere. St. James Place Museum collection.

Log Cabin drawing which was the usual signature.

251

Round vase with wide orifice, 7¾", double glazed with thick runs of secondary glaze. Log Cabin Pottery. Bailey collection.

Vase, 8½", Log Cabin, blue glaze painted over white. Rare and valuable example. Bill Ivey collection.

Vase with unusual glaze by Jonah Franklin Owen (1896 – 1966). Jonah Owen had a long and varied career. He made many of the interesting pieces we are just beginning to identify because much of his work was turned at several locations. When Jonah returned from the Army in the 1920s, he worked for his father until J.H. died in 1923. Clarence Cole asked him to join the Hunters near Guilford College in Greensboro, the pottery to be operated as Log Cabin Pottery. After it closed, Jonah worked at North State. He set up his own pottery at "Sodom" which he closed in 1940. (B.R. Hussey)

Vase, 8", variegated, thick glaze. Log Cabin Pottery. With the complexity of this operation, one never knew if an outstanding result was fortuitous or purposeful. Edwards collection.

Fluted vase, 12½", with reduction glaze, unsigned, maker unknown. Attributed to Jonah Owen early, at North State or Log Cabin. David Blackburn collection.

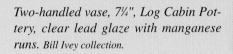

Two-handled vase, 7¼", Log Cabin Pottery, clear lead glaze with manganese runs. Bill Ivey collection.

With any collectible, judgment regarding condition of the single example is essential to the valuation process. Ascribing the importance of this parameter and factoring it into the determination of value for any particular example is, indeed, important and difficult.

The process of fashioning both utilitarian and decorative wares is complex. Mishaps can occur at each step and be expressed by variations from the expected visual appearance. We have devoted chapters to each part of this arduous journey from the clay pit to the finished bowl, vase or urn, and the consequence of each step should be considered in the valuation process.

There are certain canons in the judgment of and ascribing value to condition with any collectible. Some are reasonable and understandable, and others follow a convention, the logic of which has been lost with time. An example might be in the collection of waterfowl decoys. "Original paint" is avidly sought after while it was common practice to paint decoys at intervals to make them more useable for the intended purpose for which they were fashioned. Then why should "repaints" be devalued if they represent the standard practice of the endeavor?

Fine crackleur is acceptable for oil paintings but significant inpainting is not, for it alters the original object in an unacceptable manner. One may refurbish an antique gilded frame, but to truly restore it using different materials is quite a different manner. However, what is "significant" in painting and "restoration" in repair is a matter of judgment and should express the collective opinion of the acquirer whether to add to one's holdings or offer for resale.

To be encyclopedic in these considerations regarding North Carolina pottery is beyond the scope of this text, but a summary description of certain common problems might prove useful.

Since the process of fashioning these objects begins with the clay, defects in the wares can result from improper preparation of this fundamental material. Debris not removed in preparation can be expressed as surface irregularities. Cleaning the clay is important with utilitarian wares but especially so with art pottery. Not regulating the moisture in the clay can result in bubbles and blisters on the surface of the object and separation of the glaze. These defects may devalue the object greatly, whether it is a 15-gallon Daniel Seagle vessel or a Ben Owen vase. Whether or not it is collectible depends upon the rarity and importance of the specific example. Would you acquire a reworked Velasquez or a restored Elmer Crowell sleeping Canada goose if the price was right; we suspect so.

Separation of the glaze from the clay body is a bit like flaking in oil paintings or paint separation on antique water fowl decoys. If the separation is minimal and does not particularly affect the appearance of the object, the piece may still be collectible.

Mishaps and mistakes while the ware is in the kiln are myriad. Placement of the greenware in relative positions and appropriate distribution according to the range of kiln temperature is an art form itself. With alkaline glazes, position can result in the glistening translucent surface or, if improperly fired, a dull and lifeless one. With so-called reduction glazes such as the popular chrome red, an overfired surface can result in a dark and dull brown, and if underfired, a vapid light yellow-orange. The collector should be seeking an appearance of a reddish-orange with streaks of contrasting brown with the chrome red. However, gradations of this pattern are so commonly seen that there remain a spectrum of acceptable visual appearances with chrome red glaze.

Form, age, and importance of the potter and pottery are always factors to consider in the valuation process. Transition pieces from the late teens and early twenties reflect the change and experimentation that occurred. Most collectors accept a wider latitude in quality in these wares than ones produced later.

The glaze known as Chinese blue, developed by the founder of Jugtown Pottery, Jacques Busbee, and used by Ben Owen, master potter, may well be the best known and most avidly collected of the North Carolina glazes. The light green to turquoise primary color should be complimented by the reduction red variation from lead and iron according to Busbee's formula which he literally "took to his grave" in the 1940s. A significant amount of the oxblood color contrasted upon the more homogenous aqua or turquoise background will add significantly to the value of the piece and, if it is a Han Dynasty-inspired form or a Persian vase rather than a simple wide ovoid bowl, will enhance the value even more. Pieces that are almost solidly blue-green in appearance tend to be the least valuable. Controlling this color distribution process, as with chrome red, depended upon observation from previous kilns and experience by the potter.

Another rather common mishap that occurs is a kiln crack or separation. These fissures will have a cleft-like appearance, and there may be glaze penetrating the edges where the clay is separated. Conventional wisdom suggests that these defects are not as determinative of value as cracks and fractures that occur from usage and trauma. Logic would say that kiln defects are a part of the natural process of formation of the ware.

Admittedly this particular canon is not exactly logical, but nothing in the valuation of pottery is codified. These are truly value judgments, but they do have a tradition and have evolved over time. Do not feel absolutely compelled to adhere rigidly to them, but they should be guidelines in your acquisition posture.

Chips, fractures, and cracks are common with clay vessels, especially with utilitarian ware. The rims of bowls and vases are particularly vulnerable. Rim chips are to be expected on any cup or small flower vase that has been in use for 50 or 60 years. Yet the presence of these signs of the intended use of the object devalue it; how much is the issue. Certain purist collectors may feel that if the object is not pristine, it is unacceptable to them. They will miss the opportunity to acquire the majority of these pieces. Others reason that a stricter condition standard should be applied is if the object is to be displayed in the intimate setting of one's home rather than on a shelf in a museum at some distance from the observer. As a collector, you should seek your own comfort level. True breaks, especially in handles, will occur in pairs and may be glued but will be apparent if the glaze loss at the fracture lines is not repaired. How visually apparent the defect is makes a great deal of difference in the acceptability of the object.

A number of years ago when even the more unusual examples of North Carolina pottery were readily available, collectors were willing to postpone acquiring an example, reasoning there would be a more appropiate future opportunity. This has changed with the realization that there are a finite number of examples of certain forms and glazes, and the production of certain potters are not as available as previously believed.

Since large vases and storage crocks had a limited market and were difficult to turn, they were never available in abundance. Because of their size, they were particularly susceptible to blunt trauma as most have been compromised. While these could be purchased only a few years ago for almost nothing, today they are acquired by collectors as examples. Recently at a regional auction, a Daniel Seagle 10-gallon, four-handled storage vessel with several fractures and at least two large holes sold for over $3,000, and an A.R. Cole chrome red vase with damage for over $400.

Chips vary in importance depending upon their location and how visible they are. Rim chips of the upper opening of a vessel are given greater weight than a chip at the base. They are more determinative of the visual appearance, being in a more direct line of the observer's vision than a defect almost at the undersurface.

Hairline fractures at times are difficult to detect visually. If you suspect a hairline, look at the opposite surface of the vessel. Another ploy is to tap the surface with your finger. If there is a crack, there will be a dull sound emitted rather than the normal resonance of an intact flat surface of clay. Again what you as a collector/acquirer do with this information is dependent upon your intent. Hairlines do not tend to significantly degrade the appearance of an example, but they do render it less than structurally sound.

Repairs of pottery run the gamut just as any restoration of collectibles in general. This can be a simple filling in of a small glaze loss or reinsertion of a missing piece. More extensive repairs can involve the fashioning of handles or replacement of a rim using materials that are often not fired and applying a modern glaze that blends with the color. With the recognition of the scarcity of certain examples of North Carolina pottery, a cottage industry of restoration of collectible examples has come into being just as it has for the rare North Carolina antique waterfowl decoy. Some restorers of pottery have become so skilled that their work is difficult to detect without close inspection.

Extensive repair will significantly devalue a work, but it may not render it unacceptable as an example, especially if the defect and repair are not visibly apparent. You probably should accept a repaired labeled J.B. Cole piece or a North State first stamp ware or almost any important form by O.L. Bachelder. Our advice might be to acquire an acceptable restoration at a low price then wait and hope for a more pristine example later.

While there exist conventions and widely held beliefs regarding the implications of condition of North Carolina pottery, a collector can select his own criteria depending upon his financial commitment and the purpose for his collection.

Small jug, 5", broken handle, early North Carolina utilitarian piece. Chapel Hill Museum collection.

Lidded storage vessel (butter jar), 10¾", salt glaze, made by J.D. Craven, last quarter of the nineteenth century. St. James Place Museum.

North State vase, 13½". With rim chips which are visible and would significantly devalue this example.

Large coffee pot, 9½", by A.R. Cole, unusual double glaze. Note broken and repaired handle which greatly devalues this outstanding example. $50.00 – 75.00.

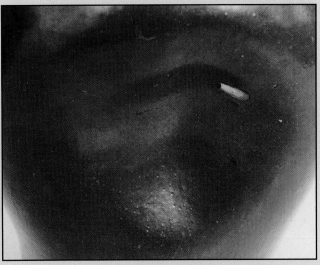

Glaze loss, mid body of pinch bottle below. The defect would only minimally devalue the example. Repair would be simple and not compromise the integrity of the object.

Detail of C.R. Auman vase. Note the very fine crackle/spidering in the glaze. "Spidering" has several explanations, one of which is inhomogeneous contraction of the clay during the firing process. It can be seen as a natural consequence of age.

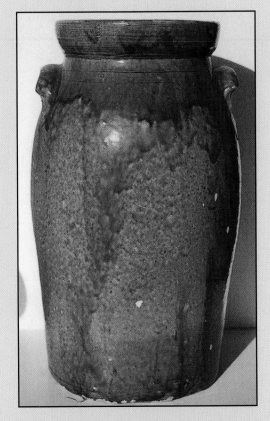

Churn with lug handles, 24", typical utilitarian shape but with art pottery glaze. Glaze defects in a rare transitional piece. $225.00 – 350.00.

Pinch bottle, Brown Pottery, Arden, North Carolina, 7¾", black. Unusual form for Brown Pottery (stamped).

Porch vase, two ring handles, 19½", J.B. Cole Pottery by Waymon Cole. Damage to rim with filler during attempted repair. This example in excellent condition would be valued at $450.00 – 600.00. In present condition, $150.00 or less.

Transition piece. Early two-handled vase with "trophy" form with rim damage. Maker of this very unusual glaze unknown. Attributed to Jonah Owen, son of J.H. Similar to signed J.H. Owen in Southern Folk Potters collection. Chapel Hill Museum collection.

Multiple areas of glaze loss in bowl, circa 1920s. Rare example of early transitional defects, would decrease value 15 – 40%.

Detail of Royal Crown bowl at right, circa 1940, almost invisible hairline fracture from rim at 10 o'clock. This will reduce the value of this elegant, desirable example of the short-lived pottery (1939 – 1942) founded by Victor Obler.

(Right) Wide bowl by Royal Crown, impressed rubber stamp (circa 1939 – 1942). This aqua glaze was popular and suited the sophisticated forms and highly reflective surfaces of Royal Crown wares. Turned by Charlie Craven and glazed by Lesley Stanley, 11".

J.B. Cole vase, ruffled rim with rim chips which would significantly reduce the value.

Brown Pottery stamp, Valdese and Alden. Note finger marks at rim in Albany slip glaze. As wares are immersed in glaze, they are held by the potter and finger marks remain. Treat this as a phenomenon, not a condition problem.

Alkaline glaze, 12¾", storage crock, wide mouth. Note multiple speckled areas in glaze due to fly ash. Also small naked areas with clay visible due to bubbles of air from clay. These do not devalue the example of Catawba Valley pottery significantly.

Transition pottery. Two-handled, 14" large opening ware with incised ring. Thought to be a mix of salt glaze on a secondary run vase which was underfired.

Candle holders, J.B. Cole, circa 1950 – 1960. Note repair to lip of right candle holder. Collector must decide upon the devaluation which would be significant.

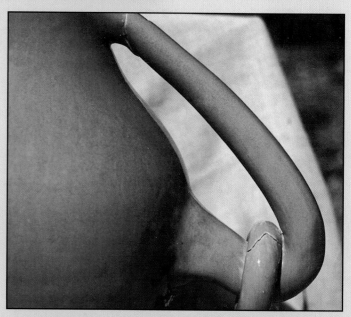

Arm of buzzard vase, Smithfield Pottery. Note kiln crack. This is a rare form and is collectible still.

Broken handle, expertly repaired. This will devalue this handsome example but it remains quite collectible. St. James Place Museum.

Kiln crack in very large porch vase by Way-mon Cole. The implication of kiln cracks isn't as negative as fractures and in-use breaks, according to collecting conventions. A vase this size in a desirable glaze is rare and would command $600.00 – 1,100.00.

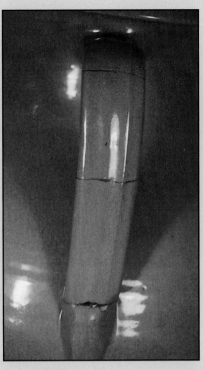

Candlestick, 8", J.B. Cole Pottery, circa 1950s. Candlesticks are a popular form and the taller ones are collectible, even with slight damage. $25.00 – 35.00. Chapel Hill Museum collection.

Joe Owen, 22" porch vase. Note repair of three cracks in the handle. The defects are obvious and would devalue the $250.00 – 350.00 vase to less than $150.00.

Two-handled vase with intricate handles (upper and lower loops). Well-proportioned double groove top handles with extra looping of lower ones. Form seen in both A.R. Cole and J.B. Cole wares. Glaze is more characteristic of J.B. Cole. Repaired handles. Chapel Hill Museum collection.

Pitcher, circa 1920, attributed to Smithfield Pottery. Note loss of glaze to rim and chip at lip of spout. These obvious signs of damage significantly devalue a fairly rare piece.

Undersurface of candlestick above. The stilt marks are present as is evidence of the J.B. Cole belt sander. Note chip at base which even on the undersurface devalues the piece.

Second stamp on vase at left is almost obscured by debris from kiln.

Ovoid vase, 8½", North State Pottery, turned by W.N. Owen. Glaze is thick white/buff with "antiquing" or crackleur. Note hairline fracture running vertically. Second stamp.

Three-handled bowl, chips on rim, otherwise intact. A.R. Cole, 1940s, 4¼". Chips devalue this example, that is collectible but not rare, by 20 – 30%.

Note fly ash from draft in wood-fired kiln and small speckle defects in glaze due to high feldspar content. Rim chips are present which affect the value of this rare transitional example. $75.00 – 100.00. Ray Wilkinson collection.

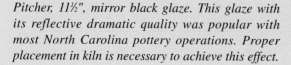

Pitcher, 11½", mirror black glaze. This glaze with its reflective dramatic quality was popular with most North Carolina pottery operations. Proper placement in kiln is necessary to achieve this effect.

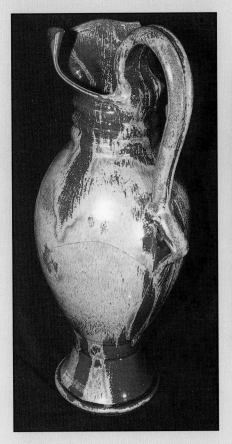

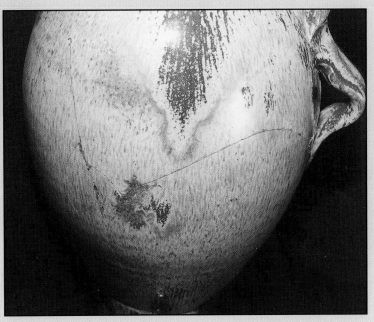

Note converging hairline fractures on Grecian (Roman) pitcher at left. This did extend to inner wall. The body is stable but the hairline is visible. Pristine example, $175.00 – 225.00; this piece, $75.00 – 100.00.

Grecian (Roman) pitcher, 14", with rutile glaze. A.R. Cole Pottery turned by General Foister Cole. This was Foister's signature piece. Note hairline fracture through body of pitcher.

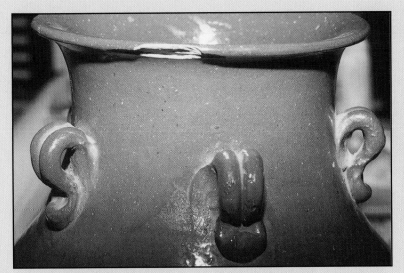

Chip in rim of unique tall vase, early Jugtown, circa 1920s – early 1930s. The rarity and inherent value of this museum piece would almost obviate the effect of this damage.

J.H. ("Jas") Owen pitcher, early 1920s, 7¼". Note rim chip. A defect of this type would render the average ware almost worthless. This is still collectible because of the piece's age and the importance of its maker. $100.00 – 125.00. Ray Wilkinson collection.

Detail of glaze loss and internal rim chip on vase at left. Glaze loss is very common with chrome red glaze. Rim chip devalues this example 15 – 20%.

Vase, 6¾", Pisgah Forest. Note the coarseness of the surface and small round openings in glaze. This may have been due to steam emerging from the clay during firing.

Vase, 11½" with fluted (or ruffled) top edge, chrome red glaze, attributed to J.B. Cole, 1930s. Small loss of glaze at base and rim chips. $125.00 – 175.00.

Two-handled vase, 11", attributed to Carolina Pottery. Note the thin application of blue glaze, with separation creating a variegated pattern.

Two-handled vase, 14¼", Pisgah Forest Pottery. Note pinhole defects due to escape of gases from clay or release of water as steam. In some areas it appears that "crawling" has occurred due to improper attachment of the glaze.

Sources and Techniques of Collecting
North Carolina Art Pottery

In discussions and texts on collection of any particular aesthetic, most of the energy and data are expended in description and espousing its virtue, and little or no emphasis is placed upon the technical aspects of the acquisition process. Throughout this text we have alluded to the shapes, forms, and particular examples the collector should seek but believe it would be useful to enumerate some of the sources we have found productive and certain modes of acquisition we believe effective.

Only a few years ago the number of collectors of North Carolina Art pottery was only a handful. Most collectors of other types of art pottery had little interest or knowledge about this particular genre. There were valid reasons for this circumstance

As we have noted throughout this text, the North Carolina art pottery movement grew from a utilitarian production in which the premise was one of usefulness and not beauty. The early attempts by the utilitarian potters were almost without consideration of aesthetic merit but with the dogged perseverance that most of them exhibited, they began to fashion wares that did have true visual appeal. However, their artistry never equaled fine vases made as one-of-a-kind or on commission by others. Most of the North Carolina production was pottery to be used in households and not as exclusively decorative items. At best, they were felt to represent collectibles and not true objects of art or antiques. Many of the larger vases were sold to florists for flower arrangements, and the heroic porch vases often held umbrellas and walking sticks.

The unit costs for most North Carolina wares were characteristically inexpensive since the premise was volume and achieving a wide geographic distribution for customers. Thus, the often-repeated statement "you might find it anywhere" has an element of truth.

Most North Carolina pottery was made in such volume that collectors could not be attracted by the rarity phenomenon at the outset for most of the production. Thousands of wares were sent to tourist areas to be acquired as inexpensive baubles to take home, memorializing the trip. Thus, the general public saw the undistinguished wares, and there came to exist a mind set that this form of pottery production was about as accomplished as the North Carolina potters were going to demonstrate. In science, this would be a "sample error," but a logical one.

Most collectors of North Carolina pottery were initially local citizens of the area, and they could acquire major examples by going to nearby auctions or sales in the counties around Seagrove, Hickory, or Asheville. One could also purchase major examples from the descendants of the early potters; even estate sales and yard sales as well as flea markets were good sources at that time and on through the 1970s and 1980s. At most local auctions, a number of pieces of pottery would be available with only a few collectors competing, and for a moderate expense even great pieces could be acquired.

If one attended an arts and crafts conference, some North Carolina pottery would be offered, and at ceramic and art pottery festivals, one might have an opportunity to acquire a piece or two with rarely a large inventory to select from. The dealers recognized that North Carolina art pottery was largely regarded as an "acquired taste," but one that in time would come to be acquired by many collectors from many venues.

In the 1920s through WWII, potters and potteries were concerned about feeding themselves and their families, and only rudimentary marketing was part of the activity. Potteries like J.B. and C.C. Cole did publish catalogs. Jugtown had a showroom in Greenwich Village and North State one near Washington, D.C.

Some pottery operations positioned themselves along Highway 1 or 301, catching the tourists moving from the cold to the sunshine. This insured that North Carolina art pottery would be well distributed from Maine to Florida along the North/South corridor at least. Western pottery had a somewhat built-in advantage for collectors in that many tourists were attracted to the Asheville area in the summertime, and families from all over in eastern United States had vacation homes there, extending as far west as Cherokee, North Carolina. The Catawba Valley area was on the path for tourists to the Blue Ridge Mountains.

One would not imply that no thought was given to the visual appeal of this fancy ware and choices were made by the various North Carolina pottery operations and shops. To receive aesthetic affirmation, Juliana and Jacques Busbee attempted to duplicate many Oriental forms that could be seen in the major museums of the world.

Jacques had trained as an artist at the Arts Students League in New York where many of our most famous American painters taught, and one can appreciate this orientation in the forms and glazes he designed. In general, Ben Owen turned at Jugtown and Busbee glazed. Concomitant with these attempts, Jugtown as did all other Seagrove and Catawba Valley potteries, made wares for use in everyday households; plates, teapots, cups, and saucers. After the very earliest stage of operation (1917 – 1920s), Jugtown wares were stamped, and quality control over the years has been good. People became aware of the Jugtown stamp just as they have of the Pisgah Forest one, and since they could associate a pottery with a form or glaze, they became interested in collecting it. You will find Jugtown Pottery and Pisgah Forest widely distributed and appreciated. If it is a rare form (like an extensive scene on a cameo piece) or a rare glaze (like Chinese blue), be prepared to make a significant financial commitment because this is an uncommon opportunity you do not want to miss. The same could be said of a sophisticated painted piece by Maude Hilton in the Catawba Valley area.

Once we were shuttling between the numerous outdoor summer fairs in Pennsylvania, a very good source of North Carolina pottery, and sighted a very large, chrome red rope-handled vase clearly visible and identifiable 50 yards away. As we approached the vendor, seeing our anticipation he announced, "It ain't Jugtown." No, but it was a 24-inch example of the artistry of Waymon Cole and, as expected, unsigned. The heroic porch vase was in almost perfect condition, and he was asking about one-tenth its value, reflecting his disappointment that it was "not Jugtown." Not Jugtown can represent an outstanding acquisition opportunity for any informed collector of North Carolina pottery.

Outside (open-air) fairs continue to be excellent sources of North Carolina pottery. One can attend the "granddaddy" of all in Brimfield, Massachusetts (three times annually) but expect to walk a great distance between opportunities there. Also, dealers of North Carolina pottery have usually made previous arrangements, and they get presented examples privately before the event. However, only last year we acquired both a major example of North State (second stamp) and an early Teague Pottery vase. The year before we had unwittingly acquired a C.B. Masten vase (neither the vendor nor we knew what it was), so a random major acquisition is still quite possible there if you are diligent. Brimfield is truly an American phenomenon appreciated at some level by many.

Certainly, one might find collectible examples of North Carolina art pottery at small fairs anywhere in the Tarheel State, but we would recommend that the novice experience Cameron, Liberty, the Charlotte Expo in North Carolina, and Hillsville just over the border, an event over Labor Day in south-central Virginia. Cameron and Liberty are projects of the small communities, and the townspeople seem glad to have you with them. They also will have several dealers specializing in North Carolina art pottery. These individuals are very knowledgeable, and, in our experience, are fair in both their descriptions, evaluations of condition, and prices. They want repeat business and thus attempt to establish a mutually beneficial relationship. Their inventories are generally excellent.

Regarding specialized dealers in North Carolina pottery, they are the first collectors and connoisseurs of what they sell. Most began as collectors, and some even finance their collecting habit by periodically selling part of their collection. More often they are "trading up" which has nothing to do with beads or wampum but acquiring funds from the sale of one example to purchase a better and more expensive one. Deaccessions from important collections may well be appropriate acquisitions for others, like acquiring a used Auburn or Dusenburg.

If you encounter a very collectible example but one slightly compromised by condition, you should probably acquire it and hope to "trade up" in the future. If that anticipated event never occurs, you as the collector still have an important example; you may not have the opportunity to ever acquire a more significant one.

This concept appears to be gaining acceptance.

Recently at an auction, a four-handled 10 gallon jug by Daniel Seagle with three large holes and other damage brought approximately $3,000; only several years before $500 would have been a winning bid. This reflected the increasing realization that these large vessel Catawba Valley wares are becoming very rare, and those in good condition are in collections and if deaccessed will bring $10,000 – $12,000. Thus, the appeal of rare examples is actually whatever you the collector feel comfortable with — only you should decide whether to acquire a piece.

At present, auctions represent the forum for the greatest available inventory of collectible North Carolina pottery. Certain auction houses, such as Robert Brunk in Asheville, Leland Little in Hillsborough, John Lambert at the Mebane auction, and many others offer several specialty auctions a year that include North Carolina pottery. The Southern Folk Potter Collectors Society operated by Billy Ray and Susan Hussey in Bennett, North Carolina, has extensive "silent auctions" several times a year. They offer vintage examples of North Carolina art pottery and memorabilia, and their catalogs contain certain unique and essential information for the collector. The catalog should be purchased even though you may not be a successful bidder. They have a phone bidding system with "call backs" that needs to be mastered if you want to acquire pots there. Do so, because their consignments are from all over America, and major examples will be offered. Billy Ray is one of North Carolina's most creative contemporary potters, and he is quite accurate in his identification and vernacular descriptions of the wares photographed for the catalog.

Did you think we were going to fail to mention the burgeoning area of E-commerce? With diligence and time, one can almost continuously view North Carolina art pottery for sale on the Internet. To date, the mixture is either big-ticket items or truly pedestrian fare. With digital technology, the images are good although true color rendition is not always perfect, and pixel density does not often equal a 35mm photo.

While this is a source that will grow exponentially over the ensuing years, it does have certain practical drawbacks. First, one does not have the opportunity for a hands-on evaluation of the proffered ware. This is especially important in judging condition. A hairline fracture could have legitimately escaped the consignor's eye and certainly would be below the resolution of the digital (even your $3,500 Nikon) camera. The wares must be shipped and, by any method, the possibility of breakage results. If it is broken, then one has to go to the expense and bother of shipping it back; even more important with a unique piece, it has been lost as a pristine example. No restoration will obviate that.

We like to give examples of North Carolina art pottery as presents to non-collectors, especially for weddings, graduations, housewarmings, and Christmas. They are not only aesthetically pleasing but along with the accompanying historical data about the genre we provide, may encourage the gift receivers to be new collectors.

Once we gave a particularly elegant vase with a fluted rim by A.R. Cole and stamped "Daison Ware" for a wedding present. We were unable to attend the event and shipped this fairly rare and relatively valuable piece. Despite an abundance of bubble wrap and appropriate choice of box and shipping instructions, it arrived literally shattered. The recipient attempted to get it "repaired" which was less than satisfactory.

We suspect that this is a worse case scenario, and hundreds of pieces are shipped every day without untoward incidents, but an event such as this has made us cautious about shipping, especially parts of our collection for exhibition as well as purchase over the Internet. Besides, had you not rather discuss the piece with your colleagues (and competitors), physically examine it, enjoy the competition of bidding, and take it home in your van on the seat beside your Labrador retriever? Collecting should be a personal endeavor and touching your CRT screen is not all that adrenaline enabling; it is warm but not fuzzy.

Antique malls five to 10 years ago in North Carolina and to a lesser extent the Southeast were excellent sources of mid-level pieces, but even then finding major examples there were rare. This is when you need to call upon your personal storehouse of knowledge. The tags will contain such vital information as "jug, vase, or bowl." Sometimes it will say "old" or "possibly North Carolina," but it may be mislabeled "Fulper, Bybee, or Frankoma" to put a name on the possible mislabel. If the shop owner does not know the value of the ware, they will often overprice it ("don't want to sell it too cheap," as if it were a possible Faberge egg) or so undervalue the piece you are tempted to inform them of their error.

In the decoy and sports card collecting worlds, in-kind exchanges are common, and organized swap meets abound. This is at present not an important phenomenon with collectors of North Carolina art pottery. The Pottery Collectors Guild, brainchild of Steve Compton and his colleagues, meets monthly in the state capital of Raleigh. Before each lecture or colloquium there is a "show and tell" session. These are very informative, and one could probably explore the fact they might exchange a pot they have for something a fellow collector has brought in for demonstration. If this occurs, it is rare; but the learning experience from this convivial group of collectors/experts is extraordinary. To date, there is no other equivalent experience except the occasional day affair at the Catawba Valley Pottery Festival, celebrations at the Southern Folk Pottery Collectors Society, or either the North Carolina Folklore and North Carolina Folk Art Society.

In the world of fine painting, "pickers" are essential to the dealer's inventory replenishment, and they may even have arrangements with a few important collectors. To date, this practice exists but does not flourish in the world of North Carolina art pottery. Fellow collectors are also a resource. Several very well-known collectors of North Carolina art pottery have booths in antique malls. One owns the mall, and this is probably a consideration of space to house his extensive collection. Others finance their trading up activities, and one changes collecting interests between genres from time to time. The inventory is usually good, accurately described, and well documented.

Thus, your North Carolina art pottery collection can come from a number of sources. These will be further diminished, as your tastes become more refined. Your research will necessarily become more focused and inclusive, but at the same time the pleasure of the process will be enhanced. Making your collecting activity a personal endeavor will also create a continual learning experience. All of us enjoy the accumulation of data if the acquisition process is pleasurable and as our competence grows, so will our confidence. The lack of predictability of this process will be both a part of its attendant's frustration but also its very singular charm; over a period of time, the former will diminish, whereas the latter will enhance and endure.

Multiglazed "tourist" pottery by C.C. Cole. Small wares were shipped to various resorts from the Seagrove area.

Two-handled, 7¼" green mottled glaze vase. Attributed to A.R. Cole. Stamped on undersurface, Toxaway Lake, North Carolina, a well-known resort. Numerous contractual arrangements between Seagrove pottery operations existed.

While there is no strict definition of tourist pottery, we thought it would be of interest to demonstrate some of the manifestations of contracts North Carolina pottery firms had with tourist resorts or with other businesses along tourist trails.

Stamped "Virginia Pottery," probably turned in North Carolina by J.B. Cole.

Stamp on pitcher at right. Williamsburg, probably the work of Cole Pottery.

Wide mouthed pitcher, 7¼". Multiglazed, circa 1920 – 1930. Stamped Williamsburg Pottery, probably made by C.C. or A.R. Cole.

Rebecca pitcher, 5½", matte finish. Form very similar to those made for Williamsburg, Virginia, by Seagrove potters, principally the Coles. $35.00 – 55.00.

Tourist pottery, all stamped with name of a resort. These are only collectible as oddities.

Wide aperture green bowl, circa 1935 – 1940, painted dogwood decoration. Attributed to Lera Dale Hilton or possibly Maude Hilton.

Tourist pottery, small cider jug, 4½", from Brown Pottery, Arden, North Carolina. Made for convention at Lake Lure, North Carolina, a well-known resort, circa 1960. St. James Place Museum.

Painted, unglazed basket, 8¾", signed E.J. Brown Pottery, Evan Javan Brown stamp. "Tourist pottery" took many forms, some more attractive than others. $60.00 – 75.00. Chapel Hill Museum.

Undersurface of the green bowl above. Lera Dale Hilton (1885 – 1969) was the daughter of E.A. and Clara Maude Hilton.

Tourist artware pair of scalloped vases, 3½", unsigned. Difficult to identify these unique wares. Some resemblance to the unglazed exterior/glazed interior "agate" or swirl ware vases of W.N. Owen. Also like work from Niloak Pottery. Benton, Ark. made of three or four clays. Possibly Brown Pottery as well.

Miniature three-handled vases, 2¾" and 2¼". J.B. Cole, attributed to Nell Cole Graves. Bailey collection.

Tourist ware. Ink stamp Mrs. Smith's, Natural Bridge, Virginia. A natural wonder, this location has been captured in countless paintings, drawings, and photographs.

Tourist pottery, unsigned paper label. Buxton is a village on the outer banks of North Carolina. The barrier islands of the Tarheel State attract thousands of tourists each year.

J.B. Cole stamp. Marion, Virginia. Marion is a town in southwest Virginia. The reason for the stamp is unknown.

Small jug, 5", stamped "Al Smith," Auman Pottery, 1928. Bill Ivey collection.

Tourist "Indian pottery," 4", unglazed, High Hampton hand etched in the side of ashtray. Of interest but not particularly collectible. Leland Little Auction.

Junction of Highway NC 705 and Busbee Road, Westmoore Community. There are over 100 potteries in the Seagrove area.

Charlie Lisk, well-recognized contemporary potter, Vale, North Carolina. Charlie is best known for his blue on white swirl ware and for his colorful personality.

J.B. Cole Pottery site, now closed. This was the most productive of the North Carolina pottery operations. Many potters turned wares there including Virginia Shelton, but the principals were Waymon Cole, Nell Cole Graves, Philmore Graves, and Bascomb King.

Jugtown Pottery is now operated by Vernon Owens, his wife Pam, and brother Bobby. North Carolina pottery is referred to by the uninitiated as "Jugtown," and people misspeak of the area of Seagrove as "Jugtown."

North Carolina Pottery Museum, Seagrove, North Carolina.

Large storage vessel at previous site of Seagrove Pottery operated by Walter and Dot Auman. Before their untimely accidental deaths, they founded the first potter's museum. Several thousand examples from their holdings are in the collection of the Mint Museum in Charlotte.

Contemporary potter Mark Hewitt at his shop near Pittsboro and Carol Wilson, collector. Note large pots for which Hewitt is very well known.

Neolia Cole Womack at A.R. Cole Pottery, identifying wares. Note the unglazed low vase that was turned at the Auman Pottery in the 1920s. Neolia Cole Womack (b.1927), daughter of A.R. Cole and sister of Celia (b. 1924) operates A.R. Cole Pottery with grandson of A.R., Kenneth George (b. 1971).

Greenware at Evans pottery, produced by Evan and Javan Brown.

Evan Javan Brown Pottery. Preparation area for weighing and shipping clay. Asheville area.

Clay preparation area. Pottery of Evan Javan Brown, now operated by his daughter.

Shelves inside kiln. Note the arching roof and the stacking arrangement.

Traditional North Carolina pottery. Note top deco-rated vase with cobalt and scroll over salt glaze. This was turned by J.H. Owen (circa 1910 – 1920). Utilitarian forms with decoration were the first examples demonstrating the transition of these potters from utilitarian to artistic imagery. J.H. Owen (1866 – 1923) was a leader in this movement and helped Jacques Busbee in the early operation at Jugtown. St. James Place Museum.

Wares made by A.R. Cole at Rainbow Pottery. Note the glaze colors of Rainbow Pottery, 1926 – 1941. Carol Wilson, Jai Jordon (formerly with the Mint Museum), and Richard McHenry, collector. Photo taken during inventory and cataloging of St. James Place Museum, circa 1994.

M.L. Owens with handle for teapot, identifying an unknown example. Older potters can often identify the maker on the basis of technical pattern and the evidence of turning and decorative methods.

Examples of early North Carolina pottery, North Carolina Pottery Museum, Seagrove, North Carolina. The museum is located in the heart of the Seagrove pottery area, houses significant archival material, and has an excellent educational program.

Ben Owen III at Seagrove Pottery Festival. Ben is the grandson of Ben Owen, master potter of Jugtown, and operates Ben Owen Pottery. Trained at the community college and East Carolina University, he has studied in Japan and exhibited at the Mint and Chrysler museums.

Seagrove Pottery Festival, annual event that is very well attended and offers demonstrations, food, an auction, and other attractions. Held in Seagrove, North Carolina.

Scheduled pottery demonstrations are given by local potters at the Seagrove Pottery Festival.

Charles "Terry" Zug, folklore scholar and former chair of studies in Folklore at the University of North Carolina at Chapel Hill, "wearing" a two-handled bowl at the Cameron Antiques Festival. Dr. Zug is author of the seminal text, Turners & Burners, UNC Press, Chapel Hill.

Pottery collectors and dealers at Hillsville, Virginia, for Labor Day Festival. No, that is not Tom Mix, it's Robert Hodgin, a well-known pottery dealer from Alamance County, North Carolina, with Mike Smith.

One may find collectible antique North Carolina art pottery at many local outdoor shows including Cameron (on Highway 1 below Sanford), Liberty (south of Burlington), the Charlotte Extravaganza, and Hillsville, Virginia, to cite only a few. So many wares were shipped out of North Carolina that one's search can be nationwide with the Washington area or Pennsylvania shows being the most productive.

Dealer/collector Quincy Scarborough at the Cameron show, author of the Auman text and a monograph on Webster Pottery.

Hillsville, Virginia, outdoor festival, Labor Day. Note the terrain, that explains the designation "hills" and reflects the challenge as well.

281

*Author A. Everette James evaluating identification
criteria on a large A.R. Cole vase.*

Author with Yvonne and Archie Teague, 1994.

St. James Place
Robersonville, North Carolina

Folk Art Museum

St. James Place

St. James Place, a restored Primitive Baptist church is located on US Hwy. 64 in Robersonville, NC which can be reached from US I-95, US Hwy. 17, or NC Hwy. 903. This quaint, pristine example of late, clapboard Gothic revival architecture serves as a museum for folk art, antique decoys, and art pottery.

Open daily and by appointment:

Town Hall	(919) 795-4006
Historical Society	(919) 792-6605
Library	(Key)
Mrs. Gene Taylor:	(919) 795-4576

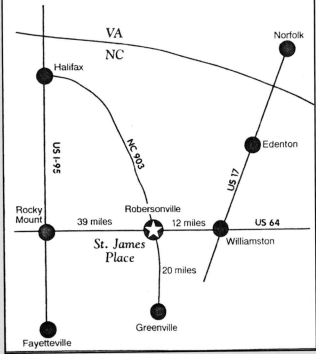

St. James Place Museum brochure.

283

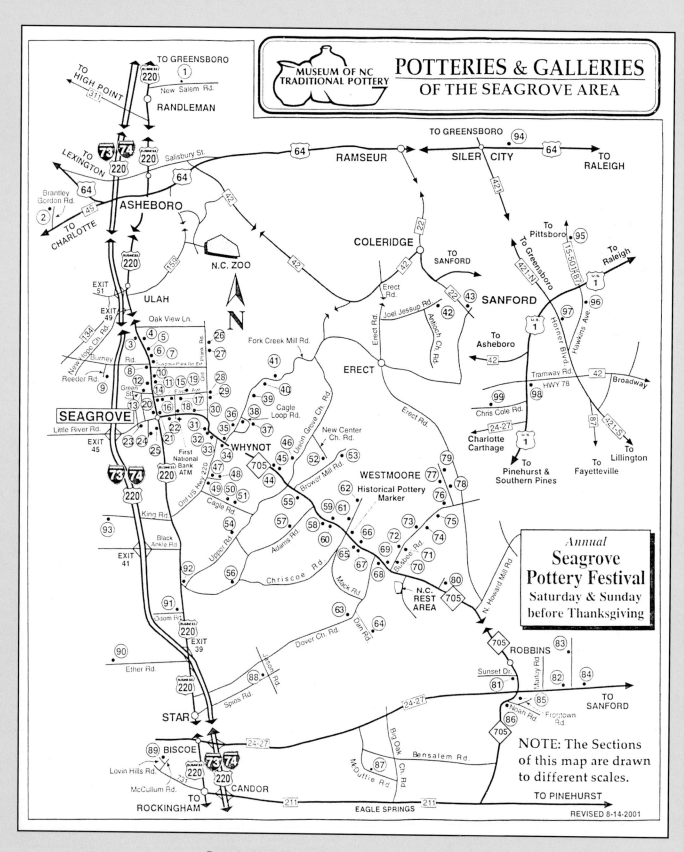

Potteries & galleries of the Seagrove area (adapted).

≋ Bibliography ≋

Auman, Dorothy, and Charles G. Zug III. "Nine Generations of Potters: The Cole Family." In *Long Journey Home: Folklore in the South*, edited by Allen Tullos, pp. 166 – 74. Chapel Hill, N.C.: Southern Exposure, 1977.

---. "Nine Generations of Potters: The Cole Family." *Southern Exposure* 5, Nos. 2 – 3 (1977): 166 – 74.

---, and Walter Auman. *Seagrove Area.* Asheboro, N.C.: Village Printing Company, 1976.

Ben Owen Pottery. Catalog of an exhibition held at North Carolina Musuem of History, Raleigh, N.C. June 1 – July 15, 1974.

Betts, Leonidas J. "Burlon Craig: An Open Window into the Past." N.C. State Foundation Gallery, exhibition catalog, 1994.

Bivens, John F., Jr. *The Moravian Potters in North Carolina.* Chapel Hill: University of North Carolina Press, 1972.

Bridges, Daisy Wade. "Ash Glaze: Traditions in Ancient China and the American South." Ceramic Circle of Charlotte Studies Volume VI. Southern Folk Pottery Collectors Society, 1998.

---. "Catawba Valley Pottery Has Unique Beauty." *Antiques Monthly* 13, No. 7 (May 1980): 13B.

---. "North Carolina Art Pottery." *1982 Mint Museum Antiques Show.* Charlotte, N.C.

----, ed. *Potters of the Catawba Valley, North Carolina.* Charlotte, N.C.: Mint Museum of History, 1980 – 81.

---. *Potters of the Catawba Valley, North Carolina.* Journal of Studies, Ceramic Circle of Charlotte, Vol. 4. Charlotte, N.C.: Mint Museum, 1980. Exhibition Catalog.

Burrison, John A. "Alkaline-glazed Stoneware: A Deep South Pottery Tradition." *Southern Folklore Quarterly* 39, No. 4 (1975): 377 – 403.

"Catawba Clay: Pottery from the Catawba Nation," N.C. Pottery Center, Seagrove, N.C., exhibition catalog, Feb. 4 – Apr. 15, 2000.

Conway, Bob. "Last of the Catawba Valley Potters." *State* 49, No. 2 (July 1981): 8 – 9.

"The Craft Potters of North Carolina: Busbee, Hilton, and Stephen: The Influence of Oscar Louis Bachelder." *Bulletin of the American Ceramics Society* 21, No. 6 (1942).

Craig, James H. *The Arts and Crafts in North Carolina, 1699 – 1840.* Winston-Salem, N.C.: Museum of Early Southern Decorative Arts, Old Salem, Inc., 1965.

Crawford, Jean. *Jugtown Pottery: History and Design.* Winston-Salem, NC: John F. Blair, Publisher, 1964.

Danielson, Leon E. "The Hilton Potteries of the Catawba Valley, North Carolina." *Potters of the Catawba Valley, North Carolina*, edited by Daisy Wade Bridges, 21 – 32. Journal of Studies, Ceramic Circle of Charlotte, Vol. 4. Charlotte, N.C.: Mint Museum, 1980. Exhibition Catalog.

Exhibition of C.R. Auman and C.B. Masten Pottery, North Carolina State University Gallery of Art & Design, Talley Student Center, Raleigh, N.C., 2001

Gilson, Richard. J.B. Cole Catalog (1932). Reprinted Holly Hill Pottery, Seagrove, N.C.

Green, David. *A Handbook of Pottery Glazes.* New York: Watson-Guptill Publications, 1979.

Greer, Georgeanna H. "Alkaline Glazes and Groundhog Kilns: Southern Pottery Traditions." *Antiques* 61, No. 4 (1977): 42 – 54.

---. *American Stonewares: The Art and Craft of Utilitarian Potters.* Exton, Pa.: Schiffer Publishing, 1981.

Harmer-Rook Galleries Absentee Auction Catalog, Georgeanna H. Greer Collection, Part 1, 1992; Part II, 1993; Part III, 5/12/93.

Henzke, Lucile. *Art Pottery of America.* Exton, Pa.: Schiffer Publishing, 1982.

Hertzman, Gay Mahaffey. *Jugtown Pottery: The Busbee Vision.* Raleigh, N.C.: North Carolina Museum of Art, 1984. Exhibition Catalog.

Hussey, Billy Ray and Susan Hussey. Southern Folk Pottery Collectors Society. Catalogs 1-19. Bennett, N.C.

Innovations in Clay: Catawba Valley Pottery. Hickory Museum of Art, Hickory, N.C. October 10, 1987 – January 17, 1988.

James, A.E. "A Century of North Carolina Pottery". *Carolina Antiques.* 1996

---. "A Visit with M.L. Owens. *Voices.* Publication of the NC Folk Art Society. 1995.

---. "Early Movement in North Carolina Art Pottery". *New England Journal of Antiques.* 2002.

---, "It is in the Clay". Seagrove Pottery Festival Annual publication. Bill Ivey, editor. 1995.

---. "Nell Cole Graves: Pioneer Potter". *Carolina Antiques.* 2001.

---. "North Carolina Pottery: A Matter of Form". *Southern Antiques.* 2001.

---. "North Carolina Art Pottery: The Glaze". *Antique Gazette.* 2002.

---. "North Carolina Pottery: The Rare and Unusual". *Southern Antiques.* 2002.

---. "The Cravens". *Carolina Antiques.* 2002.

---. The Transition Period of North Carolina Pottery (at press 2002).

Johnston, Pat H. "Omar Khayyam Pottery." *Antiques Journal* 29, No. 9 (September 1974).

---. "Pisgah Forest and Nonconnah Pottery." *Antiques Journal* 32, No. 5 (May 1977).

---, and Daisy Wade Bridges. *O.L. Bachelder and his Omar Khayyam Pottery.* Journal of Studies, Ceramic Circle of Charlotte, Vol 5. Charlotte, N.C.: Mint Museum, 1984. Exhibition Catalog.

Jugtown Pottery. Catalog of exhibition held at Salem (N.C.) College and Academy, September 10 – 28, 1972.

Leftwich, Rodney L. *Arts and Crafts of the Cherokee.* Cullowhee, N.C.: Land-of-the-Sky Press, 1970.

Lock, Robert C. with Yvonne Hancock Teague, Archie Teague and Kit Vanderwal. *The Traditional Potters of Seagrove, North Carolina and Surrounding Areas from the 1800s to the Present.* Greensboro, N.C.: The Antiques & Collectibles Press, 1994.

The Museum of North Carolina Traditional Pottery: Annual Seagrove Pottery Festival Guides. Number 1 – 17; 1982 – 1992. Seagrove, N.C.: Friends of N.C. Pottery Museum.

North Carolina Museum of Art. Jugtown Pottery: The Busbee Vision. Exhibition Catalog. 1984. Seagrove Pottery's Project Interviews: Dorothy and Walter Auman. North Carolina Department of Cultural Resources, Raleigh, N.C. and the Randolph Arts Guild, Asheboro, N.C. 1983.

North State Pottery mail order catalog, facsimile reproduction. Charlotte, N.C.: Mint Museum of History, 1977.

Norton, Robert. *Southern Antiques and Folk Art.* Birmingham, Ala.: Oxmoor House, Inc., 1976.

Owen, Ben. "Reflections of a Pottery." *The State of the Arts.* Raleigh: North Carolina Arts Council, 1969.

Owens, Vernon. "Building and Burning a Groundhog Kiln." *Studio Potter* 3, No. 1 (Summer 1974).

Parmelee, C.W. *Ceramic Glazes.* Boston: Colners Publishing Co., 1968; London: Industrial Publication, Inc., 1948.

Rhodes, Daniel. *Clays and Glazes for the Potter.* Philadelphia: Chilton Book Co., 1957; London: Pitman Publishing, 1957.

---. *Stoneware and Porcelain: The Art of High Fired Ceramics.* Philadelphia: Chilton Book Co., 1959.

Scarborough, Quincy. "Connecticut Influence on North Carolina Stoneware: The Webster School of Potters." *Journal of Early Southern Decorative Arts* 10, No. 1 (1984): 14 – 74.

---, and Robert Armfield. *Seagrove Pottery: The Walter and Dorothy Auman Legacy.* Fayetteville, N.C.: The Scarborough Companies, 1992.

Schwartz, Stuart C. *The Museum as Collector: Acquiring and Exhibiting America's Ceramic Heritage.* Charlotte, N.C.: Mint Museum of History.

---. *North Carolina Pottery: A Bibliography.* Charlotte, N.C.: Mint Museum of History, 1978.

---. *The North State Pottery Company, Sanford, North Carolina,* 1924 – 1959. Charlotte, N.C.: Mint Museum of History, 1977. Exhibition Catalog.

---. "The Reinhardt Potteries." *Potters of the Catawba Valley, North Carolina,* edited by Daisy Wade Bridges, 33 – 38. Journal of Studies, Ceramic Circle of Charlotte, vol. 4. Charlotte: Mint Museum, 1980. Exhibition Catalog.

---. "The Royal Crown Pottery and Porcelain Company, Merry Oaks, North Carolina." *Pottery Collectors' Newsletter* 3, No. 5 (February 1974): 57 – 62.

Shaw, K. *Ceramic Colours and Pottery Decoration.* New York: American Elsevier Publishing Co., 1972; London: Maclaren, 1962, revised 1968.

Smith, Elizabeth S. "Burlon B. Craig, Potter." *Tar Heel* 8, No. 1 (February 1980): 52, 54.

Smith, Howard A. *Index of Southern Potters.* Mayodan, N.C.: Old America Company, 1982, 1986.

"Southern Folk Pottery." *Foxfire* 8, edited by Eliot Wigginton and Margie Bennett, 71 – 384. Garden City, N.Y.: Anchor Press, 1984.

Southern Folk Pottery Collectors Society, References Catalogs and Society Newsletters. B.R. and Susan Hussey. Bennett, N.C.

Sweezy, Nancy. *Raised in Clay: The Southern Pottery Tradition.* Washington, D.C.: The Smithsonian Institution Press, 1984.

Terry, George, and Lynn Robertson Myers. *Southern Made: The Southern Folk Heritage.* Columbia, S.C.: McKissick Museums, University of South Carolina, 1981. Exhibition Catalog.

Two Centuries of Potters: A Catawba Valley Tradition, Lincoln County Historical Association, Lincoln County Museum of History exhibition catalog, June 4 – September 18, 1999.

"Vernacular Pottery of North Carolina." 1987 exhibition catalog, N.C. State University Raleigh.

"Wilkinson Collection of North Carolina Pottery", catalog from tag sale, June 11, 1994, collection of Raymond Smith Wilkinson.

Williams, Ben F. "The Jugtown Pottery Collections." *Bulletin of the North Carolina Museum of Art* 5, No. 1 – 2 (Fall 1964 – Winter 1965).

Zug, Charles G., III. "Pursuing Pots: On Writing a History of North Carolina Folk Pottery." *North Carolina Folklore Journal* 2, No. 2 (November 1970): 34 – 55.

---. *The Traditional Potters of North Carolina.* Catalog of an exhibition held at Ackland Art Museum, University of North Carolina, Chapel Hill, 1981.

---. *Turners and Burners: The Folk Potters of North Carolina.* Chapel Hill: The University of North Carolina Press, 1984.

Acknowledgments

No one could write a text on North Carolina art pottery without building upon the legacy of Daisy Wade Bridges, Charles "Terry" Zug, and the late Howard Smith. Other references might be made to the publications of Nancy Sweezy, Robert Lock, the catalogs and newsletter of the Southern Folk Pottery Collectors Society by Billy Ray Hussey, and the Seagrove Pottery Festival monographs by Bill Ivey.

Many persons allowed me to photograph their collections or sent me photos, and many examples are available only because they were so generous. These include George Viall, Joe and Ray Wilkinson, Boyd Owens (M. L. Owens Museum), Leon Danielson, Barry and Allen Huffman, W. D. Morton, Mick Bailey, Phillip Fulton , the L. A. Rhynes, Nowell Guffey, Bill Ivey, David Blackburn, Professor and Mrs. Leon Danielson, Tommy and Cindy Edwards, Charlotte Brown, and colleagues at the North Carolina State University Gallery of Art and Design.

I am indebted to:

Leon Danielson who not only shared with me his extraordinary Hilton collection but his incredible knowledge of the history of art pottery in the Catawba Valley.

Collector and art dealer Nowell Guffey for introducing me to the sophisticated Cherokee Indian pottery.

Charlotte Brown who not only contributed the foreword but edited several of the chapters. She and her staff made available the collection at the North Carolina State University Gallery.

Pam and Vernon Owens who contributed in many ways to the chapters on clay, glazes, and forms.

I benefited greatly by the discussions of North State Pottery with W. D. Morton.

My authorities in the identification process are thoughtful individuals who engage in the buying and selling of North Carolina pottery. I appreciate the time and expertise of Joe Wilkinson, Mick Bailey, Tommy and Cindy Edwards, Arthur Baer, Billy Ray Hussey, Kyle Bullock, Joe Foster, William Fields, and Steve Compton for assisting in the identification and evaluation process.

About the Author

Everette James, a native of rural Martin County, North Carolina, was educated at the University of North Carolina in Chapel Hill, Duke Medical School, Harvard, and the Johns Hopkins School of Public Health. Dr. James taught at Harvard, Johns Hopkins, University College London, and Vanderbilt. He has published more than 20 books and 500 articles and established St. James Place, a restored historic Primitive Baptist church exhibiting over 400 examples of North Carolina pottery. He and his wife, Dr. Nancy Farmer, have donated their collection of Nell Cole Graves pottery to the North Carolina Pottery Museum at Seagrove and a survey collection of 250 examples to the Chapel Hill Museum. They live in Chapel Hill and are active in community affairs.

❧ General Price Guide ❧

This list was derived from the inventories of three institutional collections, and the value ranges were assigned by one of the collection's curators and three noted dealers. These values are growing each year geometrically and for the major examples, exponentially; what we have listed here we offer in good faith and with the knowledge that they are relative to the publication time of this book. Pieces designated with asterisks are recognized by authorities specifically as tourist pottery.

A

Aladdin lamp, brown (handle repair), Waymon Cole (J.B. Cole)...$250.00 – 325.00

Aladdin lamp, earthenware 4½", mottled green, attributed to J.B. Cole Pottery, Waymon Cole (ca. 1950)...........$275.00 – 325.00

Apothecary jar, earthenware 4", aqua, attributed to Rainbow Pottery ....$60.00 – 80.00

Apothecary jar, earthenware 4¼", white, attributed to Rainbow Pottery...$75.00 – 90.00

Apothecary jar, earthenware 5½", green, signed Rainbow Pottery, ink stamp ....$85.00 – 100.00

Apothecary jar, earthenware 6", yellow, attributed to J.B. Cole Pottery..$80.00 – 100.00

Apothecary jar, earthenware 6½", aqua, attributed to J.B. Cole, Waymon Cole (ca. 1930s) ....$110.00 – 125.00

Apothecary jar, earthenware 6½", blue, attributed to Rainbow Pottery, ...$75.00 – 90.00

Apothecary jar, earthenware 6¾", black ankle glaze, attributed to Jugtown Pottery ....$175.00 – 200.00

Apothecary jar, earthenware 9", green over chrome red, double dipped, attributed to North State Pottery Co. ....$175.00 – 200.00

Apothecary jar, 9½", Rainbow Pottery...$125.00 – 150.00

Apple rings (4), earthenware, multiglazed, stamped A.R. Cole Pottery...$85.00 – 100.00 for all

Ash tray, earthenware 3¾", bronze green, stamped Handmade by Pine State Pottery ....$45.00 – 60.00

Ash tray, earthenware 4¾", bronze green, attributed to J.B. Cole Pottery..$45.00 – 60.00

Ash tray, earthenware 5", bronze/green, signed W.H. Owens (ca. 1970s)..$45.00 – 60.00

Ash tray, earthenware 5", yellow/bronze rim, attributed to J.B. Cole Pottery ....$40.00 – 55.00

Ash tray, earthenware 5¾", aqua/brown rim, attributed to J.B. Cole Pottery ....$45.00 – 60.00

Ash tray, fluted, earthenware 8½", bronze green, stamped A.R. Cole Pottery, Sanford, NC (small stamp) ....$45.00 – 60.00

Ash tray with match holder, earthenware 2¼" x 4", bronze green, small stamp A.R. Cole Pottery...........................$70.00 – 85.00

Ash tray with pitcher match holder, earthenware 1¼", multiglazed, attributed to C.C. Cole Pottery ....$30.00 – 40.00

B

Basket, earthenware 4", light green, cobalt runs, attributed to Auman Pottery, Masten glaze, rare ....$125.00 – 200.00

Basket, earthenware 4½" x 9", mustard, attributed to C.C. Cole Pottery, Thurston Cole (ca. 1930s),.....................$85.00 – 100.00

Basket, earthenware 5½", blue, attributed to Carolina Pottery ....$55.00 – 70.00

Basket, earthenware 5½", crystal green, attributed to A.R. Cole Pottery ....$100.00 – 115.00

Basket, earthenware 6", mauve, attributed to Rainbow Pottery ....$65.00 – 90.00

Basket, earthenware 6¼", blue, attributed to E.A. Hilton Pottery..$40.00 – 55.00

Basket, earthenware, 6½", mottled green, attributed to Seagrove Pottery ....$50.00 – 65.00

Basket, earthenware 6½", green, attributed to Joe Owen...$45.00 – 65.00

Basket, earthenware 7", multiglazed, attributed to C.C. Cole Pottery ....$40.00 – 55.00

Basket, earthenware 7½", blue, attributed to J.B. Cole Pottery ....$85.00 – 95.00

Basket, earthenware 7½", mirror black, green drips, stamped Rainbow Pottery, Handmade, Sanford, NC..............$70.00 – 95.00

Basket, earthenware 8½", brown, signed Glenn Art, foil label, attributed to Joe Owen, rare...................................$125.00 – 175.00

Basket, earthenware 9", blue, attributed to J.B. Cole Pottery, Waymon Cole, stamped Sunset Mountain Pottery ...$125.00 – 175.00

Basket, earthenware 9¾", aqua, attributed to J.B. Cole Pottery, Bascomb King (ca. 1930s) ....$95.00 – 125.00

Basket, earthenware 10½", bronze/gold, attributed to J.B. Cole Pottery, Waymon Cole ....$125.00 – 175.00

* Basket, earthenware 10½", chrome red, signed Mr Smiths, Handmade, NC Pottery, Va, ink stamp....................$145.00 – 175.00

Basket, earthenware 11", bronze green, signed Royal Crown Pottery, handmade pottery, ink stamp.......................$140.00 – 175.00

Basket, earthenware 11½", yellow, attributed to J.B. Cole Pottery, Philmore Graves (Daison Ware)......................$145.00 – 175.00

Basket, earthenware 12½", green with pink & lime mottled, attributed to Joe Owen ....$200.00 – 250.00

Basket, earthenware 13½", yellow with brown drip, attributed to J.B. Cole Pottery, Philmore Graves....................$175.00 – 225.00

Basket, earthenware 15½", light yellow with cream drip, signed Alpine Lookout, Little Switzerland, ink stamp .....$125.00 – 150.00

Basket, earthenware 16", brown, attributed to J.B. Cole Pottery, Philmore Graves ....$175.00 – 225.00

Basket, earthenware 19", aqua, signed Royal Crown Pottery, handmade pottery, ink stamp.....................................$250.00 – 325.00

Basket (low) with handle, earthenware 12", aqua, attributed to B.D. (Duck) Teague ....$95.00 – 115.00

Basket, 9" x 9", blue, Candor Pottery ....$100.00 – 125.00

Basket, stoneware 11", brown and white, signed B. Hilton ....$75.00 – 90.00

Batter dish, earthenware 5¼" x 11", bronze green, attributed to J.B. Cole Pottery, Waymon Cole ....$45.00 – 60.00

Batter jar with lid, stoneware 11", stamped Jugtown Ware 1991, signed Vernon Owens ....$175.00 – 225.00

Bean pot, earthenware 4" x 6½", brown, signed Seagrove ....$35.00 – 50.00

Bean pot, earthenware 5", brown, stamped Bolick Pottery ....$35.00 – 50.00

Bean pot, earthenware 5½", glazed inside, attributed to E.A. Hilton Pottery Co., (ca. 1920) ....$225.00 – 250.00

Bean pot, earthenware 7", lead glaze (spotting), stamped Jugtown Ware, 1st stamp ....$175.00 – 200.00

Bean pot, stoneware swirl 9", stamped B.B. Craig, (ca. 1982) ....$225.00 – 250.00

Bean pot with lid, earthenware 4" x 11", dark aqua, stamped A.R. Cole Pottery, Sanford, NC (twice)..........$70.00 – 95.00

Bean pot with lid, two-handled, earthenware 6", Albany Slip, attributed to O.L. Bachelder ....$95.00 – 140.00

Bent plate, earthenware 8½", clear lead glaze (spotting), stamped Jugtown Ware.....................................$225.00 – 250.00

Birdbath, stoneware 15" x 4", unglazed exterior, glazed interior, attributed to A.E. Hilton Pottery (Catawba Indian) ....$450.00 – 600.00

Bird, earthenware 4", salt glaze, signed A. Teague Pottery ....$40.00 – 55.00

Birdhouse, earthenware 6", apple green, attributed to J.B. Cole Pottery ....$75.00 – 90.00

Birdhouse, earthenware 7", brown, stamped Brown Pottery..$25.00 – 35.00

Bottle, earthenware 9/2", green/gray, double dipped, signed Teagues...$75.00 – 90.00

Bowl, earthenware 2½", clear lead glaze, stamped Ben Owen, Master Potter (ca. 1960) ....$125.00 – 150.00

Bowl, earthenware 2½", yellow, signed Teagues Lead..$25.00 – 40.00

Bowl, earthenware 2¾" x 11", clear glaze (green spotting), stamped Jugtown Ware, 1st stamp ....$85.00 – 110.00

Bowl, earthenware 3", glazed inside, attributed to E.A. Hilton Pottery Co. ....$65.00 – 95.00

Bowl, earthenware 3¼", black ankle, stamped Jugtown Ware, very rare ....$225.00 – 250.00

Bowl, earthenware 3¼" x 9", clear lead glaze, stamped Jugtown Ware, 1st stamp ....$175.00 – 200.00

Bowl, earthenware 4", yellow, attributed to Carolina Pottery...$55.00 – 70.00

Bowl, earthenware 4½" x 11", orange, signed Seagrove..$25.00 – 35.00

Bowl, earthenware 5" x 9½", salt glaze, cobalt decoration, wood fired, signed Ben Owen III ....$125.00 – 175.00

Bowl, earthenware 5" x 13½", green, attributed to Royal Crown Pottery ....$75.00 – 100.00

Bowl, earthenware 7 " x 13", salt glaze, sine wave and cobalt, stamped Jugtown Ware, signed Vernon Owens 1976 ....$90.00 – 110.00

Bowl, earthenware 8", alkaline glaze, signed Stop at Stumps, Rocky Mount, NC, ink stamp (rare)..............$45.00 – 60.00

Bowl, earthenware 15" x 4½", clear lead glaze, attributed to Salem (ca. 1815) ....$350.00 – 425.00

* Bowl, fluted, earthenware 2" x 6¼", multiglazed red/yellow, attributed to C.C. Cole Pottery,
   signed Skyline Drive Va., ink stamp..$30.00 – 55.00

* Bowl, fluted, earthenware 2" x 8", multiglazed, attributed to C.C. Cole Pottery...$50.00 – 65.00

Bowl, fluted, earthenware 4½", glazed swirl, attributed to Auman Pottery, C.B. Masten glaze (rare) ....$125.00 – 150.00

Bowl, fluted, two-handled, earthenware, cream/green, attributed to C.C. Cole ....$75.00 – 95.00

Bowl, footed, earthenware 3" x 7½", white, attributed to J.B. Cole Pottery..$75.00 – 100.00

Bowl, squared, earthenware 2" x 6", brown, stamped Handmade by North State Pottery................................$55.00 – 70.00

Bowl, stoneware 2" x 4½", brown glaze (interior), stamped Valor Ware 44, Brown Pottery ....$35.00 – 40.00

Bowl, stoneware 9" x 4½", blue ring decoration, attributed to A.E. Hilton Pottery ....$95.00 – 115.00

Bowl, stoneware 12½" x 6", attributed to Penland's Pottery (ca. 1890) ....$325.00 – 375.00

Bowl, three-sided, earthenware 4", white, attributed to Seagrove area (ca. 1950)...$35.00 – 45.00

Bowl, two-handled, earthenware 4" x 4½", almond, attributed to Seagrove Pottery ....$50.00 – 60.00

Bowl, two-handled, earthenware 4" x 9", aqua, attributed to Rainbow Pottery..$45.00 – 65.00

Bowl, two-handled, earthenware 5", blue, attributed to Rainbow Pottery ....$65.00 – 95.00

Bowl, two-handled, earthenware 5" x 9½", aqua, attributed to Seagrove area ....$40.00 – 55.00

Bowl with lid, attached fluted plate, earthenware 3", orange, clear lead glaze, stamped Jugtown Ware, 1st stamp ....$115.00 – 145.00

Bud vase, earthenware, 4¼", clear glaze, stamped Ben Owen, Master Potter (ca. 1960).........................$85.00 – 110.00

Bud vase, earthenware 5", tan, attributed to Seagrove Pottery...$20.00 – 70.00

Bud vase, earthenware 5", yellow, attributed to J.B. Cole Pottery..$45.00 – 55.00

Bud vase, earthenware 6½", copper green, attributed to Seagrove Pottery..$25.00 – 45.00

Bud vase, earthenware 12¼", clear glaze, attributed to J.H. Owen..$125.00 – 150.00

Butter dish, stoneware 5", swirl, stamped B.B. Craig ....$65.00 – 90.00

Butter jar, stoneware 6", stamped J.D. (Jacob Dorris) Craven, ...$200.00 – 250.00

Butter jar with lid, stoneware 8", salt glaze, J.D. Craven ....$350.00 – 400.00

Butter warmer, earthenware 1¾", bronze green, attributed to J.B. Cole Pottery, Nell Cole Graves..$65.00 – 90.00
Butter warmer, earthenware 3½", white/aqua, J.B. Cole, Seagrove, Nell Cole Graves...$25.00 – 30.00
Button ash tray, earthenware 6¼", bronze green, attributed to J.B. Cole Pottery ....$35.00 – 50.00
"Buzzard" vase, two-handled, earthenware 9¼", blue lead glaze, signed Rainbow Pottery,
    Handmade, Sanford, NC, ink stamp ....$250.00 – 350.00
"Buzzard" vase, two-handled with rings, earthenware 12½", aqua, attributed to J.B. Cole Pottery.......................................$200.00 – 235.00
"Buzzard" vase, two-handled with rings, earthenware 13", dark aqua, attributed to J.B. Cole Pottery.................................$275.00 – 325.00

C

Candle dish, earthenware 6", matte green, attributed to Seagrove Pottery...$25.00 – 40.00
Candleholder, earthenware 2", cranberry sponge, stamped A.R. Cole Pottery ....$35.00 – 55.00
Candle holder, earthenware 2", red, attributed to M.L. Owens Pottery, ...$65.00 – 80.00
Candle holder, earthenware 2½", mirror black, stamped A.R. Cole Pottery..$55.00 – 70.00
Candleholder, earthenware 4¼", aqua, attributed to Seagrove area..$30.00 – 45.00
Candle holder, earthenware 5" x 8", orange/red, attributed to Joe Owen...$65.00 – 90.00
Candle lantern, earthenware 3½", green and brown, signed Owens ....$80.00 – 95.00
Candle lantern, earthenware 4", red, attributed to M.L. Owens ....$40.00 – 60.00
Candle lantern, earthenware 5", tan with rutile separation, attributed to Seagrove Pottery ....$45.00 – 60.00
* Candle lantern, earthenware 6½", multiglazed, signed Williamsburg Handmade Pottery ....$30.00 – 35.00
Candle lantern, earthenware 6¾", bronze green, attributed to J.B. Cole Pottery ....$65.00 – 90.00
Candle lantern, earthenware 8¼", aqua, double dipped, stamped Handmade by North State Pottery,
    Sanford, NC, 3rd stamp..$50.00 – 70.00
* Candlestick, earthenware 1½", red, attributed to M.L. Owens Pottery ....$35.00 – 50.00
Candlestick, earthenware 2½", apple green, attributed to J.B. Cole Pottery...$35.00 – 50.00
Candlestick, earthenware 2½", copper-green, attributed to Seagrove Pottery ....$35.00 – 50.00
* Candlestick, earthenware 3", cream/brown rim, attributed to J.B. Cole Pottery, signed Handmade Pottery Oven Ware,
    The Handy Craftsman, Battleboro, NC (paper label), (ca. 1950s)...$45.00 – 60.00
Candlestick, earthenware 3", olive green (incised rings), stamped Evan's, Handmade..$45.00 – 60.00
Candlestick, earthenware 3", olive green, stamped Handmade (twice) - Evan's Arden (upside down)..................................$40.00 – 50.00
Candlestick, earthenware 3", red/black drip, attributed to Owens Pottery ....$60.00 – 75.00
Candlestick, earthenware 3½", Albany slip, attributed to Robert B. Keller..$90.00 – 110.00
Candlestick, earthenware 3½", chrome red, attributed to J.B. Cole Pottery, stamped North Carolina Handmade Pottery ....$45.00 – 60.00
Candlestick, earthenware 4", clear lead glaze, cobalt decoration, attributed to Auman Pottery ....$75.00 – 95.00
Candlestick, earthenware 4" x 7½", aqua/rust border, attributed to J.B. Cole Pottery, Nell Cole Graves...............................$60.00 – 75.00
Candlestick, earthenware 4½", cream/rust border, attributed to J.B. Cole Pottery, Nell Cole Graves ....$45.00 – 60.00
* Candlestick, earthenware 4½", olive green, stamped ?? Pinehurst, NC..$35.00 – 50.00
Candlestick, earthenware 5", brown/orange, stamped Handmade, Pine State Pottery..$50.00 – 65.00
Candlestick, earthenware 6", clear, attributed to Alfred Cole Pottery...$50.00 – 65.00
Candlestick, earthenware 6", salt glaze, signed A. Teague (ca. 1994)..$35.00 – 55.00
Candlestick, earthenware 8½", blue, script BH Owens..$45.00 – 60.00
Candlestick, earthenware 10", clear glaze, magnesium drip, attributed to Seagrove area ....$45.00 – 50.00
Candlestick, earthenware 14", tobacco spit brown, stamped Ben Owen Pottery ....$125.00 – 175.00
Candlestick, earthenware 10½", clear/cobalt, attributed to Auman Pottery...$125.00 – 150.00 pair
Candlestick, porcelain 5½", light green, attributed to Pisgah Forest Pottery ....$60.00 – 75.00
Candlestick, twist handle, earthenware 4½", multiglazed, attributed to C.C. Cole Pottery ....$25.00 – 40.00
Candlesticks, earthenware 5¼", gunmetal black, attributed to J.B. Cole Pottery ....$90.00 – 115.00 pair
Candlesticks, earthenware 11½", painted dark blue, attributed to Auman Pottery (ca. 1924)...$100.00 – 125.00 pair
Canister (bean pot), earthenware 9½", clear lead glaze, stamped Ben Owen Pottery Shop (straight stamp) ....$225.00 – 275.00
Canister with lid, earthenware 6", mistake crystal blue, stamped A.R. Cole Pottery...$50.00 – 65.00
Casserole, earthenware 4" x 4½", matte blue, attributed to Seagrove Pottery ....$30.00 – 45.00
Casserole dish, two-handled, earthenware 3¼" x 9", green, double dipped, stamped Handmade by North State Pottery..........$50.00 – 65.00
Casserole dish with dome lid (individual), earthenware 3½", orange, clear lead glaze,
    stamped Jugtown Ware, 1st stamp..$125.00 – 150.00
Casserole dish with lid, earthenware, brown, stamped Valor Ware, stamped Brown Pottery ....$80.00 – 105.00

Casserole dish with lid, earthenware 2½" x 8½", apple green, attributed to J.B. Cole Pottery ....$45.00 – 70.00

Casserole dish with lid, earthenware 4" x 9", clear lead glaze, stamped Jugtown Ware, 1st stamp ....$275.00 – 300.00

Casserole dish with lid (individual), earthenware 3½" x 7", chrome red, attributed to J.B. Cole Pottery, Bascomb King ....$60.00 – 80.00

Casserole with domed lid (individual), earthenware 5", tobacco spit brown, stamped Jugtown Ware....................................$275.00 – 300.00

Catfish, earthenware 7", frogskin, signed B. Yow, Seagrove, NC (circle) ....$75.00 – 95.00

Center bowl, curved handle, earthenware 3½" x 9½", mottled green, attributed to J.B. Cole Pottery ....$65.00 – 75.00

Center bowl, curved handles, earthenware 4" x 13", bronze green, stamped A.R. Cole Pottery ....$75.00 – 95.00

Center bowl, earthenware 4" x 11", brown sugar, attributed to Seagrove Pottery ....$75.00 – 100.00

Center bowl, earthenware 5" x 16", blue, attributed to Rainbow Pottery (A.R. Cole) ....$95.00 – 115.00

Center bowl, rectangular, earthenware 5½" x 15", yellow, attributed to J.B. Cole Pottery, Bascomb King ....$65.00 – 75.00

Center bowl, two-handled, earthenware 5½" x 13", multicolored (Mason stain), attributed to Rainbow Pottery...................$100.00 – 140.00

Center bowl, two-handled, fluted, earthenware 3¾" x 11", aqua, stamped Royal Crown Handmade Pottery (ink) ....$85.00 – 100.00

Chicken bowl, earthenware 2½" x 10", yellow, clear lead glaze, stamped Jugtown Ware, 2nd stamp ....$275.00 – 325.00

Chicken, earthenware 7", clear, signed Seagrove, W. Auman (Walter)..$200.00 – 225.00

Chicken, earthenware 7¼", yellow, signed Charles Moore 1979, stamped Jugtown Ware ....$175.00 – 200.00

Chicken, earthenware 10", clear, yellow, signed Owens, B.H. ....$85.00 – 10.00

Chicken, earthenware 10¾", brown, signed RA 1984, stamped Armfield Pottery...$75.00 – 85.00

Chicken, earthenware 13", brown, signed Albert Hodge ....$95.00 – 125.00

Chicken feeder, stoneware 12½", stamped B.B. Craig (ca. 1983) ....$275.00 – 350.00

Chicken feeder (waterer), stoneware 13", attributed to North Carolina (ca. 1900)...$275.00 – 325.00

Chicken pepper shaker, earthenware 4¼", salt glaze/cobalt, stamped Jugtown Ware (twice)...$75.00 – 115.00

Churn, earthenware 7", blue/light blue, stamped Joe Owen...$60.00 – 75.00

Churn, stoneware, 19", 5-gallon, attributed to J.B. Cole Pottery, Bud Luck ....$125.00 – 175.00

Churn, stoneware 21", 6-gallon, attributed to Burlon Craig, Vale, NC (ca. 1950) ....$275.00 – 300.00

Churn, two-handled (lug and strap), stoneware 15½", 4-gallon, stamped Penland's Pottery ....$250.00 – 300.00

Churn, two-handled, rings, stoneware 18½", 4-gallon (coggle) salt glaze, drips, attributed to William Henry Hancock.......$145.00 – 175.00

Churn, two-handled, stoneware 15", 3-gallon, stamped JFS (James Franklin Seagle) (ca. 1880)..$375.00 – 425.00

Churn, two-handled, stoneware 15", 4-gallon, stamped O'Henry Pottery ....$300.00 – 350.00

Churn, two-handled, stoneware 17", 3-gallon, attributed to Catawba Valley ....$150.00 – 225.00

Churn, two-handled, stoneware 17½", attributed to Hilton Pottery ....$150.00 – 175.00

Churn, two-handled, stoneware 17½", 5-gallon, stamped O'Henry Pottery (ca. 1940)...$175.00 – 225.00

Churn, two-handled, stoneware 18½", stamped Auman Pottery (3 times) (ca. 1926)..$175.00 – 195.00

Churn, two-handled, stoneware 19", 3-gallon, attributed to Union Co. ....$175.00 – 200.00

Churn with lid, one handle, stoneware 14½", 3-gallon, attributed to Burlon Craig (ca. 1950)...$150.00 – 200.00

Churn with lid, stoneware 17", unmarked ....$100.00 – 125.00

Churn with lid, stoneware 18½", 6-gallon, stamped Brown Pottery (ca. 1920)..$125.00 – 145.00

Coffee mug, earthenware 4", green/brown glaze, stamped C.C. Cole ....$20.00 – 35.00

Compote, earthenware 4½", mottled green, attributed to J.B. Cole Pottery, Nell Cole Graves...$40.00 – 60.00

Compote, earthenware 4½" x 8", orange/cream, attributed to J.B. Cole Pottery ....$35.00 – 55.00

Compote, earthenware 9", matte green, attributed to Seagrove Pottery...$55.00 – 90.00

Cookie jar with lid, earthenware 8", yellow, attributed to Rainbow Pottery..$85.00 – 110.00

Cream pitcher, earthenware 2½", yellow, signed Rainbow Pottery, Sanford, NC ink stamp ....$85.00 – 110.00

Cream riser, stoneware 6", signed Brown Pottery (ca. 1930)...$45.00 – 65.00

Cream riser, stoneware 6", stamped W. H. Hancock (William Henry) ....$225.00 – 275.00

Cream riser, stoneware 6½", stamped J.D. Craven ....$225.00 – 275.00

Cream riser, stoneware 7", attributed to Catawba Valley (ca. 1910) ....$135.00 – 175.00

Cream riser, stoneware 7", 1½-gallon, attributed to Joe Owen (ca. 1930)...$125.00 – 150.00

Cream riser, stoneware 7", stamped J.H. Spencer (twice) (Jordan Harris) ....$225.00 – 275.00

Cream riser, stoneware, 7", stamped J.F. Brower, cogglewheel in circle ....$350.00 – 550.00

Cream riser, stoneware 7¼", buff yellow, signed B. Hilton...$70.00 – 85.00

Cream riser, stoneware, 7½", 1½ gallon, attributed to Joe Owen (ca. 1930)..$100.00 – 125.00

Cream riser, stoneware 7½", stamped SLH (Sylvanus Leander Hartsoe) (ca. 1880)...$225.00 – 250.00

Cream riser, stoneware 8", stamped O'Henry Pottery (ca. 1940) ....$125.00 – 175.00

Cream riser, stoneware 9", stamped TR (Thomas Ritchie) ....$225.00 – 300.00

Cream riser, stoneware, 9", 2-gallon, attributed to Catawba Valley ....$85.00 – 125.00

Cream/sugar, candle holders/candles, earthenware 2", brown, attributed to M.L. Owens Pottery ....$45.00 – 75.00

* Cream/sugar set, earthenware 2", candles, attributed to M.L. Owens Pottery, "Scented Candle - Carolina Soap & Candle Makers,
    Southern Pines, NC" (paper label) (in original box)..$45.00 – 60.00

* Cream/sugar set, earthenware 2¼" each, blue, brown rim (matte), attributed to Seagrove Pottery.....................................$25.00 – 35.00

Cream/sugar set, earthenware 2¾", each, Chinese blue, attributed to North State Pottery Co. ....$45.00 – 55.00

Cream/sugar set, earthenware 2¾", and 3", bronze green, stamped A.R. Cole Pottery ....$45.00 – 60.00

Cream/sugar set, earthenware 3", matte blue, signed Seagrove ....$35.00 – 55.00

Cream/sugar set, earthenware 3½", and 3", yellow/brown rim, attributed to J.B. Cole Pottery ....$45.00 – 60.00

Cream/sugar set, 3½", each, clear orange/brown glaze, stamped Brown Pottery, Handmade...$30.00 – 45.00

Cream/sugar set, earthenware 3½" bowl, 4" pitcher, multicolored glaze, attributed to C.C. Cole Pottery.................................$45.00 – 60.00

Cream/sugar set, earthenware 3½" - 3", brown, stamped Joe Owen ....$45.00 – 65.00

Crock, pickle, stoneware 6½", attributed to North Carolina ....$85.00 – 100.00

Crock, stoneware, 10", attributed to Catawba Valley...$125.00 – 150.00

Crock, stoneware, 11", stamped key, George Donkel ....$175.00 – 250.00

Crock, stoneware, 11½", 2-gallon, attributed to S.L. Hartsoe (Sylvanus Leander) ....$175.00 – 200.00

Crock, stoneware 14½", attributed to Kennedy Pottery ....$225.00 – 275.00

Crock, two-handled, stoneware 11½", alkaline glaze ....$175.00 – 200.00

Crock, two-handled, stoneware 12", 2-gallon, stamped T.R. (Thomas Ritchie)...$200.00 – 250.00

Crock, two-handled, stoneware 12", 3-gallon, attributed to Catawba Valley ....$150.00 – 175.00

Crock, two-handled, stoneware 14", attributed to E.A. Hilton Pottery ....$200.00 – 225.00

Crock, two-handled, stoneware 14", attributed to Hartsoe family ....$200.00 – 225.00

Crock, two-handled, stoneware 14", stamped SLH on lug handle (SL Hartsoe) ....$250.00 – 275.00

Crock, two-handled, stoneware 16", 4-gallon, stamped Reinhardt Bros...$200.00 – 250.00

Crock, two-handled, stoneware 16", 5-gallon, stamped Reinhardt Bros...$200.00 – 250.00

Crock, two-handled, stoneware, 16½", 5-gallon, attributed to Reinhardt Pottery ....$175.00 – 450.00

Crock, two-handled, stoneware 19½", 10-gallon, stamped Brown Pottery ....$175.00 – 200.00

Cup/saucer, earthenware 3½" matte green, attributed to J.B. Cole, Nell Cole Graves (ca. 1960s)...$45.00 – 60.00

Cup with saucer, earthenware 6" and 3", tobacco spit, stamped Jugtown Ware (saucer), stamped Jugtown Ware
    (John Rare stamp) ....$120.00 – 275.00

Custard cup, earthenware 2¼", clear lead glaze, signed Ben Owen III (1983)...$95.00 – 125.00

D – F

Devil face jug, earthenware 10", signed BH (Billy Ray Hussey)...$125.00 – 150.00

Devil face jug, earthenware 10½", signed Albert Hodge ....$60.00 – 75.00

Devil face jug, stoneware 6", alkaline glaze, stamped B.B. Craig (ca. 1983)...$175.00 – 200.00

Devil face jug, stoneware 13", swirl, stamped B.B. Craig ....$250.00 – 275.00

Dinner plate, bowl, coffee mug, earthenware 10", 4½", and 3½", orange/green border, signed Seagrove (ca. 1980s) ....$110.00 – 125.00

Dinner plate, bowl, earthenware 10" and 6" blue, stamped Jugtown Ware (ca. 1976) ....$125.00 – 150.00

Dinner plate, casserole/domed lid, earthenware 10" and 3½" orange, stamped Jugtown Ware (1930s) ....$200.00 – 250.00

Dinner plate, plate, cup, earthenware 10", 5½", and 3", tobacco spit, stamped Ben Owen, Master Potter (ca. 1960s)...........$120.00 – 150.00

Dirt dish, earthenware 8", clear glaze, probably Salem...$400.00 – 500.00

Dirt dish, redware 8", possibly Salem (ca. 1830) ....$450.00 – 500.00

Dish, earthenware 7½", bronze green, attributed to J.B. Cole Pottery ....$35.00 – 50.00

* Dish, fluted, earthenware 5½", green/white, multiglazed, signed "Williamsburg Pottery, Handmade"
    (foil label), signed "Williamsburg Pottery, Handmade", ink stamp ....$30.00 – 45.00

Dogwood vase, earthenware 5½", blue, stamped Teagues, lead glaze...$45.00 – 60.00

Double face pitcher, stoneware 7", alkaline glaze, signed Jerry Brown...$60.00 – 75.00

Duckbill pitcher, earthenware 5", bronze green, stamped A.R. Cole Pottery ....$75.00 – 95.00

Duckbill pitcher, 7", Cole, matte green ....$80.00 – 95.00

Egg cup, earthenware 3½", Albany slip, attributed to Robert B. Keller ....$80.00 – 100.00

Egg cup, earthenware 3½", clear lead glaze, stamped Jugtown Ware ....$175.00 – 200.00

Face jug, stoneware 14", alkaline glaze, signed Richard Kale ....$80.00 – 85.00

Face jug, two-handled, stoneware 12", swirl, stamped B.B. Craig (ca. 1984)...$150.00 – 175.00

Faced cookie jar with lid, stoneware 11", swirl, stamped B.B. Craig ....$250.00 – 300.00

Face wig stand, stoneware 12½", swirl, stamped B.B. Craig ....$300.00 – 400.00

* Fan, earthenware 3½", multicolored, signed Williamsburg Handmade Pottery, ink stamp...........................$25.00 – 40.00

Fan, earthenware 4", multicolored, attributed to Rainbow Pottery ....$65.00 – 85.00

Fan, earthenware 6½", multiglaze, attributed to C.C. Cole Pottery ....$75.00 – 90.00

Fan vase, earthenware 5", beige/brown edge, attributed to Seagrove Pottery ....$30.00 – 50.00

Fan vase, earthenware 7", cobalt blue, attributed to North Carolina, maker unknown ....$85.00 – 110.00

Flower pot/saucer, earthenware 4", bronze green, attributed to A.R. Cole Pottery.......................................$80.00 – 90.00

Flower pot, earthenware 4", yellow/green drip, stamped Owens Pottery ....$60.00 – 75.00

Flower pot, earthenware 8", unglazed, 1½" coggle, attributed to Seagrove area..$25.00 – 35.00

Flower pot, earthenware 10½", bronze green, attributed to A.R. Cole Pottery...$55.00 – 75.00

Flower pot, earthenware 11" x 16", gray with blue cobalt drips, stamped 5, attributed to Seagrove Pottery (ca. 1967)............$70.00 – 95.00

Flower pot/saucer, earthenware 3", aqua/brown rim, attributed to J.B. Cole Pottery ....$45.00 – 60.00

Flower pot/saucer, earthenware 3", green, double dipped, stamped A.R. Cole Pottery....................................$45.00 – 65.00

Flower pot/saucer, earthenware 4", bronze green, attributed to A.R. Cole Pottery..$50.00 – 75.00

Flower pot/saucer, earthenware 4", tan, stamped A.R. Cole Pottery..$45.00 – 60.00

Flower pot, three ringed, earthenware 12", cream/rust, attributed to J.B. Cole Pottery, Waymon Cole...............$50.00 – 65.00

Flower pots with saucers (5), earthenware, multiglazed, stamped A.R. Cole....................................$30.00 – 45.00 each

Flower vase, porcelain 6", aqua/aubergine, stamped Pisgah Forest, no date ....$125.00 – 150.00

Fluted vase, two-handled, 7", J.B. Cole...$75.00 – 85.00

Frog, earthenware 2", blue, signed Teagues, Robbins, North Carolina, F. Craven (ca. 1960)........................$45.00 – 60.00

Frog, earthenware 2¼" x 6½", yellow, attributed to Rainbow Pottery (Elvin Owen)......................................$75.00 – 90.00

Frog, earthenware 3½", bronze/green, stamped A.R. Cole Pottery...$75.00 – 95.00

Frog, earthenware 3½", green, attributed to E.A. Hilton Pottery (Auby) ....$35.00 – 45.00

Frog, earthenware 4", blue, attributed to E.A. Hilton Pottery (Auby)...$35.00 – 45.00

Frog, earthenware 5", cobalt blue, attributed to Hilton Pottery, E.A. Hilton ....$100.00 – 125.00

Frog, earthenware 5¼", green, attributed to Seagrove area..$45.00 – 60.00

Frog in mug, earthenware 3½", tobacco spit, signed Seagrove "Frog in a mug"...$35.00 – 50.00

G – H

Glass, earthenware 5½", matte blue, attributed to Seagrove Pottery ....$25.00 – 40.00

Glass (tumbler), earthenware 5", white/orange rim, attributed to J.B. Cole Pottery.......................................$30.00 – 45.00

Grecian pitcher, earthenware 12 ¾", aqua, attributed to A.R. Cole Pottery...$115.00 – 135.00

Grecian urn, earthenware 17½", bronze green, stamped A.R. Cole Pottery..$125.00 – 175.00

Hanging pot, earthenware 4½", yellow, stamped Owens Pottery, handmade (ca. 1970).................................$60.00 – 75.00

Hanging pot, earthenware 5½", yellow, attributed to Rainbow Pottery..$70.00 – 80.00

Hanging strawberry pot, earthenware 9", multiglazed with blue bottom, attributed to C. C. Cole Pottery ....$45.00 – 60.00

Hanging vase, four handles, earthenware 7", tobacco spit brown, stamped Jugtown Ware ....$300.00 – 350.00

Hanging vase, two-handled, earthenware 5", clear/cobalt decoration, attributed to Auman Pottery (ca. 1920)...........$75.00 – 90.00

Honey and vinegar pitchers (4), earthenware 6½", multiglazed, attributed to C.C. Cole Pottery ....$20.00 – 30.00 each

* Honey jug, earthenware 6", multiglazed, attributed to C.C. Cole Pottery..$20.00 – 35.00

* Honey jug with cork stopper, earthenware 4½", multiglazed, attributed to C.C. Cole Pottery ....$25.00 – 30.00

* Honey jug with stopper, earthenware 6½", multiglazed, attributed to C.C. Cole Pottery..............................$25.00 – 30.00

Honey or vinegar jar, earthenware 5½" x 4", multiglazed, attributed to C. C. Cole Pottery ....$20.00 – 30.00

* Honey pitcher, earthenware 6", multiglazed, attributed to C.C. Cole Pottery..$45.00 – 60.00

J

Jar, molasses, stoneware 18", 5-gallon, attributed to JFS (James Franklin Seagle)......................................$325.00 – 450.00

Jar, preserve, stoneware 11½", attributed to Timothy Boggs (ca. 1880) ....$225.00 – 275.00

Jar, stoneware 10", attributed to Catawba Valley (ca. 1910)...$125.00 – 150.00

Jar, storage, stoneware 9½", 2-gallon, stamped H. Fox, Masonic emblem (ca. 1870).................................$350.00 – 400.00

Jar, two-handled, earthenware 6½", Albany slip, stamped OLB (Oscar Lewis Bachelder)..........................$100.00 – 135.00

Jar, two-handled, stoneware 11", attributed to Edgefield Pottery (marked 11)..$375.00 – 500.00

Jar, two-handled, stoneware 11½", 3-gallon, attributed to Catawba Valley (ca. 1910) ....$135.00 – 175.00

Jar, two-handled, stoneware 12", 2-gallon, attributed to Merritt Taylor Sugg (ca. 1870 – 1900)...........................$275.00 – 350.00

Jar, two-handled, stoneware 12", 2-gallon, stamped H. Fox (ca. 1850)...$300.00 – 350.00

Jar, two-handled, stoneware 12½", attributed to George Donkel (ca. 1880)..$225.00 – 250.00

Jar, two-handled, stoneware 13", attributed to Edgefield, SC (ca. 1840)..$300.00 – 315.00

Jar, two-handled, stoneware 13", attributed to Samuel Fenton Propst, (ca. 1900)..$165.00 – 195.00

Jar, two-handled, stoneware 13", 3-gallon, stamped J.H. Stone (1849 – present) ....$450.00 – 600.00

Jar, two-handled, stoneware 13½", 2-gallon, attributed to North Carolina...$175.00 – 200.00

Jar, two-handled, stoneware 14", salt glaze with cobalt, stamped Goodwin and Webster (ca. 1820) ....$300.00 – 375.00

Jar, two-handled, stoneware 14", stamped J.D. Craven (ca. 1860) ....$200.00 – 225.00

Jug, one handle, stoneware 11½", 1-gallon, Albany slip, stamped J.M. Yow ....$250.00 – 325.00

Jug, one handle, stoneware 14", 2-gallon, stamped NB (Nelson Bass)..$250.00 – 300.00

Jug, one handle, stoneware 15", 2-gallon, salt glaze, Moore County, maker unknown..$175.00 – 200.00

Jar, two-handled, stoneware 16", 5-gallon, attributed to Ritchie family (rings), Catawba Valley (ca. 1870).......$185.00 – 225.00

Jar, two-handled, storage, stoneware 8", attributed to Buncombe Co..$175.00 – 200.00

Jar, two-handled, storage, stoneware 12½", stamped with key by George Donkel ....$350.00 – 425.00

Jar with lid, stoneware 14½", signed WMH (Mark Hewittt), Pittsboro, NC (ca. 1980) ....$425.00 – 475.00

Jardiniere, three-handled, earthenware 8", clear/cobalt incised rings, attributed to Craven Pottery.......................$50.00 – 60.00

Jelly jar, condiment pot, earthenware 3¼", 2¾", mottled green, attributed to J.B. Cole Pottery, Nell Cole Graves.................$40.00 – 50.00

Jug, cyclops, earthenware 13", swirl, signed KE (Kim Ellington)...$65.00 – 85.00

Jug, earthenware 3", yellow, attributed to Rainbow Pottery ....$75.00 – 90.00

Jug, earthenware, 4", green, attributed to J.B. Cole Pottery ....$70.00 – 85.00

Jug, earthenware 4", Mason Stain over lead glaze, attributed to Seagrove Pottery ....$60.00 – 85.00

Jug, earthenware 4½", brown, stamped North State Pottery Co., handmade ....$65.00 – 80.00

Jug, earthenware 4½", green, attributed to Rainbow Pottery ....$70.00 – 95.00

Jug, earthenware 4½", olive green, attributed to Carolina Pottery..$50.00 – 70.00

Jug, earthenware 4¾", frogskin, stamped Jugtown Ware...$125.00 – 150.00

Jug, earthenware 5", green, attributed to J.B. Cole Pottery, Waymon Cole...$45.00 – 70.00

Jug, earthenware 7½", lavender/blue, attributed to J.B. Cole Pottery ....$65.00 – 80.00

Jug, earthenware 10½", blue, stamped Handmade by North State Pottery ....$60.00 – 75.00

Jug frog, earthenware 4½", matte tan, attributed to Seagrove Pottery ....$35.00 – 50.00

Jug, one handle, earthenware 7½", brown...$275.00 – 350.00

Jug, one handle, rings, earthenware 7½", black ....$350.00 – 375.00

Jug, one handle, stoneware 4½", Albany slip glaze, attributed to Outen Pottery, ...$225.00 – 275.00

Jug, one handle, stoneware, 8", stamped ½ (Thomas Ritchie)...$150.00 – 175.00

Jug, one handle, stoneware 8½", Albany slip, signed R.F. Outen Pottery Co. ....$225.00 – 275.00

Jug, one handle, stoneware 10", alkaline glaze, attributed to Yoder and McClure..$275.00 – 325.00

Jug, one handle, stoneware 10", attributed to J.D. Craven ....$150.00 – 175.00

Jug, one handle, stoneware 12", 1-gallon, stamped T.R. (Thomas Ritchie)...$200.00 – 250.00

Jug, one handle, stoneware 12½", 2-gallon, attributed to John Goodman ....$250.00 – 300.00

Jug, one handle, stoneware 14½", 2-gallon, coggled, stamped J.D. Craven, reed impression..................................$250.00 – 300.00

Jug, one handle (repair), stoneware 15", attributed to Seagle Pottery ....$175.00 – 225.00

Jug, one handle, stoneware 15", salt glaze, signed J. Gay, script..$325.00 – 350.00

Jug, one handle, stoneware 15¾", 3-gallon, stamped J.F. Brower, Masonic emblem, turned by H. Fox ....$350.00 – 475.00

Jug, one handle, stoneware 17", 4-gallon, stamped DS (Daniel Seagle)..$3,000.00 – 4,000.00

Jug, one handle, stoneware 17", 5-gallon, attributed to Casey Meaders ....$200.00 – 250.00

Jug, one handle, stoneware 18", 5-gallon, attributed to James F. Seagle ....$500.00 – 750.00

Jug, one handle, stoneware, salt glaze, impressed triangles, 9", stamped W.H. Hancock ....$275.00 – 300.00

Jug, stoneware, 7", ½ gallon, attributed to Seagrove area..$125.00 – 150.00

Jug, stoneware 10", stamped W. Cassidy/T. Macon, Randolph Co. (ca. 1888)..$275.00 – 350.00

Jug, stoneware, 11", Albany slip, attributed to Trull Pottery, B.R. and J.O. Trull..$325.00 – 375.00

Jug, stoneware, 11", salt glaze, signed Mack Chrisco (ca. 1980)...$200.00 – 250.00

Jug, stoneware 11", stamped E.A. Poe (ca. 1880) ....$275.00 – 325.00

Jug, stoneware 13", attributed to Hartsoe Family (SLH), (ca. 1880) ....$150.00 – 200.00

Jug, stoneware, 13", 2-gallon, stamped O'Henry Pottery (ca. 1940) ....$225.00 – 250.00

Jug, stoneware 14", alkaline glaze, attributed to Catawba Valley or Georgia (ca. 1910) ....$175.00 – 200.00

Jug, stoneware 14", stamped J.M. Hayes, Randolph Co. (ca. 1890) ....$375.00 – 425.00

Jug, stoneware, 20", 5 gallon, stamped Brown Pottery (ca. 1920)..$185.00 – 210.00

Jug, two-handled, stoneware 19", attributed to North Carolina ....$175.00 – 225.00

Jug, two-handled, stoneware 15", 3-gallon, attributed to Poley Carp Hartsoe..$200.00 – 250.00

Jug, two-handled, stoneware 16½", Albany slip ....$227.00 – 275.00

Jug, two-handled, stoneware 19", alkaline glaze, attributed to Stone family...$200.00 – 225.00

Jug with cogglewheel decoration, stoneware 20", 5-gallon, attributed to C.B. Craven (ca. 1950).......................$175.00 – 225.00

Juice glass, cup/saucer, plate, bowl, earthenware 3", 3", 6½", and 5½", yellow, stamped A.R. Cole (ca. late 1960s) ....$225.00 – 250.00

K – L

Kettle, earthenware 4½", black, attributed to Seagrove Pottery...$60.00 – 85.00

Lady figure, earthenware 8½", signed RA 1985, stamped Armfield Pottery...$125.00 – 150.00

Large pitcher with runs, 10", B.R. Hussey (early) ....$150.00 – 250.00

Lipped flower cup, earthenware 3", blue/aqua, double dipped, stamped North State Pottery Co., handmade ....$45.00 – 60.00

Loving cup, two-handled, earthenware 8", aqua, attributed to Rainbow Pottery...$60.00 – 75.00

Low bowl, cogglewheel, earthenware 4½", brown, attributed to Seagrove area ....$75.00 – 90.00

Low bowl, earthenware 2½" x 8½", blue exterior, attributed to E.A. Hilton Pottery ....$45.00 – 65.00

Low bowl, earthenware 2½", x 9½", blue, attributed to J.B. Cole Pottery, Bascomb King ....$55.00 – 70.00

Low bowl, earthenware 2¾" x 7½", blue, double dipped, stamped North State Pottery Co., handmade ....$60.00 – 75.00

Low bowl, earthenware 3¾" x 7½", chrome red, attributed to J.B. Cole Pottery ....$40.00 – 50.00

Low bowl, earthenware 4", aqua/blue, attributed to North State Pottery ....$85.00 – 110.00

Low bowl, earthenware 4" x 8", chrome red, attributed to J.B. Cole Pottery ....$35.00 – 50.00

Low bowl, earthenware 4½", clear lead, attributed to early Jugtown ....$125.00 – 200.00

Low bowl, earthenware 8", yellow, attributed to J.B. Cole Pottery, Philmore Graves ....$90.00 – 125.00

Low bowl, porcelain, 3" x 8½", light aqua, pink interior, stamped Pisgah Forest, potter's wheel, 1938 ....$125.00 – 150.00

Low bowl, two-handled, stepped, earthenware 3½" x 8¼", Royal Blue, attributed to J.B. Cole Pottery,
      stamped Sunset Mountain Pottery...$60.00 – 75.00

Low bowl, two-handled with shoulder, earthenware 4½", brown/white (multi), stamped Carolina Pottery ....$75.00 – 100.00

Low bowl with frog, earthenware 3" x 8½", multiglazed, attributed to C.C. Cole Pottery...$30.00 – 45.00

Low vase, earthenware 3¾", brown, signed Teagues Pottery..$30.00 – 45.00

Low vase, earthenware 3¾", green (matte), stamped Brown Pottery, handmade ....$30.00 – 35.00

M – N

Miniature pitcher, earthenware 2", yellow, attributed to Rainbow Pottery...$45.00 – 60.00

Monkey jug, double, earthenware 9", green, attributed to Seagrove area...$60.00 – 85.00

Monkey jug, earthenware 11", yellow, stamped H. Pugh, signed H. Pugh..$60.00 – 85.00

Monkey jug, stoneware, 10", swirl, stamped BBC (Burlon Craig) (ca. 1983)...$300.00 – 350.00

Monkey jug, stoneware, 10", swirl, stamped B.B. Craig ....$65.00 – 85.00

Monkey jug, 12", blue ....$70.00 – 95.00

Mug, earthenware 3½", frogskin, stamped Ben Owen - Master Potter...$125.00 – 175.00

Mug, earthenware 4½", blue, stamped North State Pottery Co., handmade ....$45.00 – 60.00

Mug, earthenware 4½", brown, attributed to M.L. Owens Pottery ....$45.00 – 60.00

Mug, earthenware 5½", unglazed, E.A. Hilton Pottery, Catawba Indian Pottery ....$100.00 – 110.00

Mug, earthenware 6", clear lead, attributed to Seagrove area (ca. 1920) ....$30.00 – 45.00

Mug, porcelain 3", olive green, stamped Pisgah Forest (no date) ....$45.00 – 60.00

Nut dish (double), earthenware 3" x 7", bronze green, stamped A.R. Cole Pottery ....$45.00 – 60.00

Nut dish, earthenware 3½" x 7¾", mistake crystal blue, stamped A.R. Cole Pottery..$45.00 – 60.00

Nut dish, earthenware 4½" x 5", matte green, attributed to Seagrove Pottery ....$30.00 – 45.00

O

Open bowl, 6" x 8", blue, Smithfield...$75.00 – 90.00

Oriental wide vase, earthenware 6", Chinese blue, stamped Jugtown Ware, 1st stamp..$750.00 – 975.00

Ovoid vase, earthenware 3¾", blue, double dipped, stamped North State Pottery Co. ....$55.00 – 70.00

Ovoid vase, earthenware 4½", Chinese blue, stamped Jugtown Ware, 1st stamp ....$600.00 – 800.00

Ovoid vase, earthenware 4¾", orange/green, double dipped, stamped Handmade Pine State Pottery ....$55.00 – 75.00

Ovoid vase, earthenware 6½", Albany slip, stamped Ben Owen Pottery Shop ....$75.00 – 90.00

Ovoid vase, footed, earthenware 7½", white glaze, stamped North State Pottery Co., handmade ....$95.00 – 120.00

Ovoid vase, earthenware 7¾", Chinese blue, stamped Jugtown Ware, 1st stamp ....$1,600.00 – 1,800.00

Ovoid vase (egg), earthenware 4", Chinese blue, stamped Jugtown Ware, 1st stamp ....$275.00 – 325.00

Ovoid vase (egg), earthenware 4¼", white, stamped Jugtown Ware, 1st stamp...................................$175.00 – 225.00

P

Pansy jug, earthenware 3½", gray, stamped A.R. Cole Pottery ....$40.00 – 55.00

Pansy jug, earthenware 4½", purple, attributed to Royal Crown Pottery....................................$65.00 – 75.00

* Pansy pot, earthenware 3", multiglazed, attributed to C.C. Cole Pottery, signed Blue Ridge, Va., handmade, ink stamp .....$30.00 – 45.00

* Pansy pot, earthenware 3½", multiglazed, attributed to C. C. Cole Pottery, signed
    Blue Ridge Pottery Handmade Va., ink stamp ....$45.00 – 50.00

* Pansy pot, earthenware 5½", blue, signed "Mr. Smiths - Handmade", ink stamp ....$60.00 – 75.00

Pansy vase, earthenware 3", blue, attributed to Carolina Pottery....................................$40.00 – 60.00

Pansy vase, earthenware 3", green, double dipped, attributed to North State Pottery Co....................................$50.00 – 65.00

Pansy vase, earthenware 3½", blue, attributed to Carolina Pottery....................................$45.00 – 65.00

Pansy vase, earthenware 4½", brown/green, double dipped, stamped Pine State Pottery, handmade....................................$70.00 – 85.00

Pansy vase, earthenware 5", green, attributed to Royal Crown Pottery ....$60.00 – 75.00

Pansy vase, earthenware 5½", brown, attributed to J.B. Cole Pottery, Philmore Graves ....$65.00 – 85.00

Pansy vase, earthenware 6", green/brown, double dipped, stamped Handmade by North State Pottery ....$55.00 – 70.00

Pie pan, fluted, earthenware 10", aqua, stamped A.R. Cole Pottery, Sanford, NC (small stamp) ....$65.00 – 90.00

Pie plate, fluted, earthenware 2" x 9", cream/rust, attributed to J.B. Cole Pottery, Nell Cole Graves....................................$45.00 – 60.00

Pinch bottle, earthenware 8", unglazed, attributed to A.E. Hilton Pottery (Catawba Indian)....................................$125.00 – 175.00

Pinch bottle, earthenware 8½", green, attributed to J.B. Cole Pottery ....$75.00 – 150.00

Pinch bottle, earthenware 10½", chrome red, attributed to J.B. Cole Pottery ....$95.00 – 115.00

Pinched tumbler, earthenware 6", bronze green, stamped A.R. Cole Pottery ....$60.00 – 75.00

Pinch vase, earthenware 3½", aqua, double dipped, attributed to North State Pottery Co. ....$70.00 – 95.00

Pinch vase, earthenware 3½", green, double dipped, stamped Handmade by North State Pottery....................................$75.00 – 100.00

Pinch vase, earthenware 6", cobalt blue, stamped Brown Pottery ....$75.00 – 95.00

Pinch vase, two-handled, earthenware 6½", yellow, attributed to J.B. Cole Pottery, Waymon Cole ....$60.00 – 75.00

* Pitcher, earthenware 1¼", multicolored, attributed to C.C. Cole Pottery ....$25.00 – 30.00

* Pitcher, earthenware 2", Chinese blue, attributed to North State Pottery, signed "Fort Raleigh, NC", ink stamp ....$45.00 – 60.00

Pitcher, earthenware 3", chrome red, attributed to J.B. Cole Pottery ....$45.00 – 60.00

* Pitcher, earthenware 3", multiglazed, unmarked ....$20.00 – 45.00

Pitcher, earthenware 3¼", blue, attributed to Carolina Pottery ....$50.00 – 70.00

* Pitcher, earthenware, 3¼", multiglazed, attributed to C. C. Cole Pottery, signed
    Blue Ridge Parkway, Va., Handmade, ink stamp....................................$25.00 – 30.00

Pitcher, earthenware 3½", brown, stamped Brown Pottery, handmade ....$30.00 – 45.00

Pitcher, earthenware 3½", clear lead glaze, attributed to Jugtown Pottery (ca. 1920)....................................$225.00 – 275.00

Pitcher, earthenware 3½", clear glaze, stamped Jugtown Ware, 1st stamp....................................$200.00 – 250.00

Pitcher, earthenware 3¾", clear lead glaze, attributed to Jugtown Pottery ....$200.00 – 250.00

Pitcher, earthenware 4", Albany Slip, attributed to Robert B. Keller....................................$90.00 – 110.00

Pitcher, earthenware, 4", multiglazed, attributed to C.C. Cole,....................................$30.00 – 45.00

Pitcher, earthenware, 4", orange, attributed to Seagrove Pottery ....$35.00 – 45.00

Pitcher, earthenware 4¼", clear lead glaze, stamped Jugtown Ware, 1st stamp....................................$225.00 – 275.00

Pitcher, earthenware 4¾", clear lead glaze (spotted), attributed to Jugtown (ca. 1920s)....................................$225.00 – 275.00

Pitcher, earthenware 5", swirl, signed B. Hilton ....$60.00 – 75.00

Pitcher, earthenware 5¼", aqua, stamped Handmade by North State Pottery....................................$65.00 – 95.00

Pitcher, earthenware 5½", black/green, iridescent, attributed to North State Pottery Co....................................$50.00 – 70.00

Pitcher, earthenware 6", chrome red/green, double dipped, stamped Log Cabin (drawing)....................................$95.00 – 110.00

* Pitcher, earthenware 6", multiglazed, unmarked....................................$25.00 – 30.00

Pitcher, earthenware 6", white, attributed to J.B. Cole Pottery ....$35.00 – 45.00

Pitcher, earthenware 6¼", yellow, attributed to Rainbow Pottery ....$45.00 – 60.00

Pitcher, earthenware 6½", aqua (ca. 1940s), stamped A.R. Cole Pottery ....$100.00 – 125.00

Pitcher, earthenware 6½", cobalt, salt glaze, stamped Jugtown Ware, 1st stamp ....$95.00 – 115.00

Pitcher, earthenware 6½", green, attributed to J.B. Cole Pottery ....$60.00 – 80.00

Pitcher, earthenware 7", clear/cobalt decoration, attributed to Auman Pottery ....$75.00 – 90.00

Pitcher, earthenware 7", green, attributed to Royal Crown Pottery ....$85.00 – 100.00

Pitcher, earthenware 7", stamped O'Henry Pottery, handmade, E.J. Brown ....$195.00 – 225.00

Pitcher, earthenware 7¼", clear glaze, (spotting), stamped Jugtown Ware ....$275.00 – 350.00

Pitcher, earthenware 8", glaze flaking, attributed to North Carolina (ca. 1890) ....$25.00 – 35.00

Pitcher, earthenware 8", green/cobalt blue, attributed to C.C. Cole Pottery ....$60.00 – 75.00

Pitcher, earthenware 8", green double dipped, stamped Handmade by North State Pottery...........................$70.00 – 95.00

Pitcher, earthenware 8", matte brown, stamped M.L. Owens ....$115.00 – 150.00

Pitcher, earthenware 8¼", unglazed, E.A. Hilton Pottery, Catawba Indian Pottery ....$110.00 – 125.00

Pitcher, earthenware 8½", black, attributed to Smithfield Art Pottery...$125.00 – 175.00

Pitcher, earthenware, 9", yellow, signed Seagrove (ca. 1950s)..$65.00 – 90.00

Pitcher, earthenware, 9½", alkaline glaze with glass runs, signed BH 1990 (Billy Ray Hussey)...................$95.00 – 110.00

Pitcher, earthenware 9½", clear lead glaze (spotting), attributed to Jugtown Pottery (ca. 1920)...................$175.00 – 200.00

Pitcher, earthenware, 10", dark green, attributed to Smithfield Art Pottery..$95.00 – 125.00

Pitcher, earthenware 10", salt glaze/blue border, stamped M.L. Owens Pottery ....$135.00 – 195.00

Pitcher, earthenware 19", crystal blue, attributed to J.B. Cole Pottery, Waymon Cole ....$125.00 – 175.00

Pitcher (Futura design), earthenware 10", aqua, attributed to J.B. Cole Pottery ....$75.00 – 90.00

Pitcher, juice glasses (3) and small pitcher, earthenware 8", 4", 4½", aqua/brown rim, attributed to J.B. Cole Pottery,
    signed VS (Virginia Shelton)...$175.00 – 200.00

Pitcher, side handle, earthenware 3", white, attributed to A.R. Cole Pottery..$40.00 – 55.00

Pitcher, sine wave decoration, earthenware 7½", crystal blue, attributed to J.B. Cole Pottery, Waymon Cole ....$60.00 – 75.00

Pitcher, stoneware, 5", attributed to Burlon Craig (ca. 1930) ....$110.00 – 145.00

Pitcher, stoneware, 10", attributed to Propst Pottery (ca. 1890)..$125.00 – 150.00

Pitcher, stoneware, 11", attributed to Ritchie family, Catawba Co. (ca. 1890)...$135.00 – 175.00

Pitcher, stoneware 11", blue band, attributed to E.A. Hilton Pottery ....$175.00 – 250.00

Pitcher, stoneware 11½", 1½-gallon, gray/brown ....$75.00 – 100.00

Pitcher, swirl, stoneware 7", attributed to Enoch Reinhardt..$225.00 – 275.00

Pitcher vase, earthenware 7¼", green, signed Teagues ....$40.00 – 55.00

Pitcher with lid, earthenware 4½", frogskin, stamped Jugtown Ware, 1st stamp ....$150.00 – 200.00

Pitcher with lid, earthenware 8", speckled brown, stamped Brown Pottery, handmade ....$40.00 – 60.00

Pitcher with lid, stoneware 6½", stamped B.B. Craig ....$225.00 – 250.00

Plate - dinner, earthenware 8¾", clear lead glaze, stamped Jugtown Ware, 1st stamp.....................................$65.00 – 195.00

Plate, earthenware 3¾", bronze green, stamped A.R. Cole Pottery ....$35.00 – 55.00

Plate, earthenware 5½", clear lead glaze, stamped Ben Owen - Master Potter..$150.00 – 175.00

Plate, mug, earthenware 8", 4", yellow, attributed to J.B. Cole Pottery (ca. 1960s)...$80.00 – 110.00

Plate, 7", Jugtown (ca. 1930 – 1940)..$100.00 – 125.00

Plate, juice cup, earthenware 7", 3", uranium yellow, stamped A.R. Cole Pottery, Sanford, NC (ca. 1960s)..........$45.00 – 80.00

Plates (3), earthenware 7", clear glaze, attributed to Jugtown Pottery (ca. 1930s) ....$375.00 – 425.00

Platter, fluted, earthenware 14", bronze green, attributed to J.B. Cole Pottery ....$65.00 – 80.00

Platter, two-handled, earthenware 15", aqua, attributed to Rainbow Pottery...$100.00 – 140.00

Porch vase, double, two-handled, earthenware 20½", painted blue, parrot decoration, attributed to Auman Pottery (ca. 1924)....$425.00 – 500.00

Porch vase, rat tail handles, earthenware 16½", orange/manganese, stamped "3",
    attributed to North State Pottery Co., Jonah Owen..$125.00 – 200.00

Porch vase, two-handled (double), earthenware 18½", bronze green, stamped A.R. Cole..............................$375.00 – 500.00

Porch vase, two-handled, earthenware 16", yellow, attributed to J.B. Cole Pottery ....$120.00 – 200.00

Porch vase, two-handled, earthenware 17", orange/green runs, cogglewheel design, attributed to Joe Owen.......$200.00 – 250.00

Porch vase, two-handled, earthenware 17½", clear lead glaze, cogglewheel, attributed to Joe Owen ....$150.00 – 250.00

Porch vase, two-handled, earthenware 18", green, attributed to Royal Crown Pottery ....$250.00 – 350.00

Porch vase, two-handled, earthenware 18½", bronze green, attributed to A.R. Cole Pottery..........................$100.00 – 125.00

Porch vase, two-handled, earthenware 19", chrome red, stamped Rainbow Pottery, handmade ....$225.00 – 275.00

Porch vase, two-handled, earthenware 22½", glazed interior, black exterior, painted scene,
    attributed to E.A. Hilton Pottery ....$300.00 – 375.00
Porch vase, two handled, earthenware 23", chrome red, attributed to J.B. Cole Pottery, Waymon Cole ....$425.00 – 600.00
Porch vase, two lug handles, earthenware 20½", aqua, attributed to J.B. Cole Pottery, Waymon Cole ....$275.00 – 400.00
Porch vase, two rope handles, earthenware 18", gunmetal gray, attributed to J.B. Cole Pottery, Waymon Cole ....$350.00 – 450.00
Punch bowl, earthenware 5½" x 13", aqua, attributed to Rainbow Pottery ....$125.00 – 150.00

R

Rebecca pitcher, earthenware 4½", matte green, attributed to Seagrove Pottery ....$40.00 – 55.00
Rebecca pitcher, earthenware 5½", yellow ....$65.00 – 80.00
Rebecca pitcher, earthenware 6½", bronze/green, stamped A.R. Cole Pottery.......................................$65.00 – 90.00
Rebecca pitcher, earthenware 6¾", multiglazed, attributed to C.C. Cole Pottery................................$75.00 – 95.00
Rebecca pitcher, earthenware 7", brown sugar, attributed to Seagrove Pottery....................................$55.00 – 65.00
* Rebecca pitcher, earthenware 7", gunmetal, "Souvenir of North Carolina" (paper sticker) ....$35.00 – 40.00
Rebecca pitcher, earthenware 7¼", aqua, attributed to Virginia Shelton ....$85.00 – 95.00
Rebecca pitcher, earthenware 7½", aqua/multiglazed, attributed to Rainbow Pottery ....$65.00 – 80.00
Rebecca pitcher, earthenware 7½", green, stamped Handmade by North State Pottery, Sanford, NC (3rd stamp) ....$60.00 – 85.00
Rebecca pitcher, earthenware 8¼", brown, stamped Brown Pottery, Handmade Arden, NC........................$70.00 – 95.00
Rebecca pitcher, earthenware 8½", chrome red, attributed to C.C. Cole Pottery ....$60.00 – 85.00
Rebecca pitcher, earthenware 8½", light aqua, attributed to Rainbow Pottery ....$50.00 – 75.00
Rebecca pitcher, earthenware 8½", matte green, attributed to Seagrove Pottery....................................$60.00 – 75.00
Rebecca pitcher, earthenware 8½", multiglazed, attributed to Seagrove Pottery...................................$60.00 – 75.00
Rebecca pitcher, earthenware 8¾", multiglazed, attributed to C.C. Cole Pottery...................................$60.00 – 75.00
Rebecca pitcher, earthenware 9", aqua/brown rim, attributed to J.B. Cole Pottery ....$70.00 – 85.00
Rebecca pitcher, earthenware 9", bronze green, attributed to J.B. Cole Pottery ....$70.00 – 85.00
Rebecca pitcher, earthenware 9¾", aqua, double dipped, attributed to North State Pottery Co. ....$60.00 – 75.00
*Rebecca pitcher, earthenware 10½", green, stamped Virginia Pottery ....$35.00 – 45.00
Rebecca pitcher, earthenware 11¾", aqua, attributed to Rainbow Pottery ....$60.00 – 75.00
Rebecca pitcher, earthenware 13", matte green, attributed to Joe Owen ....$75.00 – 100.00
Rebecca pitcher, earthenware 13", unglazed, attributed to Seagrove area ....$75.00 – 100.00
Rebecca pitcher, earthenware 13½", yellow, attributed to Joe Owen ....$110.00 – 250.00
Rebecca pitcher, earthenware 13¾", multiglazed, cogglewheel, stamped Joe Owen ....$90.00 – 115.00
Rebecca pitcher, earthenware 17½", cream, cogglewheel, attributed to Joe Owen ....$90.00 – 115.00
Rebecca pitcher, earthenware 19", painted black, attributed to Seagrove area ....$125.00 – 175.00
Rebecca pitcher, earthenware 20¾", yellow, attributed to J.B. Cole Pottery......................................$95.00 – 125.00
Rebecca pitcher, earthenware 21", clear/green/yellow, cogglewheel decoration, attributed to Joe Owen ....$75.00 – 95.00
Rebecca pitcher, 7", C.C. Cole ....$65.00 – 75.00
Rebecca pitcher, 9", Gen Foister Cole at A.R. Cole Pottery ....$125.00 – 150.00
Rebecca pitcher, 17", magenta, J.B. Cole...$200.00 – 225.00
Rebecca pitcher, saucer (attached), earthenware, matte green, attributed to Seagrove Pottery ....$60.00 – 80.00
Rebecca pitchers (2), earthenware 6" and 5", Mason stain, attributed to Seagrove Pottery......................$30.00 – 45.00
Refrigerator jar, earthenware 7½", cobalt blue, attributed to J.B. Cole Pottery, Bascomb King (ca. 1930s) ....$125.00 – 175.00
Refrigerator jar, earthenware 8½", chrome red, attributed to J.B. Cole Pottery, Bascomb King.................$125.00 – 150.00
Refrigerator jar (elephant trunk), earthenware 8½", orange, attributed to M.L. Owens Pottery, M.L. Owens................$75.00 – 90.00
Relish dish, earthenware 4½", tobacco brown, signed Seagrove ....$25.00 – 40.00
Reverse buzzard vase, 8", blue, A.R. Cole...$225.00 – 250.00
Ring frog, earthenware 1¼", multiglazed, attributed to C. C. Cole Pottery...$35.00 – 50.00
Ring jar, two-handled, sine wave, earthenware 16½", cream/light green, attributed to Duck Teague Pottery, Farrell Craven ....$85.00 – 110.00
Ring jug, earthenware 8½", clear glaze, attributed to Shenandoah Valley (Va.)....................................$60.00 – 70.00
Roman pitcher, earthenware 5½", mirror black, stamped A.R. Cole Pottery ....$50.00 – 65.00
Runlet, stoneware 4¾", swirl, stamped B.B. Craig..$80.00 – 95.00

S

Salt keeper, earthenware 8¾", salt glaze/cobalt, stamped Jugtown Ware, 2nd stamp (ca. 1975)............................$150.00 – 200.00

* Side pitcher, earthenware 2¼", multiglazed, attributed to North State Pottery...$30.00 – 40.00

Small jug, North State Pottery, second stamp ....$100.00 – 125.00

Snake jug, stoneware 13½", alkaline glaze, signed Michael Crocker...$125.00 – 175.00

* Soap dish, earthenware 2¼", brown sugar, attributed to M.L. Owens, signed Terrys, Buxton, NC (paper label) ....$30.00 – 45.00

Soap dish, earthenware 3", green, attributed to Seagrove Pottery..$35.00 – 50.00

Storage jar, stoneware 10¼", salt glaze, stamped J.M. Hays, 1-gallon ....$275.00 – 325.00

Storage jar, stoneware 11", attributed to North Carolina (ca. 1900) ....$85.00 – 145.00

Storage jar, stoneware 11", stamped J.R. Crisco (ca. 1890)...$250.00 – 300.00

Storage jar, two-handled, incised rings (3), stoneware 11", stamped 1-gallon, salt glaze/runs, attributed to Webster family ....$225.00 – 275.00

Storage jar, two-handled, stoneware 12¼", 2-gallon, salt glaze/runs, stamped P. McCoy ....$275.00 – 325.00

Strawberry jar, earthenware 7", mottled green, attributed to J.B. Cole Pottery ....$60.00 – 75.00

Strawberry jar, earthenware 7½", green, signed W.N. Owens (ca. 1970s) .... $45.00 – 65.00

Strawberry jar, earthenware 10", multicolored, attributed to Rainbow Pottery ....$80.00 – 115.00

Strawberry jar, earthenware 12", unglazed, unmarked. ....$85.00 – 95.00

Strawberry jar, earthenware 14¾", multiglazed, attributed to C.C. Cole ....$125.00 – 150.00

Strawberry jar (pair), earthenware 14½", multiglazed, attributed to C.C. Cole Pottery ....$325.00 – 375.00

Strawberry pot, earthenware 4¾", multiglazed, attributed to C.C. Cole Pottery ....$25.00 – 40.00

Strawberry pot, earthenware 7½", chrome red, attributed to J.B. Cole Pottery, Bascomb King ....$45.00 – 60.00

* Sugar bowl, earthenware 3", multiglaze, attributed to C.C. Cole Pottery, signed "Blue Ridge Parkway, Va.,
    handmade" ink stamp ....$25.00 – 35.00

Sugar bowl, earthenware 3½", blue/lavender, attributed to Teague Pottery ....$30.00 – 45.00

Sugar bowl, earthenware 3½", clear lead glaze, stamped Jugtown Ware ....$125.00 – 150.00

Sugar bowl (mustard jar), porcelain, 3½", aqua, stamped Stephen 1947...$60.00 – 85.00

Sugar bowl with lid, earthenware 4", blue, attributed to Smithfield Art Pottery ....$40.00 – 60.00

Sugar/cream set, earthenware 4", 31/", green, stamped M.L. Owens (ca. 1950s).......................................$45.00 – 65.00

T – U

Tall bud vase, 15" (rare), J.B. Cole ....$100.00 – 125.00

Tall bud vase, 17", A.R. Cole...$100.00 – 115.00

Tall pitcher, patterned, earthenware 7¼", bronze green, stamped A.R. Cole Pottery..................................$75.00 – 100.00

Tall vase, earthenware 9½", orange/black drip, stamped A.R. Cole Pottery, Sanford, NC (1st stamp) ....$275.00 – 350.00

Tall vase, earthenware 11¾", yellow, stamped A.R. Cole Pottery, rare ....$85.00 – 150.00

Teacup, earthenware 3", yellow, signed E. Owen (Elvin)..$30.00 – 45.00

Teacup/saucer, earthenware 2½", clear lead glaze, cobalt decoration, attributed to Auman Pottery..............$50.00 – 65.00

Teague pitcher, 7", brown/frogskin ....$85.00 – 95.00

Teapot, earthenware 5½", green, attributed to J.B. Cole Pottery, Nell Cole Graves.....................................$95.00 – 115.00

Teapot, stoneware 7½", blue and white swirl, signed Charles Lisk..$150.00 – 200.00

Teapot with lid, earthenware 6", yellow, signed Rainbow Pottery (twice), ink stamp ....$95.00 – 125.00

Teapot with lid, earthenware 6½", black and tan, stamped Cole Pottery, signed Neolia Cole (1982)................$100.00 – 135.00

Teapot with lid, earthenware 7", light blue, stamped Teagues, stamped C.B. Craven (ca. 1970s) ....$65.00 – 90.00

Teapot with lid, earthenware 8", mirror black, attributed to M.L. Owens Pottery, M.L. Owens (ca. 1950) ....$110.00 – 125.00

Teapot with lid, earthenware 12", painted dogwood, unglazed, attributed to Auman Pottery (ca. 1924)................$100.00 – 145.00

Tea set (miniature), earthenware, gray, heart decoration, stamped Owens, signed NB ....$45.00 – 60.00

Trumpet vase, earthenware 10", multiglazed, buff and green, attributed to C.C. Cole Pottery ....$65.00 – 100.00

Trumpet vase, two-handled, earthenware 6", green, attributed to Philmore Graves, stamped J.B. Cole Pottery ....$75.00 – 100.00

Tumbler, earthenware 4½", brown/blue drips, signed Teagues ....$60.00 – 100.00

Urn, two-handled/rings, cogglewheel decoration, earthenware 11", pink underglaze with green/black,
    attributed to Joe Owen ....$145.00 – 175.00

V

Vase, cameo, porcelain 8", olive, green, blue with white cameo, signed R.A. Leftwich.................................$35.00 – 50.00

Vase, (Chinese), earthenware 5¼", aqua, attributed to J.B. Cole Pottery ....$35.00 – 50.00

Vase, decorative handles, earthenware 6½", mistake crystal blue, stamped A.R. Cole Pottery, Sanford, NC (small stamp).........$45.00 – 60.00

Vase, double-handled, earthenware 9", blue (periwinkle), attributed to J.B. Cole Pottery, Philmore Graves.........................$75.00 – 90.00

Vase, double-handled, earthenware 9½", dirty white, attributed to J.B. Cole Pottery, Philmore Graves ....$95.00 – 110.00

Vase, earthenware, clear/cobalt blue, stamped North State Pottery Co. Handmade, Sanford, NC, 2nd stamp ....$75.00 – 100.00

Vase, earthenware 4", beige/green, stamped North State Pottery Co., handmade ....$50.00 – 65.00

Vase, earthenware 4", blue, attributed to Carolina Pottery...$45.00 – 60.00

Vase, earthenware 4", mirror black, attributed to J.B. Cole Pottery...$50.00 – 65.00

Vase, earthenware 5", green, attributed to Smithfield Art Pottery ....$65.00 – 75.00

Vase, earthenware 5½", green, attributed to J.B. Cole Pottery ....$60.00 – 75.00

Vase, earthenware 6½", aqua, stamped Rainbow Pottery - Handmade, Sanford, NC, ink stamp......................................$75.00 – 90.00

Vase, earthenware 6½", blue with yellow/red/green, signed Royal Crown Pottery, handmade pottery, ink stamp.................$85.00 – 100.00

Vase, earthenware 6½", gray, signed Log Cabin (drawing)..$90.00 – 115.00

Vase, earthenware 6½", green, attributed to Royal Crown Pottery...$65.00 – 80.00

Vase, earthenware 6½", yellow, signed Log Cabin (drawing)..$85.00 – 110.00

Vase, earthenware 7", chrome red, attributed to J.B. Cole Pottery ....$65.00 – 75.00

Vase, earthenware, 7½", salt glaze/cobalt, stamped North State Pottery Co., handmade..$60.00 – 75.00

Vase, earthenware 8", blue, stamped O'Henry Pottery, handmade, E.J. Brown..$40.00 – 50.00

Vase, earthenware 8", blue/salt glaze, attributed to J.B. Cole Pottery ....$60.00 – 75.00

Vase, earthenware 8", green, attributed to O.L. Bachelder ....$225.00 – 750.00

Vase, earthenware 8¼", blue speckle, attributed to Teague Pottery ....$55.00 – 70.00

Vase, earthenware 8½", swirl (painted), attributed to North State Pottery Co..$85.00 – 110.00

Vase, earthenware 9", chrome red, stamped Handmade by North State Pottery, Sanford, NC, 3rd stamp ....$60.00 – 75.00

Vase, earthenware 9", green/brown underglaze, attributed to Carolina Pottery..$60.00 – 75.00

Vase, earthenware 9", yellow/cobalt run, attributed to J.B. Cole Pottery (1920s) ....$120.00 – 145.00

Vase, earthenware 9¼", matte yellow, stamped Carolina Pottery..$75.00 – 100.00

Vase, earthenware 9½", blue/green speckle, attributed to Teague Pottery ....$60.00 – 75.00

Vase, earthenware 10", clear glaze/cobalt, attributed to Seagrove area ....$45.00 – 60.00

Vase, earthenware 10", clear (orange), glaze, manganese/yellow drips, stamped North State Pottery Co.,
    Handmade, Sanford, NC, 1st stamp (very rare)..$350.00 – 500.00

Vase, finger grooved, earthenware 10", bronze green, attributed to J.B. Cole Pottery ....$75.00 – 95.00

Vase, fluted and stepped, earthenware 5½", mottled green, attributed to J.B. Cole Pottery, Waymon Cole...........................$45.00 – 60.00

Vase, fluted, earthenware 5¾", brown sugar, attributed to J.B. Cole Pottery, Nell Cole Graves ....$35.00 – 45.00

Vase, fluted, earthenware 5¾", multiglazed, attributed to C.C. Cole Pottery ....$35.00 – 55.00

Vase, fluted, earthenware 6", crackle white, attributed to Rainbow Pottery (rare) ....$125.00 – 140.00

Vase, fluted, earthenware 7", swirl, attributed to North State Pottery Co...$95.00 – 145.00

Vase, fluted, earthenware 7½", bronze green, attributed to J.B. Cole Pottery ....$45.00 – 65.00

Vase, fluted, earthenware 7½", gray/green, double, attributed to Teagues Pottery ....$40.00 – 55.00

Vase, fluted, earthenware 7½", green, attributed to J.B. Cole Pottery, Philmore Graves ....$45.00 – 60.00

Vase, fluted, earthenware 8¾", blue, attributed to Smithfield Art Pottery..$50.00 – 70.00

Vase, fluted top, earthenware 5", multiglazed, attributed to C.C. Cole Pottery ....$50.00 – 65.00

Vase, fluted, two-handled, earthenware 5", green, attributed to Seagrove Pottery ....$35.00 – 55.00

Vase, 4", C.C. Cole...$35.00 – 50.00

Vase, 8", blue, Candor Pottery ....$75.00 – 90.00

Vase, fluted, earthenware 9", chrome red/brown, double dipped, attributed to North State Pottery Co................................$95.00 – 125.00

Vase, fluted, earthenware 9½", blue/green runs, attributed to J.B. Cole Pottery, Philmore Graves ....$95.00 – 115.00

Vase, fluted, earthenware 12", green, attributed to A.R. Cole Pottery, signed "Daison Ware," paper label ....$235.00 – 350.00

Vase, (Futura), earthenware 6½", yellow, attributed to J.B. Cole Pottery ....$45.00 – 65.00

Vase, incised rings, earthenware 8", blue, attributed to Smithfield Art Pottery...$100.00 – 125.00

Vase, Moravian handles, finger impressed, earthenware 10½", multicolored (Mason stain),
    attributed to Rainbow Pottery ....$175.00 – 225.00

Vase, one handle, fluted, earthenware 7½", chrome red, attributed to J.B. Cole Pottery, Philmore Graves (ca. 1920s)...........$80.00 – 100.00

Vase, Pisgah Forest, porcelain, 5¼", aqua, stamped Potters Wheel ....$65.00 – 95.00

Vase, porcelain 4½", aqua, stamped Pisgah Forest 1949 ....$90.00 – 115.00

Vase, porcelain 5½", aqua/aubergine, stamped Pisgah Forest (no date)...$90.00 – 115.00

Vase, porcelain 9", aqua/aubergine, stamped Pisgah Forest, Potters Wheel 1939...$125.00 – 175.00

Vase, porcelain 10", aqua, stamped Pisgah Forest, Potters Wheel 1930..$95.00 – 125.00

Vase, rat tail handles, earthenware 8½", chrome red, attributed to Royal Crown Pottery, Jack Kiser ....$85.00 – 110.00

Vase, rope handles, earthenware 13¾", black underglaze, blue overglaze, attributed to Smithfield Art Pottery ....$175.00 – 225.00

Vase, sine wave decoration, earthenware 12¼", clear/cobalt, signed Log Cabin (drawing) ....$175.00 – 250.00

Vase, split handles, earthenware 15", aqua, Mason stain, attributed to Rainbow Pottery...................$150.00 – 200.00

* Vase, stoneware, 6", swirl/cogglewheel, signed Chimney Rock, NC ....$35.00 – 45.00

Vase, stoneware, (transitional piece), stamped Penlands Pottery...................$125.00 – 150.00

Vase, strawberry jar, earthenware 3¾", mottled green, attributed to J.B. Cole Pottery...................$50.00 – 70.00

Vase, swirl handled, earthenware 7", blue/black, double dipped, attributed to J.B. Cole Pottery, Bascomb King ....$80.00 – 100.00

Vase, swirl handled, earthenware 9", aqua, attributed to J.B. Cole Pottery, attributed Daison Ware...................$75.00 – 95.00

Vase, swirl handles, earthenware 11", dark aqua, attributed to J.B. Cole Pottery, Bascomb King...................$95.00 – 115.00

Vase, swirled handles, stoneware 7½" (transitional piece) ....$100.00 – 125.00

Vase, three-handled, earthenware 4¾", aqua, attributed to A.R. Cole (turned), Pisgah Forest type glaze ....$125.00 – 150.00

Vase, three-handled, earthenware 6", brown/green, double dipped, stamped A.R. Cole Pottery,
   Sanford, NC (small stamp)...................$95.00 – 115.00

Vase, three-handled, earthenware 7", blue/green, attributed to J.B. Cole Pottery or Rainbow Pottery ....$100.00 – 110.00

Vase, three-handled, earthenware 9", black green/iridescent, attributed to North State Pottery Co. ....$125.00 – 160.00

Vase, three-handled, earthenware 9", teal, attributed to A.R. Cole Pottery, "Daison Ware" ....$110.00 – 135.00

Vase, three-handled, earthenware 13¾", aqua, attributed to Rainbow Pottery ....$175.00 – 200.00

Vase, three-handled, earthenware 14", blue, attributed to Teague Pottery...................$145.00 – 185.00

Vase, two-handled, band, earthenware 11", clear/cobalt, attributed to Daniel Z. Craven (ca. 1920s)...................$225.00 – 275.00

Vase, two-handled, coggle wheel, earthenware 10", clear/cobalt, attributed to Craven Pottery...................$200.00 – 250.00

Vase, two-handled, earthenware 4½", bronze green, attributed to J.B. Cole Pottery...................$45.00 – 60.00

Vase, two-handled, earthenware 5", matte green, attributed to Seagrove Pottery...................$45.00 – 95.00

Vase, two-handled, earthenware 5½", blue, attributed to Carolina Pottery, Wren Cole...................$60.00 – 75.00

Vase, two-handled, earthenware 5¼", aqua, attributed to Carolina Pottery, Wren Cole...................$65.00 – 80.00

* Vase, two-handled, earthenware 6", dark yellow, attributed to J.B. Cole Pottery, stamped Sunset Mountain Pottery ....$40.00 - 55.00

Vase, two-handled, earthenware 6", matte blue, attributed to Seagrove Pottery...................$35.00 – 50.00

Vase, two-handled, earthenware 6½", bronze, attributed to J.B. Cole Pottery ....$40.00 – 55.00

Vase, two-handled, earthenware 6½", green, attributed to J.B. Cole, Philmore Graves...................$55.00 – 70.00

Vase, two-handled, earthenware 6¾", chrome red, stamped Handmade by North State Pottery ....$50.00 – 65.00

Vase, two-handled, earthenware 7", aqua, double dipped, stamped Handmade by North State Pottery ....$70.00 – 85.00

Vase, two-handled, earthenware 7½", green speckled, attributed to Seagrove area (ca. 1930s) ....$35.00 – 50.00

Vase, two-handled, earthenware 7½", mottled blue/white, stamped North State Pottery Co. ....$60.00 – 75.00

Vase, two-handled, earthenware 7¾", green/orange, attributed to Seagrove area ....$50.00 – 65.00

Vase, two-handled, earthenware 8", blue and white spatter, attributed to Rainbow Pottery...................$70.00 – 95.00

Vase, two-handled, earthenware 8", cream, green, blue, triple dipped, attributed to Log Cabin Pottery ....$95.00 – 125.00

Vase, two-handled, earthenware 8", green, attributed to Seagrove area ....$45.00 – 60.00

Vase, two-handled, earthenware 8", mauve, attributed to Rainbow Pottery ....$90.00 – 120.00

Vase, two-handled, earthenware 8½", chrome red/green, double dipped, attributed to Seagrove area ....$125.00 – 165.00

Vase, two-handled, earthenware 8½", yellow, attributed to Rainbow Pottery...................$65.00 – 90.00

Vase, two-handled, earthenware 9", aqua, attributed to Rainbow Pottery ....$45.00 – 60.00

Vase, two-handled, earthenware 9", matte green, stamped North State Pottery Co., Sanford, NC, 2nd stamp...................$45.00 – 65.00

Vase, two-handled, earthenware 9", pink, attributed to Rainbow Pottery...................$85.00 – 110.00

Vase, two-handled, earthenware 9", unglazed exterior, attributed to E.A. Hilton Pottery (Catawba Indian)...................$200.00 – 325.00

Vase, two-handled, earthenware 9½", blue, attributed to Smithfield Art Pottery ....$90.00 – 110.00

* Vase, two-handled, earthenware 9½", painted swirl ....$45.00 – 60.00

Vase, two-handled, earthenware 9¾", blue, attributed to E.A. Hilton Pottery...................$45.00 – 60.00

Vase, two-handled, earthenware 10", green/yellow/red, attributed to Rainbow Pottery...................$90.00 – 175.00

Vase, two-handled, earthenware 10", orange, green, over glaze, attributed to Joe Owen...................$85.00 – 105.00

Vase, two-handled, earthenware 10½", multiglazed, attributed to C.C. Cole Pottery ....$40.00 – 55.00

Vase, two-handled, earthenware 11", pink/green runs, attributed to C.C. Cole Pottery ....$110.00 – 150.00

Vase, two-handled, earthenware 12", aqua, attributed to J.B. Cole Pottery, Waymon Cole,
   stamped Sunset Mountain Pottery...................$60.00 – 75.00

Vase, two-handled, earthenware 121", clear (yellow) blue/green, decoration, attributed to J.B. Cole Pottery
(1920s – 1930s), stamped J. Palmer, Handmade Pottery, ink stamp ....$125.00 – 140.00

Vase, two-handled, earthenware 12", yellow, attributed to Seagrove area (ca. 1930) ....$110.00 – 135.00

Vase, two-handled, earthenware 13¾", chrome red, attributed to J.B. Cole Pottery, Waymon Cole ....$85.00 – 275.00

Vase, two-handled, earthenware 14", variegated blue/white, attributed to J.B. Cole Pottery, Waymon Cole (ca. 1930s)........$80.00 – 100.00

Vase, two-handled, earthenware 14½", unglazed, painted, attributed to E.A. Hilton Pottery ....$75.00 – 95.00

Vase, two-handled, fluted, earthenware 6", mottled green, attributed to J.B. Cole Pottery, Philmore Graves ....$75.00 – 95.00

Vase, two-handled, fluted, earthenware 7", gunmetal, attributed to J.B. Cole Pottery, Philmore Graves ....$70.00 – 95.00

Vase, two-handled, earthenware 7½", yellow, attributed to Seagrove area (ca. 1940) ....$60.00 – 85.00

Vase, two-handled, 18" (repair), Cole Pottery...$95.00 – 125.00

Vase, two-handled, 18½", glazed inside, attributed to E.A. Hilton Pottery Co. (ca. 1920), ...$200.00 – 250.00

Vase, two-handled, fluted, earthenware 7¾", white, attributed to J.B. Cole Pottery, Philmore Graves ....$55.00 – 75.00

Vase, two-handled, lug, earthenware 8½", chrome red, attributed to Smithfield Art Pottery, Herman Cole ....$75.00 – 85.00

Vase, two-handled, porcelain 5¾", blue/green, stamped Aunt Nancy ....$70.00 – 95.00

Vase, two-handled, rings, earthenware 5", multiglazed, attributed to C.C. Cole Pottery, ...$50.00 – 65.00

* Vase, two-handled/rings, earthenware 7½", dark aqua, unmarked ....$25.00 – 35.00

Vase, two-handled, 13", Smithfield..$175.00 – 225.00

Vase, two rings, earthenware 6", orange/brown, attributed to Seagrove area...$75.00 – 95.00

Vase, two vertical handles, earthenware 9½", lavender, attributed to Rainbow Pottery...$95.00 – 100.00

Vase with shoulder, earthenware 4½", multiglazed/green, signed Log Cabin (indistinct) ....$75.00 – 90.00

Vases, earthenware 4", multiglazed, attributed to C. C. Cole Pottery...$30.00 – 45.00

Vases, two-handled/rings, earthenware 23", painted green and white, attributed to E.A. Hilton Pottery (ca. 1920) ....$95.00 – 125.00

W

Wall pocket, earthenware 8", unglazed, attributed to E.A. Hilton Pottery Co. (Catawba Indian Pottery).................................$65.00 – 75.00

Water pitcher with ice keeper, earthenware 7¼", brown-green glaze, signed Teagues ....$75.00 – 95.00

Water pitcher with lid, earthenware 8", mottled green, attributed to J.B. Cole Pottery, Nell Cole Graves ....$85.00 – 175.00

Weed pot, earthenware 7¾", brown/black, stamped A.R. Cole Pottery..$85.00 – 100.00

Weed pot, earthenware 8", multicolored, stamped A.R. Cole Pottery ....$90.00 – 110.00

Weed pot, earthenware 8", speckled ivory, stamped A.R. Cole Pottery, Sanford, NC (straight 3 lined stamp), rare.............$125.00 – 145.00

Weed pot, earthenware 19", gunmetal, stamped A.R. Cole Pottery..$60.00 – 75.00

Weed vase, earthenware 5", brown, signed Teagues lead glaze..$45.00 – 60.00

Wide vase, earthenware 5½", green, attributed to Seagrove area ....$25.00 – 45.00

Wide vase, porcelain 4½", aqua/aubergine, stamped Stephen 1946 ....$65.00 – 90.00

Wide vase, porcelain 5¼", gold, stamped Pisgah Forest 1981..$60.00 – 80.00

Wide vase, two rings, earthenware 11", green/blue, attributed to J.B. Cole, Waymon Cole ....$75.00 – 90.00